Building Socialism in Bolshevik Russia

THOMAS F. REMINGTON

Building Socialism
in
Bolshevik Russia

Ideology and Industrial Organization

1917–1921

UNIVERSITY OF PITTSBURGH PRESS

Series in Russian and East European Studies No. 6

Published by the University of Pittsburgh Press, Pittsburgh, Pa., 15260
Copyright © 1984, University of Pittsburgh Press
All rights reserved
Feffer and Simons, Inc., London
Manufactured in the United States of America

Library of Congress Cataloging in Publication Data

Remington, Thomas F., 1948–
Building socialism in Bolshevik Russia.

Includes index.
1. Soviet Union—Economic policy—1917–1928.
2. Industrial organization—Soviet Union—History.
3. Industry and state—Soviet Union—History. I. Title.
HC335.2.R46   1984   338.947   84-3603
ISBN 0-8229-3809-X

Contents

Preface

THIS IS A STUDY of the efforts by the Bolshevik government to "build socialism" during the first three and one-half years of the revolution, from the moment of triumph in October 1917, when the Bolsheviks seized power from the Provisional Government and declared a workers' and peasants' government, to the Tenth Communist Party Congress, in March 1921, when the regime turned course sharply by instituting the New Economic Policy. I am specifically concerned here with the Bolsheviks' efforts, conducted under the most desperate circumstances, to construct institutions for planning and administering industry. Theoretically literate, immensely articulate, intent on describing the larger meaning of each act, Bolshevik writers of the day poured out a great quantity of material reporting, analyzing, challenging, and defending the actions I am discussing. Newspaper, periodical, and book publications of the period form the immediate basis for this study, but research in the Soviet Union and in the West has contributed an abundant literature on these topics as well. A final well from which I have drawn data, harder to handle but no less essential, has been the memoir and eyewitness literature, which must be treated as an indispensable primary source at least until Soviet archives are open to Western scholars. Still, despite this wealth of information, it remains a challenge to determine how the schemes of the central leaders were carried into practice and to understand the forces acting on them.

What were the particular imperatives that shaped the structure of political authority in the early Soviet regime? The Russian Revolution has been studied from many standpoints and its outcome explained by a variety of theories. While acknowledging that no single explanation may ever be wholly adequate, this book will argue that the construction of socialism contained within it two disparate and ultimately incompatible projects: the overturning of capitalism and its replacement with a socialist society, and the organization of a cohesive state apparatus. Through mobilization the Bolsheviks sought to place all the resources of society at the disposal of the new state, with the consequence that society, by 1921, had become a field of fragmented, individualized forms of endeavor surrounding the garrison of party-state power. The organization of industrial administration offers an excellent test case of the proposition that it was the attempt to build the new state by means of mobilizing society that prevented the regime from establishing the self-sustaining social institutions on which a socialist regime depends.

The vast and vital problems of the peasantry and the outcome of the civil war—which might justly be considered the most burning issues of the time—generally do not fall under the scope of this inquiry. Rather, focusing on the efforts to "build socialism" in the industrial sphere, I treat the relations between the regime and the working class; the framework of administration; the emergence of a developmental ideology for the state; and the persistent dissipation of nominally centralized political authority, which ultimately prompted Bolshevik writers to envision alternatives to the model of concentrated power.

In the last chapter I extend the discussion to the present. The structural theory that I elaborate asserts that a mobilization regime reaches a point at which order breaks down as a consequence of the center's unredeemable claims to control society; the model therefore envisions a dynamic process of system change through a sequential alternation of regime types. Since the dilemma of political order and social control in the Soviet state acquired its fundamental outlines during the early period of Soviet power, I argue that subsequent transformations in the relations of state and society represent successive adaptations of the commitments originally made by the regime in these years.

My obligations to others for advice and support in the production of this study are considerable. Begun as a doctoral dissertation at Yale, it benefited at different times from suggestions by H. Ray Buchanan, Zygmunt Bauman, Paul Cocks, Alexander Erlich, Gregory Grossman, Peter Scheibert, Frederick Starr, and Robert C. Tucker. My readers at Yale offered numerous helpful comments as chapters appeared: the late Raymond Powell, David Cameron, Leon Lipson, and Charles E. Lindblom. Three individuals have been particularly helpful. From the inception of the project, Stephen F. Cohen has been a generous and wise guide, repeatedly taking time to offer advice and encouragement. It is very largely to his splendid biography of Bukharin that I owe my interest in early Soviet history. David Apter has shared the excitement and provocativeness of his ideas with me and his advice has been consistently acute. As is evident, the influence of his developmental theory, and especially his concept of the mobilization system, is deeply imprinted on this book. Finally, I want to record my deep appreciation to Frederick C. Barghoorn, who served as my dissertation advisor. He has been unfailingly magnanimous in sharing the benefit of his experience, his extraordinary bibliographic knowledge, his scholarly judgment, and his command of the field. Throughout, he has been a good teacher and friend.

I would like to record my appreciation to the political science department of Emory University for its support during the long gestation period of the book. In addition, I am indebted to the institutions which have aided the research materially. Yale University's Council on Russian and East European Studies made funds available for summer study. A fellowship from the International Research and Exchanges Board made it

possible to spend six months in the Soviet Union doing research in the published materials bearing on the topic. The
Hoover Institution deserves special mention both for the excel-
lence of its collections and the helpfulness of its librarians. The
staff at the University of Pittsburgh Press, and particularly
Catherine Marshall, merit warm thanks for their considerate
and skillful treatment of the manuscript.

Above all, my wife Nancy has my deepest gratitude for her
confidence and her honesty. She has put up with the manuscript for many years with unselfish support and has aided it
with her editorial judgment. To her I affectionately dedicate
the book.

Building Socialism in Bolshevik Russia

CHAPTER ONE

The Bolshevik Mobilization Regime

WRITERS ON THE RUSSIAN REVOLUTION have left two competing impressions of Bolshevik policy in the hard years immediately following October 1917. Some depict the period principally as a drama of class revolution carried out in the teeth of war and ruin. Others focus their attention on the external pressures confronted by the regime as it struggled to maintain its power; they hold that the intensity of the civil war gave the regime no choice but to pursue a course of fierce militarization of authority. Because the Bolsheviks themselves provided ad hoc theoretical explanations of their actions as they went along, they rationalized many decisions according to the logic of proletarian dictatorship.[1] Only after the Tenth Party Congress declared a New Economic Policy in March 1921 did Lenin offer the half-ironic name of "War Communism" for the period just passed, suggesting both that the early illusions of a shortcut to communism had faded and that the end of civil war and of foreign embargo and intervention could allow the regime to adopt a more moderate course.[2] (See table 1 for dates of national congresses.)

Although scholars have differed in their interpretations of the period—some stressing the ideological and revolutionary impetus in the regime's actions, some the military and social constraints on its freedom—they have generally agreed on the main elements of War Communism. Possessing strong political support in most centers of working-class organization—the soviets, the factory committees, the local branches of the party

3

Table 1
National Congresses, 1917–1921

	Party		Soviet		Trade Union		Sovnarkhoz
1917 (o.s.)	6th[a] 26 July–3 Aug.	1st[b]	5–11 June			1st	25 May–4 June
		2nd	25–26 October				
		3rd	23–31 December			2nd	18–27 December
1918 (n.s.)	7th[c] 6–8 March	4th	15–16 March	1st	7–14 January		
		5th	4–10 July				
		6th	6–9 November				
1919	8th 18–23 March	7th	5–9 December	2nd	16–25 January		
1920	9th 29 March–4 April	8th	22–29 December	3rd	6–13 April	3rd	23–29 January
1921	10th 8–16 March	9th	22–27 December	4th	17–25 May	4th	18–24 May

a. RSDRP(b)
b. RSFSR
c. RKP(b)

itself—the Bolshevik leadership, we now recognize, lacked the means of effective control over any of them.[3] It was therefore imperative for the new government to consolidate its power without losing its working-class backing. The Bolshevik leaders were conscious of their tenuous position. Accordingly, their initial policies combined expedience with redress of the most immediate grievances of the workers, soldiers, and peasants.

The first of these elements was the adoption of grain requisitioning. The program under which peasants were encouraged to seize land and regard themselves as individual proprietors, viewed as a cynical and opportunistic gesture by Menshevik opponents, re-created the problem of food shortages that had been felt acutely under the tsarist and Provisional Government regimes during the war. The devaluation of the currency and shortage of manufactured goods discouraged the peasants from marketing their surpluses; the conscription of as many as fourteen million men had depleted the labor force on the land; and the tendency of the peasants to divide up the land into tiny family parcels had reduced productivity. For these reasons, the Bolsheviks had no realistic grounds for hoping that a sufficient supply of foodstuffs would be available until they could restore production in nonmilitary branches of industry and reestablish trade between the city and the countryside. When its attempt to stir the lowest stratum of the peasants—the *bednota*—against the richer strata failed, the regime turned to forced requisitions of grain, as preceding governments had done.

Second, the severe shortage of most subsistence goods had already upset most regular channels of commerce, stimulating speculation and illicit trade. The new regime placed the distribution of basic goods on a rationing system, by which it could punish its enemies, reward supporters, and maintain control over the work force. Third, it nationalized nearly all manufacturing and instituted short-term command planning to set production targets so as to satisfy its most pressing needs. Finally, the regime sought to place the entire labor force at the immediate service of the central authorities by extending the principle of military mobilization as widely as possible, through labor conscription, restrictions on political and economic rights, and appeals for voluntary sacrifice. These policies were not all introduced at once, but they came to define the most fundamental principles of War Communism.

These points appear in the characterizations of the period provided by most analysts. Peter Wiles, who called the 1918–1921 period that of "naive communism," asserted that it consisted of three basic strands: the total nationalization of production and trade, except in agriculture; the subordination of workers' councils to the trade unions; and the beginning of a planning system by which production orders were issued to enterprises. Throughout, the regime's policies were aimed at maximizing communization and centralization in the economy. Recently the Soviet historian E. G. Gimpel'son presented a slightly more elaborate scheme. Gimpel'son considers the period's distinctive features to have been the reliance upon grain requisitions as a means of forcing peasants to relinquish their products; a pace of nationalization in industry and commerce that was accelerated by the pressures of the civil war, which also forced the regime to nationalize smaller enterprises; tendencies to pay wages in kind and to level wage differentials; the militarization and centralization of administrative authority in the economy; and the mobilization of labor. Gimpel'son argues that the centralization of authority in itself was not a distinctive feature of War Communism, since this was envisioned as an essential form of socialist construction by the Marxists all along. Rather, what gave the period its special character was the forced pace at which the transformation of the economy took place owing to the urgency of war needs.[4]

The Soviet historian David Baevskii also considered War Communism a system composed of interrelated measures: grain requisitions; the government's demands that even medium- and small-scale industries sell to the state rather than to the market; rationing of goods, with its inherent tendency to reduce income disparities; and the mobilization of labor. Like

Gimpel'son, Baevskii considered these measures to have been forced on the regime by the outbreak of civil war in the spring and summer of 1918, so that only with the easing of the military threat did it become possible to return to the mixed forms through which Lenin had initially intended to guide the transition to socialism.[5]

These Soviet interpretations represent the views of post-Stalinist historiography, lines of argument which either formed in the more liberal years of Khrushchev's rule or which had remained discreetly out of view under Stalin. By stressing that Lenin had at first hoped for a more moderate course, in which some compromise with the bourgeoisie was to have played a significant part, these historians could suggest that the Bolsheviks were not ideologically opposed to a gradual and peaceful transition to socialism. They took their cue from Lenin's own call, in the spring of 1921, for a return to the interrupted policies of early 1918 and his dismissal of the intervening excesses as folly incited by the desperation of the time.

This line of interpretation is plausible and appealing, because it emphasizes the pragmatic side of Bolshevik rule. Modern intellectuals might well wish to offer this value a retrospective tribute. But, although it makes attractive politics, it is unsound history. We should recall that an earlier school of Soviet historians looked to War Communism to find prefigurings of the policy directions of the Stalin era. Since Stalin revived many of the practices and goals of War Communism, it was important for Stalinist historiography to demonstrate their Leninist pedigree. The Soviet historian I. A. Gladkov, for example, cited Lenin's call, in the spring of 1918, for placing stress on autarky, intensive industrial development, and the primacy of electrification and heavy industry as evidence that War Communism had undertaken but not completed the most important tasks of building socialism.[6] Characteristic of this older school is its concern with two institutions created in the early period that were glorified anew under Stalin: Gosplan, the state planning agency, and Goelro, the master plan for the electrification of Russia. In short, again for its own political reasons, Stalinist historiography emphasized those features of the period, such as central planning and industrial development, in which continuity could be established between War Communism and Stalin's "revolution from above."

The Hungarian economist Laszlo Szamuely also saw in War Communism a system based on the current ideological conception of socialism. The Bolsheviks had acquired their theoretical understanding of the political economy of socialism from Kautsky and other German Social Democrats, and this was not jettisoned when the Bolsheviks renounced Social Democracy over the war issue. Their early policies in many respects embodied the prewar concept that socialism was a consummation of "organized capitalism." In turn, this final stage in the development of capitalism consisted of the maximum extension of state ownership of the means of production through nationalization; the forced allocation of labor; a high degree of centralization of administration of production and distribution in the economy; egalitarianism in the distribution of goods; and the attempt to place the entire economy on a nonmarket basis so as to eliminate the commodity character of production and exchange. In short, Szamuely's stress on the ideological side of War Communism fully coincided with the view of the more ardent Bolsheviks, such as Lev Kritsman, who himself had helped to shape War Communism and who wrote its most famous retrospective apologetic: "Geroicheskii period Velikoi Russkoi Revoliutsii" (The heroic period of the Great Russian Revolution), which first appeared in 1924. Both Szamuely and Kritsman argued that the Bolsheviks had been guided in their policies above all by an ideological determination to overcome the anarchic capitalist marketplace.[7]

Leaving aside for the moment the argument over whether the war or the leaders' ideological principles exerted the greater influence on the creation of policy in this period, it is reasonable to conclude that the extension and centralization of the state's authority in industry and the mobilization of society form integral parts of a consistent course. Throughout the period, the regime was not only adapting resources for the accomplishment of its policy goals, it was also exercising what power it had to create an administrative apparatus through which it would govern. The regime was taking over the existing framework of state power as well as building up its own newly organized bodies, seeking to reassemble the splintered fragments of political authority from the old state and from society into a responsive and accountable machinery of power. In part, the success of this process of state-building depended on the elimination of political opposition in order to prevent any weakening of the Bolsheviks' control. But the revolutionaries' ambitions went far beyond simply calling a state into existence. Class revolution meant the overturning of capitalist economic relations and their replacement with collective ownership, control, and administration. In order for the Bolsheviks to hold on to power, as Lenin had foreseen, they had to satisfy the workers' expectations and their own promises of a socialist policy. In short, they had to begin building a socialist society.

The construction of socialism, however, confronted the regime with enormous challenges. Eliminating market relations required them to set and enforce targets for industrial output and supply; to organize a new system of managerial and administrative bodies loyal to the regime; to decide the priority of central branch boards as opposed to the local soviets in the regions; to settle the meaning of "workers' control"; to identify a role for trade unions; to fix the course of development for Russia's natural resources. Abolishing capitalist relations among economic producers and consumers meant that all those centers of private economic power which by their individual actions had determined how goods would be produced and exchanged were now, except for the smallest actors, to be administered as a part of the state. To the extent that the marketplace had been an integrating force in Russian society (and the war had gravely weakened the national market), political power would now replace it.

By taking over the administration of all large and medium industry, the Bolsheviks were expanding the state's power into domains from which even the autocracy had kept its distance, and they were doing so at the same time that they had to create the very conditions of statehood. The Bolsheviks scarcely realized the enormity of this enterprise or the limits of their capacity to succeed in it. To be sure, the territory over which they could claim effective control for any extended length of time scarcely began to approach the immense span of the tsarist empire; at times it consisted of no more than thirty-odd provinces in European Russia. However, the war they fought against White Guard forces and foreign contingents, while pressed by isolation and embargo, represented a net drain on their capacity to build administrative institutions. War, as Herodotus put it, may be the father of all, but it exacts a terrible tribute from its progeny.

It may be helpful to suggest a recent parallel. In December 1981, Poland was put under military rule; its Communist party was overshadowed, if not swallowed, by a military Council of National Salvation, which governed both through naked force and through appeals for order and national survival. This extraordinary and provisional arrangement was unique in the experience of communist systems. Neither in the zones of Communist rule during the Chinese civil war nor in Bolshevik Russia did the authority of party leaders give way to the rule of the army. While party and military leaders formed a combined center of authority in these periods, the revolutionary cause was always uppermost and the party represented the interests of that cause. Thus in contrast to the emergency Polish regime, the Bolsheviks strove to construct a civilian and essentially socialist state as the vehicle of their rule, not a provisional military dictatorship. They tried to do so by concentrating vast and immediate power over their administrative agencies in the hands of a few supreme bodies, such as the Council for Workers and Peasants Defense (later called the Council for Labor and Defense), the Supreme Council of the National Economy, and, of course, the Council of

People's Commissars. These bodies sought to build their central-ized power by placing as many of society's resources as possible on a footing of military subordination to the central authorities, a system we call a *mobilization regime*. The Bolsheviks failed to recognize until late in the period that there were limits to the ability of a central government to rule society directly.

To understand Bolshevik policy in this period, therefore, it is necessary to go beyond the old conflict of explanations and to recognize that building socialism entailed two simultaneous processes: the spread of social relations based on cultural norms of solidarity and nonmarket forms of economic ex-change; and the establishment of authoritative political institu-tions through which to make and carry out policy. The princi-pal mechanism by which the Bolsheviks attempted to generate the power to construct socialism was mobilization.

Mobilization is a process by which a central authority subjects the resources of a society to its command. It subordinates the ordinary purposes to which resources such as labor or loyalty are otherwise put to a common and overriding cause. Devotion to this cause takes on a quasi-religious quality, lending values associated with its service a consummatory character.[8] It ex-tends over the society a binding authority, fusing diverse lines of subordination and power into a single solidaristic hierarchy. Paradoxically, however, mobilization systems emphasize the solidarity of the group rather than the distinctions of hierarchi-cal rank.[9] Mobilization erases ordinary safeguards against offi-cial power, but at the same time it tends to make everyone equal, enlisting their willing and autonomous participation in the struggle. It sets aside legal or customary guarantees of those shares of discretionary authority that citizens and institu-tions possess in favor of a single, all-encompassing goal. To the extent that the regime mobilizes society, a generalized authority shared between society and the state tends to subsume any distinctively state power.

For example, during World War II in the United States, the

government, which had been able to slight business interests during the New Deal years, had to defer to business once society was mobilized for war.[10] A more pertinent example is the mobilization of Russian society in World War II, when Stalin was compelled to make concessions to such traditional institutions as the church.

In constrast to the conversion of social resources to the state's purposes through mobilization, state-building requires the delegation of fixed and regular powers to state organs, and this means isolating a sphere of authority identified by a general and exclusive principle of "state-ness" or statehood (in Russian, *gosudarstvennost'*). As chapter three will detail, the state-building process for the Bolshevik regime entailed reintegration of the fragmented centers of government power left by the collapse of the tsarist and Provisional regimes. State power had broken down primarily along two lines of fissure: the class conflict, which had brought about the unstable dualism of soviet and tsarist institutions, and the territorial breakup of the empire, under which national regions as well as local authorities in Russia proper acquired de facto autonomy. The new Bolshevik state required unitary political institutions with fixed powers, possessing exclusive jurisdiction across the territory that the revolutionary regime claimed to control.

For the Bolsheviks, the mobilization of society was more than a temporary expedient required by the civil war. The regime saw in mobilization the means to draw the independent initiative and organizational authority of working-class and industrial bodies into the new state and to place them under its formal authority. Doing so deprived the regime of the support that social institutions outside the state such as independent factory committees, industrial managers, trade unions, educational institutions, professional associations, newspapers, and the like might have given it. In early 1921 the Bolsheviks were forced to abandon the mobilization model when the system they were seeking to establish collapsed, and they demobilized society by restoring market relations. The socialist sector remained weak and entirely dependent on the state. Virtually no socialist institutions, cultural or economic, remained outside the state to sustain it—factory workers' militia, soviets, and communications media had all been absorbed into the state itself. The consequence, therefore, of building a socialist state through societal mobilization was that only through a renewal of mobilization could the state resume the construction of socialism. This method of state-building prevented the Bolsheviks from creating the socialist society to which their doctrine pointed and on which their legitimacy depended.

In short, where revolutionaries seek to mobilize society as a means of building a new state, the result is likely to be self-defeating: either the creation of an autonomous state makes the state the sole source of power and purpose, or the state concedes power to the social institutions which join the cause. Not uncommonly in those countries today where new institutions fail to take enduring form, neither a state nor an overriding cause succeeds in capturing the political resources of the society, and power is splintered among multiple factions and centers.

The Bolsheviks took power lacking a political theory that might have helped them to grasp the functional requirements of the state they intended to found. They were all too willing to assume that the fusion of state and societal authority had already been largely accomplished under prewar state capitalism and in particular through the mobilization of society during the war. Many Bolsheviks were certain that the organizational transformations wrought by imperialism and war in the structure of society would facilitate the transformation of society under a proletarian dictatorship, which only needed to grasp the levers of the centralized and streamlined economic machine that capitalism had bequeathed it.

Confidence in the ability of collectivism and planning to reconstruct society ran strong in the earlier months of the revolution and endured in most quarters of the party until 1921. At the outset many leading Bolsheviks believed that socialism represented all the answers to the problems created by the war's devastation. The young party leader G. I. Lomov (Oppokov) asserted that although socialism in Russia must be built under circumstances of ruin rather than prosperity, Russia's future was bright because of the greater rationality of a planned economy—a prospect he contrasted to the doom awaiting the shattered economies of the capitalist West.[11] Karl Radek flatly declared in May 1918 that only socialism could guarantee recovery from war.[12] In December 1918, after the needs of civil war had grown to overshadow reconstruction, the deputy chairman of the Supreme Economic Council, V. P. Miliutin, called for further socializing measures, "even in the conditions of civil war."[13] In speeches and articles by Miliutin, Bukharin, Larin, Kritsman, and many other economic policymakers, it remained a stock argument, even in the dark years of 1919 and 1920, to claim that the superior techniques of social organization possessed by socialism were the surest means of averting total breakdown.[14]

How then did the party propose to construct socialism? As they rebuilt industrial relations, the Bolsheviks' implicit goal was to embody the unity of the proletarian cause in a structure of political authority that would transmit commands from the supreme organs of the center to all other central and local agencies of Soviet rule, including organs inherited from the old state and institutions that were formerly voluntary. In this model, the authority that enabled the center to exercise power on such a scale ultimately resided in the unified will of the nation, at least in that part of it in whose name the party ruled.

However, the Bolshevik regime was at least as much shaped by the actual mobilization of society during World War I as by the idea of a unitary state. Historically, the model of national mobilization was a distinctively modern contribution made by the world war to politics in our century. The resources of an entire nation-state were brought to bear on the accomplishment of a single transcendent purpose: victory in war. To that end, for the first time in history, governments placed entire national populations on a military footing, claiming that the nation itself was fighting the war. By eliciting the putative consent of the population to active participation in the war effort, governments everywhere raised popular expectations about the rewards of war to an impossibly high pitch. After the war national populations sought to redeem those promises through expanded participation in politics. Some national armies began breaking down in mutiny and disorder. At one time over half the hundred divisions France had fielded refused to conduct offensive operations.[15] In Britain and America campaigns for the expansion of the franchise brought universal adult suffrage almost immediately after the conclusion of hostilities. Farther east in Europe—in Russia, Austria, Germany, Hungary—the demands spilled out into popular insurrection.

Moreover, the war called upon the most advanced techniques for managing large-scale organizations and tested each combatant state's ability to field huge armies, supply them, reinforce them, direct them, coordinate their movements, and arrange in advance for the production and provision of all necessary materiel. More than any war before or since, World War I was conducted by commanders placed at a vast distance from the field of operations, connected to the front by the modern products of the steam age, telegraph lines and railroads.[16] At the same time, sustaining so immense a war machine required public support, and, as the war dragged on far longer than anyone imagined possible, public enthusiasm had to be nurtured and preserved. However, the warring governments had provided for this exigency early in the war by organizing—again on a greater scale than ever before—propaganda campaigns and methods for controlling the flow of information about the war through the mass media to the mass public. Earlier than most social scientists, Harold Lasswell saw in the deliberate manipulation of communications by wartime governments a portent of modern politics, devoting his doctoral thesis to the subject.[17]

The regimentation of society by militarizing the civilian sector and stimulating the masses' enthusiastic participation in the

war effort generated a freedom of action for modern governments that absolute monarchs might have envied. Its effect was
to merge the private power of social organizations, such as
business corporations, churches, and communications media,
with the compulsory and public authority of government. The
distinction between voluntary and compulsory participation became blurred. Ordinary goals of action were deferred or subordinated to the one common goal of victory. Again, Lasswell saw
in such total war a terrible danger that governments would
never be required to commit themselves to any particular set of
war aims, with the result that the carnage might be prolonged
past any reasonable limit.[18] The concentration upon victory affected the system of values throughout the society, giving the
war effort a transcendent character, sanctifying it through a
cult of victory and lending a sacred purpose to the hardships
endured in the course of daily life.

By fostering national unity on such a scale, the combatant
governments centralized their control over the economy, enabling them to plan and oversee production, distribution, supply, transportation, and the allocation of the work force. To
Marxists, the extent of this control, its evident tendency to replace the market relations prevailing under normal capitalism
with planning and in-kind exchange, the conscription and direction of labor on a national scale, the administration of industry by centralized branch boards, were extremely suggestive of
socialism. Some of them employed the term *war socialism* to
refer to these features of the war economy.[19] Others insisted
that the war pushed certain organizational tendencies of capitalism to their ultimate extent, but that the very destructiveness
of the war proved that its economic foundation could not out-
last it. Bukharin, in a dispute with Lenin over the meaning of
the term *state capitalism,* argued that the bureaucratized, op-
pressive leviathan spawned by the war—which he colorfully
described as "the final type of the contemporary imperialist
robber state, an iron organization which envelops the living
body of society in its tenacious, grasping paws"—could have

nothing in common with proletarian socialism. Lenin, however, took a milder view of state capitalism. After all, it performed the great historical service of squeezing out the petty bourgeoisie, which he knew to be the greatest threat to a socialist government in Russia, and it integrated smaller units of production into great national syndicates and trusts. As he put it, "state capitalism is something centralized, calculated, controlled and socialized, and we lack this."[20]

In short, the Bolsheviks saw in the wartime societies of Germany and the other combatants an organizational model of fused and centralized power which might be employed by a proletarian dictatorship for the construction of an entirely new society. Throughout his career, Lenin had insisted that the capture of political power stood as the cardinal goal of the revolutionary movement. Those social institutions that the working class had organized during its preparation for the revolution, such as the soviets, trade unions, factory committees, newspapers, and militias, were to be employed, first of all, as instruments with which to break the power of the old state. After the revolution, the Bolsheviks would make them instruments for the generation of a combined societal-state dictatorship which would eliminate its class enemies and create the economic, cultural, and political environment for socialism. Under such a theory it was easy for the Bolsheviks to mistake the unity of the state they sought to construct for the imputed solidarity of the social interest which ultimately was the source of its power; to confuse, as had the French Revolution before, *le pouvoir constitué* for *le pouvoir constituant*.[21] Further, the war fostered the illusion that the unity of the armed camp merely reflected the uniformity of society's interests. The existing theory of socialist construction, however, in denying any need for a "public space" *outside* the state in which political interests might be articulated and satisfied, blinded them to the possibility that officialdom would acquire an interest in preserving its status and power which it would satisfy at the expense of all other social claims.

The Bolsheviks took power poorly equipped to resolve the central theoretical issue of their revolution: what should be the relationship of the organized working class to the institutions of the state? Under proletarian dictatorship, the interests of the laborers were supreme, but the laborers themselves were subordinate to the state managers in whose collective person they were said to be represented. Mobilization deprived their organizations of any power but that which was exercised on behalf of the state, although it was impolitic to point this fact out too bluntly. Most Bolsheviks recognized that the state could not assume all responsibility for protecting the working class's interests. Eventually all the working-class organizations that had formed before the revolution were absorbed either into the trade unions or the state, but the trade unions retained a certain independence while they exercised practical administrative functions for the state, such as personnel recruitment, social welfare, and the enforcement of discipline. All the same, the logic of the mobilization regime required that their small area of political autonomy be eliminated and that they be merged into the state. Efforts to carry this principle into practice did provoke, as we know, heated controversy in the late months of the War Communism period. The trade unions enjoyed scarcely more than the right to petition the authorities for material benefits, but they kept it at the price of acknowledging that political control over the means of production was vested securely in the state rather than in society. The reintegration of social and political authority occurred, not through the reabsorption by society of its own alienated power, as Marx had envisioned, but by the reverse process: the absorption of society by the state.[22]

The extension of state power into industrial administration posed inevitably political questions.[23] The forms of administration had to be decided: To what extent would the members of each enterprise's labor force be able to determine the conditions of their work, their wages, and the targets of production? How much power would subnational levels of government have over the economies of their jurisdiction? What mixture of worker and specialist representatives should make up the boards managing industry at each level? Who would plan new construction? Issues such as these strained the regime's ability to make and carry out decisions from the center. One answer was to turn to experts. The Bolsheviks maintained a surprisingly strong faith in scientific reason, unshaken by the bloodletting of the war which had so disillusioned Western intellectuals about the promise of technical progress. The Bolsheviks carried rationalism in politics to fantastic lengths. They assumed that technology was neutral toward particular interests much as the state was; ends could be deduced from science, while reason, married to power, could accomplish marvels thought impossible under the tsars. Many within the party were ready to give scientific and technical elites substantial amounts of power and status in the new order in return for their cooperation with the state in planning grand development projects.

The urge to ground political choice in something other than politics, whether technology, or, in the popular term, "life itself," to escape the burdensome obligation to choose among alternative courses of action, recurred throughout the early period. At the same time, the Bolsheviks accepted as an inheritance from the autocracy a sense of responsibility for state-directed social modernization. They cultivated an ideology of technological modernism which linked the accumulation of national power to the liberation of society's resources from underdevelopment. Lenin, in particular, translated the older socialist ideals of justice and equality into formulas of collective power through industrial progress. Industrialism provided the mechanistic images of Lenin's vision of society: a society grown into the state, a state in which, to be sure, power was itself shared with the masses and social choice was disaggregated into millions of discrete but automatic responses.[24] Soviet democracy would be based on the participation of the masses in discussing policy, in carrying it out, and in selecting leaders. But no chaos would be tolerated. Total unity of will and clockworklike coordination would be required.[25]

Neither solidarity nor freedom was the inspiration of this concept of socialism. Socialist rationalism reached its height in the application of knowledge to power, power to develop backward Russia, to transform the peasant hinterland (what Trotsky called the "muzhik periphery") and enlighten the dark masses, and to bring the advances of modern large-scale machine technology to every town and village. If in March 1918 Lenin posed as the "Chief Task of Our Days" the requirement to learn from the Germans not only discipline and organization, but also the technology of modern industry, by 1921 he described the importance of electrification as follows:

1. Contemporary technology.
2. Restoration of productive forces. Their increase.
3. Centralization-maximum.
4. Communism = Soviet Power + electrification.
5. General and unitary plan: centralization of the attention and strength of the people.
6. A rise in culture (of the laborers).
7. Not simple literacy.[26]

For all the emphasis on democratic participation, then, Lenin twice notes here that this modernizing socialist state demanded maximum centralization of power. Absorbing proletarian civil society into the state for the purpose of building the state had the unintended effect, however, of leaving the state without a social base—"hanging in the air," to cite the ancient Byzantine image which Bukharin translated into a picture of the nemesis of Soviet rule.[27] As a result, the bureaucracy of the party and the state became the equivalent of a social class, monopolizing control over the allocation of resources through its access to political power.

State-building through social mobilization had two principal sets of consequences. Within the garrison of state power, over-centralization prevented party leaders from maintaining centralized control over the chaotic sprawl of official agencies. As the overlapping bureaucratic organs of Soviet rule fought vigorously for their independence from oversight, whether from above or from below, the regime became progressively less capable of responding to progressively greater crises. The second set of effects took place in society: as the regime stripped away the working class's political autonomy, groups of workers organized countermobilizations in protest. Working-class opposition, combining economic and political demands, became so widespread in February and March of 1921 that the regime was forced to relax its grip over society. Far less dramatic but equally important was another change in society, the shift of a large part of production and exchange to a sphere outside the state's command, where private, small-scale organization was the rule. From the perspective of party rulers, this was the domain of the ineradicable petty bourgeois, who lived, as Lenin once put it, in the souls of a great part of the working class. For all that the regime sought to suppress it, this sphere came to provide the bulk of production and trade on which not only peasants and many workers, but also many state agencies, depended for their subsistence.

Thus the mobilization regime created a particular kind of "dual society." One society was the walled fortress of state power, with its official doctrine and its bureaucratic solidarity; the other was the "little world" outside the state made up of individualized endeavor and reward, of small-scale production and trade, of hermetic pockets of unauthorized culture. Over the decades of Soviet rule, the more that the regime has sought to realize its early dream of a fused and centralized authority stretching across state and society, the greater the bifurcation between the realm in which the state held sway and that of private action. When the regime has moderated its efforts at the mobilization of society, the fundamental diversity of the interests of its bureaucratic organs comes to the fore and defeats the leaders' hopes for coherent policymaking.

It might be argued that to put the case this way is to overstate the influence of theoretical imagination, and to understate the power of circumstances, in determining the choices that the

Bolsheviks made. But, as should become clear, there is ample evidence that the Bolsheviks took quite seriously the aims that we, and they, later called fantastic. Close examination of Bolshevik writings and speeches of this period reveals a strong tendency to rely at critical junctures in the argument upon figurative devices to represent the supposed unity of society and state. In an era when artists and politicians alike believed that all things were being made anew, the party was neither concerned nor able always to discriminate before the fact between fantasy and practical reason. It had been fantasy, Lenin said in one of his summing-up speeches about the period, to have expected to create the foundation of socialism in a rural economy in three years—yet the party had included many such dreamers. And where is the harm? he asked. "How could one begin a socialist revolution in a country like this without fantasists?"[28]

[CHAPTER TWO]

The Factory Committees and Workers' Control

AMONG THE POLITICAL ISSUES over which the new leaders had to reach an accommodation with the working-class organizations that supported Soviet power, none was more delicate than the delineation of the powers of those bodies created by the workers for the monitoring, and sometimes the management, of their enterprises.[1] Through 1917, workers across Russia had created organs of "workers' control" which asserted various rights of oversight. The Bolsheviks came to power upholding the ambiguous principle of workers' control but, as observers at the time commented, there was no clear agreement among workers and party leaders about the meaning of this term. Nevertheless, to honor the principle, the regime had to recognize that self-forming, elective organizations in each workplace were empowered to carry out some form of supervision over the operations of their enterprises. From the standpoint of the leaders' interest in constructing a workable state administration, the need to regularize the function of workers' control required that they distinguish the powers of control and of management. At the same time, confronting the issue practically meant that some institutionalized relationship between the new state agencies and the national network of factory committees had to be established.

In a broader sense, the issue of workers' control lies at the heart of the theory of social democracy in industrial society. Socialists have repeatedly debated where the most appropriate site of democratic control over the economy should be located.

Is it sufficient for citizens to direct a socialized economy through their individual choices as consumers and as voters? Or is the most effective control that exercised over each enterprise from within, through participation by the work force in its management? Each viewpoint represents a long-standing position in the history of socialism. On one side stand the centralizers, who hold that the way to progress in modern economies lies through the maximization of central planning and coordination; for them control over the economy can best be exerted through the centralization of political power in the society either in a revolutionary party or through liberal constitutionalism. On the other side stand the advocates of one or another form of self-management or shop-floor democracy. They hold that workers can become just as alienated from the products of their labor under the rule of state socialism as under capitalism and can be as badly exploited, and that without their *direct* participation in the decisions made by the firm, the concept of democracy is hollow. If centralizers claim that each enterprise is merely one particularistic interest, the demands of which must be weighed against all other claims on society's goods, the self-managers regard participatory democracy in the workplace as universally desirable. In our time this controversy has been given force by Yugoslavia's experiments in worker self-management after rejecting the Soviet solution.[2] In the months following the October Revolution, the Bolsheviks established their own answer to this theoretical problem.

Defining workers' control in a way compatible with the construction of a centralized state required the utmost tactical skill on the part of the Bolshevik leadership. The factory committee movement in 1917 had been one of the most important sources of support for the party, and the party had endeavored to draw as close to it as possible without encouraging the impression that the Bolsheviks approved of anarchism or syndicalism. However, the party's penetration of the movement was so complete by the summer of 1917 that some regarded the Bolsheviks as radical decentralizers, an illusion strengthened by some of the utopian passages in Lenin's tract of the same period, *The State and Revolution.*

In actuality, whatever the positions of some local enthusiasts in the committee movement, there are no grounds for supposing that Lenin ever envisioned the proletarian dictatorship in the form of a decentralized self-managing society. For him, the committee movement was a valuable base of political support, a vehicle for asserting proletarian power over private property, and a training ground for future proletarian managers, but not in itself the embryo of a future state administration over industry. This is not to say, of course, that the rapid expansion of party membership in 1917 did not allow many whose orientation was anarchist or syndicalist to enter the party and, particularly after October, to press for a universalist interpretation of workers' control.

A variety of factors explains the particular importance the factory committee movement acquired in 1917. In the exceptionally fluid setting of the revolution, the factory committees were capable of responding instantly to each turn of events, now taking over responsibility for providing fuel and materials, now organizing an armed guard to defend their revolution against a Kornilov. They were organized by no one party and arose spontaneously to fill vacuums of authority. As the soviets in many cities turned their attention primarily to political issues, the factory committees responded to the breakdown of management and supply in industry; in some cities, especially smaller ones, the functions of factory committees were performed by local soviets. In fact, by the time of the October Revolution, nearly half the 123 soviets in Russia were engaged in economic supervision by looking after production, combating speculation, and arranging food deliveries to the cities.[3] The trade unions, slow to take form and define their role, did not compete with the factory committees for power in guiding the daily administration of individual enterprises.

In Petrograd, the concentration of machine-building industries (especially those producing armaments and other war materiel), the massing of radicalized and disciplined workers in a relatively few large enterprises, and the extensive scope of state ownership of industry all gave the factory committee movement immediate access to the centers of industrial and governmental power. The factory committee movement in Petrograd soon led the movement throughout the country, both because Petrograd was the seat of imperial power and because it was a center of defense production. Moreover, because of its distance from the sources of the raw materials and fuel its industries needed, the city suffered particularly from the disruptions in supply caused by the breakdown of the overburdened transportation system. Before the war Petrograd depended on coal, ore, and pig iron from the south; by the time of the February Revolution these supplies were drying up. Petrograd had depended upon imports of machinery and coal as well, but the outbreak of war had shut off nearly all foreign supplies. And, of course, it was afflicted with the severe inflation that cursed Russia during the war and prevented even sharp wage increases from keeping pace with prices. Thus Petrograd was ripe for intense class conflict between private and government owners on the one hand and an organized, revolutionary proletariat on the other.[4]

Factory committees had sprung up in both private and state firms in the spring of 1917, but for somewhat different reasons. Often the workers intervened in management in state-owned plants in order to keep production going despite the collapse of political authority occasioned by the February Revolution. In private firms, intervention seems often to have resulted from class conflict. As wages fell behind prices, workers pressed for higher wages and shorter hours; owners resisted and, in some cases for objective economic reasons and in others in order to break the workers' action, closed the factory doors.[5] The formation of factory committees was a common response to both kinds of problems.[6]

Although in the state's defense plants the committees worked from the beginning to coordinate their efforts to maintain production, while in private industries the committees continued to press for material gains, the available evidence does not suggest any conflict between the two types of committees. Their common interests in seeing to the supply of fuel, raw materials, and production orders; in protecting workers against the hostile state bureaucracy and manufacturers' associations; and in forming a common organization stretching across the city (and later throughout the entire country) mitigated any differences.

Observers at the time tended to concur that the committees were as often pulled into being by economic necessity as they were pushed by theory.[7] While the Bolsheviks eventually endorsed the slogan, "workers' control," which was the general banner of the movement, Solomon Schwartz (then a Menshevik active in trade union work) was probably correct in recalling that workers' control as understood in the factories and as used in Bolshevik resolutions "were two different things."[8] Broadly speaking, *after* October, when the party finally fixed a standard definition, the Bolsheviks intended control to contribute to the establishment of the proletarian state by weakening the power of capitalists and enabling the central authorities to take over industry. But *before* October, workers' committees in Petrograd, Khar'kov, the Urals, and other industrial centers where workers actively intervened in managing production took Bolshevik support for the slogan as encouragement to take over their enterprises and even to declare them nationalized.

Judging the factory committee movement tactically, Lenin found cause for concern that the workers, by assuming responsibility for the administration of production, transport, procurement, and the like, would lose their revolutionary temper. At the same time he approved of the spontaneous initative shown by many soviets and factory committees. The draft resolution he presented at the party's April Conference in 1917 reflects this ambivalence. Out in the localities, it stated, the workers can advance the revolution by direct means, by intervention into the economic crisis. The center, however, should build up its forces for the final political struggle. Characteristically, the resolution distinguished the quotidian efforts of the local committees from the decisive work of the center. Lenin praised the educational and experimental value of the interventions into management, but he refused to endorse explicitly the notion that workers' control *meant* intervention. When a delegate asked him, toward the end of the conference, whether control meant state-centered or enterprise-centered power, Lenin answered that the question had not yet been settled and allowed that "living practice" would determine the answer.[9]

At the time of the April Conference, the Bolsheviks had not officially accepted workers' control as a slogan. Shortly afterward, the Menshevik minister of labor acknowledged the right of factory committees to exercise certain kinds of oversight in their factories and laid out their legal powers to do so. In mid-May Lenin explicitly called for soviets, parties, and factory committees to exercise workers' control over production and distribution.[10] Two weeks later the party's representatives repeated the slogan at a conference of factory committees. It is hard to escape the conclusion that it was the party's political needs which dictated this change in its position. Indeed, in 1918, the Left Bolshevik N. Osinskii explicitly acknowledged that "workers' control" had been a weapon against the Mensheviks' demand for "state control."[11] Similarly, we should recall that after the July days, when the leaders of the Petrograd Soviet had turned to the right and the Bolsheviks withdrew their support for the demand "all power to the soviets," Lenin suggested that the party should concentrate its attention on the factory committees and make them, rather than the soviets, the organs of the uprising.[12] Soon afterward, of course, the Bolsheviks gained a majority position in the soviets in the wake of the Kornilov affair, and the slogan "all power to the soviets" was revived.

At the Sixth Party Congress (26 July–3 August 1917), V. P. Miliutin offered the main report on the economic situation. Workers' control, he asserted, was the means of combating economic breakdown: where it existed, it was already producing improvements. Workers' control gave the workers an opportunity to move directly into regulation and management of industry. In its first stage it referred to the oversight of production and the prevention of closings. Later it would become more direct supervision of production, and finally it would come to refer to the provision of raw materials and fuel. If it were necessary, he concluded, workers' control bodies could even run an entire branch of industry.[13]

Miliutin's conciliatory report was attacked from both sides. One group, the centralizers, disputed Miliutin's positive assessment of workers' control, considering the slogan to be out of tune with the times. Instead, they argued, the proletariat must first take power and *then* organize the regulation and management of production.[14] The most prominent spokesmen for this position were intellectuals: Osinskii, Sergeev, and Savel'ev. The other view belonged to working-class Bolsheviks active in the factory committee movement, such as N. A. Skrypnik, who argued that the factory committees, which stood closer to production than soviets, parties, and trade unions, should be named first among the bodies called upon to exercise control; his amendment to this effect was defeated. He also proposed that the party explicitly state its opposition to making the factory committees into technical organs for raising productivity, but Miliutin claimed that the point was not germane (it was introduced as an amendment to a resolution calling for general labor conscription) and it was dropped. A further motion to drop the labor conscription point altogether was also defeated.[15]

The final resolution offered a formula on workers' control which reappeared in Bolshevik resolutions at subsequent factory committee conferences through the summer and fall. It affirmed the utility of workers' control and called for developing it, by "gradual measures," into the state-wide regulation of production under proletarian rule.[16] For the party leadership, the unstated implicit premise of the resolution was that as the scope of control expanded, its powers would be taken over by state administrative bodies.

Once the Kornilov affair gave the Bolsheviks their first intimations that power was coming within reach, official party representatives dealing with the subject of workers' control began to allow cautionary notes to sound more audibly. They now warned against the danger from the anarchists, who called—"prematurely"—for the transfer of the factories to the workers.[17] At the All-Russian Factory Committee Congress, opening in Petrograd on 17 October, Miliutin again reported on the issue of workers' control. He now stressed the need for close ties between the factory committees and the Soviet state, since control was to be exercised on a state-wide scale. Using a phrase oddly consonant with the condemned Menshevik slogan, he called for "state workers' control." This, he said, would give the workers "hegemony" over industry while allowing local initiative "only up to a certain point."[18] The haziness of these ideas reveals Miliutin's desire to downplay the shift in the Bolshevik position toward a greater emphasis on centralism and statism.

Another reporter for the Bolsheviks at the same conference, M. Larin, took a much bolder stand against the decentralizing interpretation of workers' control. Larin, whose real name was Lur'e, possessed a passionate and impatient imagination. In poor health, lame, he worked indefatigably throughout the War Communism period in a variety of capacities, always pressing for the most radical centralizing measures in the face of enormous obstacles. In his enthusiasm for revolutionary socialism he was capable of outrageous arbitrariness of action and utterly unrealistic assessments of the regime's prospects. He irritated and he amused, but never grew discouraged. Together with Lev Kritsman, with whom he collaborated in a number of organizational initiatives, he worked tirelessly to create socialism out of the ruined economy the Bolsheviks inherited. It was his good fortune to die in 1932, before the terror destroyed most of his colleagues of the War Communism era, including Kritsman; he was buried with honor at the Kremlin wall.

Larin stood for uncompromising centralism. He entered the lists over workers' control in order, at first, to make workers' control seem a natural and compatible partner of central economic planning. Later, when this position was no longer tenable, he offered less charitable opinions about workers' control. But at the All-Russian Factory Committee Congress, he claimed that planning was the very heart of workers' control. Planning was to be carried out by a Supreme Economic Council (this was a month before such a body was officially conceived), and workers' organs of what he called "self-management" would carry out the plan in the enterprises. One might compare his attempt to reconcile these two institutions with the similar efforts in Yugoslavia some thirty-three years later to combine workers' councils with command planning. Larin defined control now as the duty to ensure that work went according to the central plan.[19]

The factory committee leader V. Ia. Chubar' objected to Larin's novel but prescient theses on the grounds that they relegated the committees to a bureaucratic and subordinate role: they would become no more than *tolkachi* (expediters), would lose their autonomy, and be cut off from the working masses. Skrypnik proposed amending Larin's point that workers' control was to serve the interests of the whole nation by stating instead that it was a task of workers only. In his reply, Larin defended his belief that workers' control must be linked to planning and state industrial administration, which must indeed serve the *whole* society. The factory committee, for example, had no right to sequester a factory. In the brief span of his remarks, he refered favorably to the German Kriegswirtschaftsrat (Military Economic Council) and its associated system of factory councils no fewer than three times. On the basis of his report, the congress passed a resolution reflecting these new points: workers' control expressed workers' democracy; it represented the workers' initiative in production; it preserved the normal flow of work and thus served society; and it was to ensure workers' self-discipline and to raise productivity.[20]

Larin's resolution accurately spelled out the logic of the Leninist model of centralized authority linking the formerly separate domains of state and society. But his point of view diverged in crucial respects from the position that was gradually coming to be articulated by working-class Bolsheviks in the factory committee movement. The underlying issue was whether civic, that is, nonstate, organizations had any right to an independent existence and to power derived from the voluntary wills of their members. The instructions on workers' control issued by the Petrograd Central Council of Factory Committees in November, after the Bolshevik seizure of power, indicated a different conception of the relations between workers' control bodies and the state from that of Larin or Lenin. This document envisioned that public control (*obschchestvennyi kontrol'*) would replace the existing forms of management and administration and asserted that "control must be regarded as a *transition stage* in organizing the entire economic life of the country on a social footing [*na sotsial'nykh nachalakh*], as the first necessary step in that direction, taken from below and in parallel with the work of the central economic organs above."[21]

As we shall see, the ways in which the Bolshevik leaders sought to organize control did not differ greatly in detail from the model proposed by the factory committee leaders. But the two conceptions pointed in opposite directons. Lenin, Larin, and other Bolshevik leaders regarded control as a function for the state, one that initially enabled the soviets to seize power from the propertied classes and then constituted a form of power exercised in conjunction with planning and management. Organs of workers' control would be subordinate and accountable to state bodies.[22] But the factory committee leaders understood control as a power exercised by the new proletarian society, through which workers gained genuine responsibility, not merely "experience." This was something other than syndicalism, for which the committees had picked up a certain notoriety. It was a different solution to the dilemma of social reconstruction from Lenin's, and one close to that toward which the party's own Democratic Left groped in the successive waves of discontent in 1918, 1919, and 1920; the Democratic Left, however, was always careful to oppose autonomy for factory committees after the initial excesses that workers' control had provoked. Only late and with considerable qualification did the Workers' Opposition of 1920–1921 return to the notion of control from below as an antidote to the overcentralization of the regime.

What justification did the committee movement have in seeking to become the core of the new regime's administrative apparatus? In the course of 1917 it had acquired extensive political and administrative experience. By October the factory committee movement had become an organized force of major proportions. In fifty cities the committees had formed city-wide organizations.[23] It had acquired a good deal of experience in coordinating production and supply, and reached into most of the larger enterprises of the large cities. Despite the fact that it came around to Bolshevik positions in the spring and summer, it was able to collaborate with the Provisional Government to keep the factories operating. A government ruling on 23 April recognized the committees as bargaining agents for the workers and did not dispute the resolution accepting the committees which the Petrograd Soviet had adopted on 10 March.[24]

For a time, the tendency of the committees to claim broader powers had not upset this arrangement. In fact, the committees cooperated with the government in several areas to cope with the econome crisis. In July the government established regional supply councils and later a Central Supply Council. It also formed regional conferences on defense (known as factory conferences), half of whose members came from the revolutionary "democracy"—the soviets, the trade unions, and the factory committees. The other half was drawn from the owners. This half-and-half system of representation, anathema to the Bolsheviks, was advanced by the Mensheviks in conjunction with their program of "state control": organs regulating the economy would comprise in equal numbers the "franchised" population (*tsenzovye* elements, or the representatives of public organizations and propertied classes) and the "democracy." The factory committees' participation in these bodies continued into September and October and was greatest in the "regional metal supply conference," formed 14 July, where the workers obtained a majority of the seats.[25]

Cooperation between the government and the factory committee movement began to give way to conflict in the summer, as the factory committees increasingly accepted the Bolshevik political program and confronted owners over basic property rights. Owners stiffened their resistance to the committees. In August the All-Russian Conference of Entrepreneurial Organizations declared that interference by factory committees in management was intolerable.[26] All over Russia, owners' associations joined with the Petrograd and Moscow manufacturers' associations in refusing to permit interference with management. On 22 August the Special Conference on Defense announced that it would withhold orders from enterprises where workers interfered with production; governmental bodies such as the Chief Military Commissariat joined the industrialists by threatening to place their orders with more tractable provincial factories.[27]

The owners increased their pressure on the Provisional Government to take legal steps against the committees. On 22 August the League of United Industry met with the Menshevik minister of labor, Skobelev, and demanded that the government prohibit committees from interfering with hiring and firing and from meeting on company time. The committees would be allowed to represent the workers of a given enterprise, but only the trade union could speak for a region, and soviets were to have no jurisdiction at all over factory matters. On the following day Skobelev duly issued an instruction to this effect, following it with a supplementary instruction five days later. The factory committees quickly denounced these instructions as further evidence that the socialist members of the government had sold out to the bourgeoisie. Both the Petrograd and Moscow city organizations of factory committees condemned the Skobelev circulars, and one hundred thousand Moscow leather workers went out on strike.[28] Soon after this, the threat of a coup by General Kornilov, bringing with it the Bolshevik tide that eventually swept the party to power, reinforced the autonomy and radicalism of the factory committees. When the crisis erupted, the committees actively participated in organizing the defenses of Petrograd, sending men to dig trenches and cooperating with the garrison.[29]

As the movement grew in strength, it integrated its network of city-wide councils and then united these into an all-Russian organization. Factory committees in given districts formed district councils, and city organizations were created from these. By the beginning of October, Petrograd had twelve district councils, tied to the corresponding district soviet and Bolshevik organizations, and these in turn supported the Petrograd Central Council of Factory Committees.[30] The Central Council created its own specialized commissions for the particular functions it performed: accounting, resolving conflicts, and preparing for the demobilization of industry.[31]

With the intensification of class conflict in the summer, the Central Council was called upon to intervene in regulation and management; correspondingly, disputes over purely material issues declined in number. Factory committees engaged in supervising production, overseeing the flow and storage of materials, preventing sabotage, supervising layoffs, auditing books, controlling procurements and sales, and firing uncooperative administrators. The Central Council itself was inundated with requests for assistance that it often could not provide. Short of manpower and expertise, constantly lacking material resources, it later reported that it had nonetheless conscientiously attempted to investigate every complaint and adjudicate every dispute brought to it.[32]

Moreover, it attempted to begin planning for the coming conversion of the economy to peacetime production. This issue affected Petrograd acutely, as the great metal and machine-building plants had been turned to producing war materiel. The goals of the demobilization were twofold: to avoid massive unemployment when war orders ceased, and to resume production of agricultural machinery. The Central Council had a section for organizing the supply of farm implements to the countryside. As the city's already critical food supply further dwindled, this section sent out an appeal to all factory committees to begin making agricultural equipment out of old scrap metal and broken machines. Some limited efforts along these lines had begun by October.[33]

By autumn, the Central Council had developed an extensive organization, with links to the Ministry of Labor, the Petrograd soviet organizations, and several public and state bodies concerned with supply. It had ten commissions and departments handling such matters as liaison with factory committees in other cities and its own district councils, the supply of raw materials and fuel, the settlement of factory disputes, the organization of production, and planning for demobilizaton.[34] It was not always effective in overcoming the chaos of the industrial economy, but it compensated for the absence of governmental and public authority capable of doing so. In 1922 A. L. Lozovskii, a trade-union leader who had consistently opposed the committee movement, wrote that at the time of the October Revolution, the Central Council of Factory Committees was actually running the industry of Petrograd.[35]

Probably the most important achievement of the factory committee movement was to strengthen the workers' confidence that they could take responsibility for running industry. Through the movement, working-class activists rose to positions of leadership; many factory committee leaders became senior state officials under the Bolshevik regime. The factory committees contributed substantially to the triumph of the Bolshevik party by strengthening the political awareness and morale of the working class at the same time they gave it a durable and flexible organization. Securely Bolshevik in its political affiliation, the movement nevertheless revealed over and again that its vision of industrial administration in a proletarian state was democratic. At the brief All-Russian Congress of Factory Committees, held on the eve of the Bolshevik uprising and dissolved abruptly by it before its deliberations were finished, the delegates passed a resolution once again formulating this ideal. The All-Russian Center elected at the congress would serve as the department regulating the entire economy although it would do so while serving *under* the Central Trade-Union Council. This curious and contradictory compromise between trade-union claims to supremacy at the state-wide level and factory committee desires for a unified state administration based on factory-level bodies never was realized. Nor did the resolution succeed in subordinating the factory committee movement to the trade unions, since the Bolshevik group rekindled the movement's aspirations to become the primary vehicle for state-wide industrial administration. The Petrograd Central Council, in fact, rather than the all-Russian center hastily formed at the congress, continued to serve as a de facto national center of the control movement thanks to its experience and prestige and to the general uncertainty about the future of control that the revolution engendered.[36]

The factory committee movement had penetrated industry throughout Russia to an impressive degree. By October, the factory committees were nearly as ubiquitous as the soviets. The 1918 survey of industry showed that at the time of the October Revolution, 22.5 percent of all factories, and 68.7 percent of all factories employing over two hundred workers, had factory committees. The survey discovered that the more modern and specialized the firm, the earlier its committee had formed. The survey also found that nearly two-thirds of the committees, and 79 percent of those in enterprises of over two hundred workers, were taking an active part in management.[37] Since it was so common for the committees to broaden their earlier activities from examining the books and checking the decisions of management into the direct management of the

enterprises themselves, there were strong pressures "from below"—sometimes anarchist or syndicalist in origin, but probably more often inspired by the revolutionary temper of the
times—for the committees to run each enterprise without regard for those outside the gates. However, the leadership of
the committee movement opposed such parochialism and held
to its model of a single pyramidal organization of administrative organs, in which workers' control would be but one of
several functions.

On three occasions in the first months of Soviet power, the
committee leaders sought to bring their model into being. At
each point the party leadership overruled them. The result was
to vest both managerial *and* control powers in organs of the
state which were subordinate to the central authorities, and
formed by them.

The first of these occasions came on the day after the October uprising, when the leaders of the Petrograd Central
Council of Factory Committees called on Lenin at Smolny to
propose a scheme for overseeing industry through a system of
factory committee organizations. They proposed the creation
of a Supreme Economic Council whose membership would be
proletarian. Workers would enjoy a majority in the organizations under this council, and factory committees rather than
trade unions were to be the main vehicle of power. Aware that
workers' control could no longer serve as a sufficient definition
of the powers of factory workers, they sought a role for the
committees which was compatible with the larger project of
building socialism.[38] Their proposed Supreme Economic Council would coordinate four areas of work: workers' control, management, the distribution of consumer goods, and general economic policy.[39]

Lenin was very interested in their proposal and asked many
questions about it. He particularly liked the name they proposed to give the new body. But when the Central Council
leaders asked that their plan be published as a decree, Lenin
merely laughed, promising instead to send a party leader to

help rewrite their scheme, with its crude circles and arrows, in the form of a proper decree.[40]

Lenin did not in fact have this proposal recast as a decree, either on workers' control or on general economic regulation. Where the proposal sought to integrate the functions of control and administration, Lenin separated them. Where the proposal would have based the new organs of industrial regulation on the factory committees and their network of councils, Lenin effectively deprived the factory committee movement of its raison d'être by creating brand new hierarchies, answerable to the government, for workers' control and industrial administration. This process occurred in the months between the October uprising and early 1918, when the committee movement largely dissolved itself into the trade unions and the state's new bodies, and although it did not pass entirely unnoticed, it provoked no protest.

To understand how the dissolution of the committee movement happened, we must remember that the October Revolution released fragmenting forces of every kind throughout Russia. Not only working-class grievances, but also local interests exploded into revolutionary action. Workers' groups and local authorities interpreted "workers' control" as a signal to take over their factories.[41] Workers voiced slogans such as "the Urals to the Uraltsy" and "the Volga to the Volgari."[42] In places, the takeovers degenerated into blind plunder.[43] The industrial survey of 1918 confirms the impression of a widespread and spontaneous movement of local seizures. Between November 1917 and March 1918, 836 enterprises were nationalized; three-quarters of the orders of expropriation emanated from local organs such as factory committees, trade unions, local soviets, and local economic councils. Only 5 percent were nationalized by the center—by the Council of Commissars or the Supreme Economic Council.[44] Alarmed by the dissipation of order, the party and trade unions searched for ways to restrain it without alienating the workers. From the outset of the revolution, the leadership had to reverse the decentralizing definition commonly attached to workers' control and reconcile the existing control bodies with the new state structures it hoped to establish.

Among party leaders, therefore, it was understood that although the new supreme economic organ had to enjoy the workers' support to succeed, it could not be a creature of any of the competing interests which had staked claims in the field of industrial policy. Lenin commissioned three young party intellectuals, Osinskii, Smirnov, and Savel'ev, to prepare a draft decree creating a new supreme council.[45] Although their conception of the task was hazy, they grasped that the factory committees could not be the form taken by state economic administration, and they therefore rejected the proposal offered by the Central Council of Factory Committees. Instead, they decided to base the new organization upon the inherited organs of the Provisional Government in order to be able to build on a going concern. These bodies had been virtually ineffectual, however, and the further blow of the employees' strike after October meant that all the new Supreme Economic Council took over was some furniture.[46]

Prevented from turning the apparatus of factory committees into the basis for the new Supreme Economic Council (SEC), the factory committee leaders next attempted to shape the decree formally defining workers' control which the Bolshevik government issued soon after taking power. At about the same time that he charged his party colleagues with organizing a state economic council, Lenin attended a large meeting of workers' representatives to discuss the future of workers' control. Both factory committee and trade-union delegates were present. Draft bills were proposed by Lenin, by Larin, by the Petrograd Central Council of Factory Committees, and by the Metalworkers' Trade Union.[47] Discussion centered on the two antithetical proposals offered by Larin and by the factory committees. In a sense, they served to neutralize each other. Larin's draft would have restricted both the functional authority and the organizational scope of control, while that of the factory committees sought to form a state regulatory organ relying on the committees.[48]

Lenin took an intermediate position. In this controversy, as in the trade-union dispute of 1920–1921, he allowed the provocative stand of a colleague with whom he substantially agreed to draw the fire of working-class spokesmen seeking to preserve some measure of autonomy from the state. Here his Trotsky was Larin. Striking a pragmatic note, Lenin observed that the mass of seizures that had already occurred could not be ignored, and he cited the positive value of workers' control in fighting bourgeois sabotage.[49] However, Lenin's draft was silent on certain basic points: what was the relationship of management to control at the national level, and what were the powers of control bodies in the factories over management?[50]

The trade unions' draft was defeated, as was Larin's. The factory committees withdrew their proposal in favor of Lenin's, which then became the basis for the final draft. The trade unions and the Commissariat of Labor proposed certain changes, such as the creation of an All-Russian Council on Workers' Control. While seeming to bow in the direction of the idea advanced by the factory committees, that there be some state-wide body overseeing the enterprise control bodies, this provision in fact deflected the issue by leaving the very real Central Council of Factory Committees with no official function, while creating a supervening state body with unspecified powers ostensibly to coordinate control. The new All-Russian Council never took actual form and became, in effect, a sounding board for Larin, the archopponent of workers' control. A short time later, it was absorbed into the Supreme Economic Council.[51]

The promulgation of the decree on 16 November 1917 did not resolve the outstanding questions about the scope of workers' control. Although it called for a national hierarchy of enterprise, local, and state councils of workers' control, these did not, for the most part, materialize. Moreover, the uncertainty about the meaning of workers' control led to a proliferation of competing "official" clarifications. Numerous local committees and soviets justified their attempts to break out of the restrictive fetters of capitalism by reference to the decree, and it became the basis for many retrospective analyses of early Bolshevik policy as being decentralizing and even syndicalist in intent.[52]

Yet, as we have seen, Lenin and his colleagues had certainly not wished to encourage disorderly assertions of local factory interests. Larin insisted that the decree was directed *against* localism and separatism.[53] The decree, in actuality, was the regime's acknowledgment of a *fait accompli,* of the fact that, as Miliutin put it in urging the adoption of the decree, "life has outpaced the decree and in fact workers' control is being realized in a great many localities."[54]

At this point various official commentaries on the decree began to appear. A bewildering interpretation appeared in a *Pravda* editorial on 19 November. Bearing strong suggestions of Larin's casuistical style, it sought to give workers' control two contradictory definitions simultaneously. Control, it observed, could mean either active or passive oversight. In the active sense it meant domination (*gospodstvo*). And this was the sense intended now. But of course, the article added, lower organs of control only controlled in the passive sense; clearly they could not regulate, since *general* plans must issue from the center.[55]

With incoherent commentaries such as this for a guide, it is scarcely surprising that local committees continued to interpret control according to their own lights. A conference of factory committee organizations in Petrograd held in mid-November, just at the time the decree was adopted, heard a report on the decree by Zhivotov. He explained that it allowed the workers "free creativity" in overseeing production, served as a "school" for training future worker managers, and formed part of the overall state apparatus, specifically responsible for fighting bourgeois speculation and sabotage.[56] The textile workers' union in Moscow informed its members that, thanks to the decree, they were now the organizers of production by right and could take an active role in regulation.[57]

Now a competition developed between trade unions and local soviet economic councils over rights of control; in effect, the issue was whether the factory committees would be placed under trade-union or state auspices. From the trade unions' perspective, the factory committee movement had outlived its historical usefulness. It was senseless and even harmful for committees to continue taking over managerial functions, and the parallelism of factory committee and trade-union organizations at the city and national level had to be eliminated. Likewise some soviets attempted to make the factory commmittees into executive organs of the soviets with the responsibility of overseeing production and raising worker productivity.[58]

Gradually two main lines of interpretation emerged. One took the "broad" view of control, seeing control as a charter for planning and managerial functions. For example, the Urals provincial conference of factory committees, meeting in early December, assigned sweeping responsibilities to workers' control bodies in developing the Urals minerals industries and planning for the demobilization of industry.[59] The other view gave control a "narrow" definition, usually concerned with auditing an enterprise's books, maintaining the flow of production, and upholding labor discipline.[60]

The attempt by the Petrograd Central Council of Factory Committees to set its own stamp upon the controversy over the meaning of control represented the third and last of its attempts to put industrial administration upon the democratic basis of workers' control. Shortly after the adoption of the workers' control decree, the Central Council worked out its own set of guidelines on control. In them it explicitly contrasted the broad and narrow views of the term: in its narrow sense it referred to inspection and verification (*reviziia*) of the correctness of managerial decisions, while in the broad sense it meant intervention into management itself. The council chose the latter sense, interpreting the current tasks of workers' control as consisting in the organization of production, the amalgamation of smaller enterprises, and the coordination of production across branches nationally. The essential conditions of the full exercise of workers' control, therefore, included the complete nationalization of industry, the horizontal integration of branches into syndicates, and universal labor conscription.[61]

In mid-January 1918 the Central Council issued a new set of guidelines for factory committees in response to instructions, apparently official, emanating from the largely dormant All-Russian Workers' Control Council. These latter rules had placed committees under trade unions and restricted them to overseeing the fulfillment of production norms laid down from above. Consistent with its earlier position, the Petrograd Central Council claimed that committees could interfere with managerial orders if these conflicted with the vital interests of the firm. Not a state body, the Central Council lacked the authority to annul the competing guidelines. Accordingly, it sent a delegation to meet with Lenin. They later recalled that Lenin gave them "fatherly advice" to the effect that the workers should base their action not on law but on life, and that "life soon showed" how correct Lenin's pragmatic approach was.[62]

At that point the debate ended. Neither set of guidelines was endorsed by Lenin or Sovnarkom (Council of People's Commissars). "Life," however, did indeed decide the issue, choosing the narrow view of control, perhaps by invoking party discipline sometime between mid- and late January. After January, the factory committees no longer claimed that workers' control was an autonomous power of society.

Workers' control had been the principal rationale for the factory committee movement. When it was given a merely technical role, while state-wide administration was situated in the new Supreme Economic Council, the factory committee movement lost its right to an independent existence. Responsibility for control in the enterprises—verifying and auditing accounts, raising productivity, and maintaining discipline—now passed to the trade unions. The various committees and commissions elected by the workers came under trade-union auspices. The power of control over the state itself—auditing books of state agencies, approving government budgets, supervising all administrative organs—fell prey to an internecine contest among a variety of organizations, including the trade unions, the SEC, and the inherited State Control Commissariat.[63] Ultimately, the State Control Commissariat emerged the victor in this struggle.

Over a period of several months in the early part of 1918, the Central Council on Factory Committees dissolved and reformed under the regional state economic council, while the factory committees themselves merged into the trade unions. On 22 January the sixth and last Factory Committee Conference of Petrograd convened jointly with the trade-union organization of the city and decided to merge the factory committees with the trade unions by making each committee the cell of the industrial union representing the firm's workers. What were called the "active" functions of control, that is, management, were said to fall under state jurisdiction. The Petrograd Soviet approved the conference's decision the next month.[64] For a time the Central Council went on with its coordinating and advisory activities until the metalworkers, whose representatives made up two-thirds of the Central Council's members, pulled out.[65] Then the Central Council dissolved itself as an independent organization, and, at the end of March, joined the new Northern Economic Council (the regional branch of the SEC responsible for Petrograd and its environs) as a department for control.[66] The Central Council played a major role in founding this body. Its district councils were formed from those of the factory committees and the trade unions, and it recruited several leaders from the Petrograd Central Council of Factory Committees to serve on its board.[67] Although Viacheslav Molotov, then a twenty-eight-year-old party organizer with a technical education but no experience in industrial administration, was named chairman, several other members of the presidium had served on the Central Council: V. A. Ivanov, a worker, became deputy chairman; Artur Kaktyn' became secretary; and N. I. Derbyshev, an old revolutionary and a machinist by trade, joined as well.[68] In June this new council took over the publication of the organ of the Central Council, *Novyi put'* (The new path) and continued to publish it under the same name.

Many observers at the time commented that the rapid and painless disappearance of the Central Council of Factory Committees suggested that the entire organization had been a Bolshevik contrivance from the start. However, this is refuted both by the clear evidence of the committee leaders' pressure within the party for greater power and by the continuing manifestations of localized factory loyalties. In the Urals and elsewhere, the spirit of regional or enterprise autonomy still frustrated state power.[69] As late as August 1919, a national conference of metalworkers resolved that a certain "duality" existed between factory committees and management. In some cases, workers' demands for "passive" control powers, such as access to the books and to board meetings, were denied by the government as a "misunderstanding" of state policy.[70]

By degrees the government made it clear the neither localism nor factory autonomy was tolerable. Although it never succeeded in fully bridging the gap between state-centered and public forms of control, by the spring of 1921, the organs of state control had reached an accommodation with the trade unions over the powers proper to each. The state had eliminated any grounds for interpreting "workers' control" as a charter for entering the sphere of managerial prerogatives, which belonged to the state. What remained were opportunities for workers, through enterprise bodies, to serve as auxiliaries in carrying out the state's directives, and as individuals to rise in the state administrative bureaucracy.

Through the factory committee movement, the organized working class had built a substantial network of democratic institutions with an autonomous claim to social authority. The new regime largely succeeded in making workers' control a function of the state but it did so by marking off the sphere of the state's powers from that in which a voluntary and democratic principle of social organization could operate. What I shall examine next is the formation of the new organs of state administration and management of industry. The primary issue here was not the mobilization of public and voluntary institutions into a binding system of state authority, but the regime's capacity to create an apparatus for running nationalized industry.

CHAPTER THREE

Organizing Industrial Administration

AS THE BOLSHEVIK GOVERNMENT set about to create an administrative system to integrate the inherited public and governmental bodies overseeing production and supply, it was faced with the task of rebuilding authority across two lines of cleavage. It had to resolve the conflict between workers and employers at the same time that it reintegrated the territories belonging to the old empire. In both respects, the fragmentation of production and exchange had to be brought to an end, if not by the restoration of a national market, then by means of hierarchical authority.

In the last chapter I discussed the breakdown of private and governmental authority in industry through 1917 and the class revolt that led the factory committees to intervene in management. The fracturing of the territorial unity of the empire was scarcely less profound. A number of regions in which non-Russian ethnic groups predominated, including the Ukraine, declared their independence of the Russian center. Various regions of Great Russia itself formed autonomous governments, such as the Siberian Republic or the Southeastern Union. The disintegration of the empire proceeded so rapidly that Richard Pipes was led to conclude that "at the beginning of 1918 Russia, as a political concept, had ceased to exist."[1] But in rebuilding a centralized state, the new leaders found that local and regional Soviet governments soon began to compete for power with the new central bureaucracies organized along branch lines.

No blueprint guided the Bolshevik leaders in devising the new system. The ideas they followed consisted either of generalized images of an ideal system or of improvised responses to particular dilemmas. In the first instance the Bolsheviks brought to bear a conviction that only socialism could solve the current crisis of social disintegration; as we saw, they envisioned socialism as a perfectly centralized state supplemented by the solidarity of the working masses, a hierarchy the units of which lacked any particularistic self-interest.[2]

Otherwise their ideas consisted of the ad hoc proposals that various comrades would make, generally about the need for an organization *created* to perform one or another job. The establishment of new organs thus tended to be casual, with the result that the number of nominally authoritative state bodies grew by leaps and bounds. These competed for favor and recognition and many fell by the wayside. As we shall see later in more detail, the apparatus became cumbersome and anything but centralized as a consequence of this system of "ad hoc-ery."

To be sure, certain principles were recognized to be essential features of a socialist organization of society. At the party's Sixth Congress (July–August 1917), the economic platform called for the compulsory combination of industries into syndicates and trusts.[3] Nationalization of industry was another such point, although the leaders themselves were divided on how rapidly they should press to expropriate private capital. As Lenin explained to the First Congress of Economic Councils in May 1918, before seizing power the party had not known what the forms or the pace of the transformation would be; it was only clear that private owners would eventually be expropriated.[4]

The necessity of general labor conscription in order to rebuild the economy was a third point that had been established well before October. As we shall see in the next chapter, a call for a universal obligation to labor was embodied in several early decrees of the regime. In general, even if the regime lacked a clear understanding of the steps that would lead to socialism, the fact of proletarian rule encouraged many to be-

lieve that the socialist transformation would occur in the immediate future. V. P. Miliutin cited Kautsky himself as stating that
"once the proletariat takes power, the result of that must already be in itself socialism."[5]

The principal element in the Bolshevik vision of socialism
was the centralization of political control. Centralized authority
would be required to direct and coordinate the system of state
organs and to regulate private as well as nationalized enterprises. No one sympathetic to Bolshevik rule expressed any
support for the restoration of market relations, even among
socialist producers. The concept of "market socialism" would
have been utterly incomprehensible to the Bolsheviks, as it
would have been to their opponents. Very likely the factory
committee movement, had its vision of a worker-based and
democratically formed administration been realized, would
soon have come to grips with the issue of how goods in a
self-managed economy would be allocated. Perhaps it might
have accepted some mixture of central planning and marketplace principles. In the event, the issue was academic. Russian
economic thought, both radical and academic, assumed that
state direction of the economy was an indispensable condition
of rational social development.[6]

As a practical matter the center exercised effective control
only over the two capital cities and their environs in the first
months of revolution. From the beginning, nevertheless, the
leaders labored to centralize economic control through branch
rather than territorial organs. The center's burden could have
been lightened, and its ability to direct the economy improved,
had it been willing to permit local Soviet governments to coordinate the local activities of central organs. But until early in
1920 local organs were enjoined from adjudicating the competing claims of branch agencies on local resources. Officials both
at the central and local levels often attributed the resulting
tension between center and locality to an insufficiency of coordination at the center. In response to the center's continuing
inability to exercise effective control, many local officials called

for the deconcentration of authority to local soviets. The demand for reform grew stronger as the competition among state hierarchies over a dwindling supply of resources became more acute.

In the first section of this chapter I examine the nationalization of industry. In the second, I trace the demand by local governments for a greater measure of autonomy from the center and the regime's partial retreat from full centralism at the end of 1919. The third section touches on the economic aspects of the reunification with Great Russia in the socialist "federation" of those land that came under Soviet rule during the civil war.

1 : Nationalization and Central Control

During the first months of the revolution Lenin, at least, did not doubt that socialism was practicable. In posing the question "Will the Bolsheviks Retain Power?" (1 October 1917), Lenin wrote that capitalism had so simplified the functions of accounting and control that any literate person could execute them; the proletarian state would make all workers accountants.[7] Evidently Lenin had been influenced by a series of articles Larin had written during the war on the subject of German state capitalism, because shortly after the October uprising, Lenin asked Larin to examine for the Bolsheviks the same questions he had studied in the German war economy.[8] Larin had painted an exaggerated portrait of the centralized organization of German industry, its workers' councils and labor conscription, seeing in them nascent features of socialism. Lenin shared with Larin and many other Bolshevik leaders the assumption that a centralized economic organization could be realized in Russia simply by taking over and converting the administrative system created by the war.

At least initially, attaining central control over industrial organization was of greater importance to the leaders than establishing state ownership of all the means of production. The nationalization of banking and of the large trusts and syndicates was considered an essential immediate step, but the regime did not intend to squeeze out all capitalists at one stroke. Although Lenin did seriously entertain the idea of nationalizing all stock companies in a proposal that he urged upon the Supreme Economic Council in mid-December 1917, he seems to have turned away from it early in 1918, embracing the concept of "state capitalism" instead.[9] While his meaning was never entirely clear, we may take "state capitalism" to refer to a provisional compromise with capitalism in order to consolidate production in a few large firms over which the state would exercise general supervision.[10]

To be sure, by 1914, several major branches of Russian industry had reached a high degree of concentration, a tendency that the war initially intensified. Soviet writers have pointed out that the syndicates in metallurgy, copper, oil, and coal even before the war controlled approximately 80 percent, 90 percent, 50 percent, and 75 percent, respectively, of the market in their fields.[11] The outbreak of war stimulated state control over certain necessities such as fuel, where the government attempted to enforce the priority of defense by imposing mandatory fulfillment of defense-related orders, militarization of labor, centralized distribution, and later a state monopoly over all production. However, the weak basis for such highly centralized administration was soon revealed when neither the autocracy nor the public boards overseeing basic industries could prevent private profiteering and severe disorganization.[12] By the later stages of the war it was not concentration but a breakdown in the coordination of production, transportation, and supply that resulted, revealing the helplessness of the autocracy in the face of powerful private interests and organizational bottlenecks. After Russia's military reverses in April 1915, the government's inability to provide needed supplies to the army and the defense industries led to successful public demands for a "mobilization of industry," which was led by liberal industrialists and politicians. Lenin's belief that the syndicates were the levers of economic power thus ignored the dominant realities of the war period: the weakness of intrabranch integration, the failure of the state's regulatory efforts, and the emergence of new public, nongovernmental authorities that regulated markets.

Moreover, Lenin's view of the wartime economy failed to take into account the fact that in much of Russia capitalism had scarcely penetrated the surface of the economy. The war's catastrophic impact on Russia owed much to the inability of its weakly developed capitalist institutions to bear the heavy burdens of military supply. The country was peculiarly vulnerable to the disruptions caused by war because of its imbalanced mixture of highly specialized and concentrated industrial complexes, weak domestic market, and primitive agriculture. Dependent on imports of industrial capital and expertise, Russia was ill prepared to substitute native capital when its principal foreign suppliers were lost.[13] Russia's economy displayed the inadaptability of a system so tightly fitted to special environmental conditions that it lacks flexibility in the face of radical environmental change.

Nevertheless, the Bolsheviks believed that these were the calamities which befell a capitalist world system in its death throes and that, accordingly, only socialism could extricate society from them. "For the first time in the modern history of civilized nations," Lenin wrote, governing the state "deals preeminently with economics rather than with politics."[14] A logical contradiction underlay this premise. Either capitalism had paved the way for socialism or not; if not, then socialism required an enormous amount of preparatory organizational work before it could be realized, suggesting the need for a lengthy period of coexistence with bourgeois and other classes which opposed proletarian dictatorship. If it had, then the transition to socialism should be smooth and straightforward. Although all the evidence weighed against them, the Bolsheviks were initially inclined to assume that the task of carrying out the socialist transformation posed no major difficulties.

For example, the leaders recognized that as they disengaged

Russia from the war and prepared to convert the economy to peacetime production, the demobilization and redirection of industry had to be planned. The government failed to organize the conversion, however. Demobilization proceeded spontaneously, in such chaos that it left industry seriously weakened when remobilization for civil war became necessary in the summer and fall of 1918. In the Obukhov and Putilov works of Petrograd, shops equipped for military production were broken up, destroyed, or sold off.[15] Nonetheless, Lenin considered a plan for demobilization a matter of simple technical calculation. At a 27 November 1917 meeting of the Council of Commissars, he proposed assigning the job of devising a general demobilization plan to a few engineers. The same sense of offhandedness pervades the notes he jotted down at the same meeting about socializing the economy: he proposed the creation of a special commission to work out measures for the nationalizaton of the banks and the syndicalization of industry. In mid-December Lenin suggested that a commission of technicians (*praktiki*) be formed to collect and distribute peacetime orders to reopen closed factories. In this labor, Lenin urged that they be guided by "the general economic plan of the Supreme Economic Council," although not the faintest outline of such a plan yet existed.[16] At Lenin's urging, the government did create a "commission of technicians" whose job it was to find and distribute orders to factories. However, what little order in the demobilization did exist owed less to this commission, of which the literature provides no further mention, than to the factory committee plans which were prepared even before October.[17]

Centralized control over complex organizations requires a stream of accurate and appropriate information about the performance of the organization and the state of its environment. The Bolshevik leaders possessed only fragmentary information about the state of industry at the time of the revolution. They compensated for their lack of knowledge in various ways. One was to issue open appeals for information—requesting, for example, that all factories which had resumed manufacture of agricultural equipment to notify the government thereof, so that it could organize distribution to the villages. Another means of compensating lay in promulgating unenforceable orders; for example, in early December the government urged all workers to begin turning out civilian goods at full speed until a general plan of demobilization was issued.[18]

Since there was no plan or mechanism for disaggregating general goals into specific production targets for individual enterprises, coordination was achieved haphazardly by direct bargaining between particular producers and consumers. Factories sent out delegations to commissariats and other potential buyers to seek orders and, if possible, advances. One celebrated instance of this practice occurred when the workers at the Obukhov plant in Petrograd sent two engineers out to secure an order and an advance from the government. They returned in triumph with an order for ten thousand tractors. Since tractors had never been produced in Russia before, the project had immense symbolic value as the revolution's first attempt to bring the machine age to the Russian peasant. But the order was conditional: further advances were contingent on Obukhov's success in turning out at least one prototype by August 1918. If successful, Obukhov was promised a state monopoly on tractor production; otherwise, the order would be canceled. When the two engineers announced the proposition at a general meeting of the factory, another engineer objected that Obukhov possessed neither the fuel nor the finances to fill the order. But the workers overruled him and gladly accepted the challenge. When word about the deal got out, it occasioned much criticism of Obukhov for collecting orders it could not fill. Other factories noted that Obukhov had simultaneously contracted with another government agency to perform capital repairs on locomotives, although it lacked shops, equipment, parts, and expertise for the job.[19]

The government was initially in the position of being unable to restrain the spontaneous wave of seizures of factories by the workers. It had to recognize the legal validity of local acts of expropriation while making it clear that all nationalized enterprises were to be guided by central plans. The absence of any central planning or coordination of production meant, however, that the workers' committees in the expropriated industries determined themselves what they would produce. Later, when the government had consolidated its control over local soviets and workers' organizations, it slowed the pace of nationalization and called instead for state capitalism, emphasizing the need for labor discipline. The sweeping nationalization decree of 28 June 1918, effectively declaring all stock companies to be state property, was prompted not by any ideological motives, but rather by the fact that Russian owners of private firms were evading government control by transferring formal title to German interests who by the provisions of the peace treaty were exempt from expropriation. In the main, then, the regime's attitude toward nationalization was tactical, being dictated by its assessment of how best to build centralized control over industry.

In some cases the central authorities declared firms nationalized simply in order to prevent their closing. There was little coordination at this stage. A variety of central bodies issued such orders, starting with the Military-Revolutionary Committee, the command post of the Bolshevik seizure of power. As the first center of civil authority in the revolution, the MRC was drawn into such tasks as requisitioning food from the provinces, distributing scarce goods, settling strikes, paying workers, and confiscating factories.[20] After the formation of the Council of Commissars, Lenin signed a huge number of nationalization orders on its authority. Likewise, once it was established, the Supreme Economic Council, as well as several of its organs acting independently, also claimed the right to nationalize.

The great majority of the first acts of nationalization were initiated, however, by workers' groups immediately involved in industry: factory committees, trade unions, and local soviets. In a large number of cases, the action was prompted by a desire to keep the factories open by calling upon the political resources of the proletarian revolution. Between November and March, of the eight-hundred-odd enterprises taken over from private owners (formally through nationalization, confiscation, or sequestration—although in actuality these legal distinctions bore no practical significance), the Council of Commissars and the Supreme Economic Council together had accounted for only 5 percent.[21] A case typical of the time was the nationalization of the Petrograd Electro-Technical and Machine Factory, where in late November the workers wrote the district soviet that the owner had fled, leaving the plant without funds or administrative staff, and explained that the factory committee had been forced to assume managerial responsibility. In turn the district soviet sought advice from the Central Council of Factory Committees, which provisionally acknowledged the factory committee as legal manager.[22] In 17 percent of the nationalizations, factory committees themselves seized the plants. Of these, over two-thirds involved enterprises employing fewer than fifty persons. By contrast, of the enterprises that the center nationalized, nearly two-thirds employed over one thousand persons.[23]

This finding points to a persistent pattern in the scope of state control. The central authorities controlled the large-scale units of organization. But their hope that the economy would be integrated through a relatively small number of national branch organizations proved idle. The center could not penetrate the smaller corners of economic activity. To a large extent this gap reproduced the old disjunction between town and countryside. Most of the expropriated enterprises were located in rural areas; they were small plants processing primary products such as wood, food, and leather.[24] As will become evident, many such enterprises failed to enter the channels of state direction for the entire 1917–1921 period.

In fact, the center, preoccupied with the consolidation of control over the larger firms, did not grasp the full extent of nationalization. Throughout 1918, the SEC's figures on the size of the state-owned sector greatly understated the number of expropriated enterprises. At a plenary session of the SEC in September 1918, SEC Chairman A. I. Rykov reported that approximately eight hundred enterprises were known to have been nationalized and another two hundred or so were presumed to be nationalized but were not registered as such. In fact, well over two thousand enterprises had been taken over by this time.[25] At the end of 1918, the SEC's figures erred by an order of magnitude of nearly three.[26] The discrepancy, of course, is explained by the large number of local takeovers of crafts and other small industries, about which the center's information was sketchy at best. The extent of the center's ignorance may be judged from the fact that in December 1918 Rykov expressed the hope that the state would be in a position to nationalize and run small industries by the following summer.[27] Only by the end of 1919 did the center realize how many small industries had already been seized locally when the SEC presidium heard a report that many local economic councils were running small industries without having registered the acts of nationalization. Upon hearing the report, the presidium voted to defer further nationalization of small enterprises on the grounds that the center was incapable of running them any better than they were being run already.[28]

Frequently the soviets, trade unions, factory committees, and local economic councils which initiated the early nationalization acts turned to the center for post facto approval.[29] Their petitions placed the leaders in a difficult position. Centralization was impossible without ratifying local actions, since the center had no other means of bringing industry under Soviet rule. On the other hand, local nationalization placed immediate control in the hands of various bodies that the center could not effectively oversee. Lenin recognized that, as Lomov put it, the will of the workers could not be resisted. But, Lomov recalled, as Lenin signed the sheafs of nationalization orders brought to him, he invariably sighed that it was easier to nationalize than to run the enterprises.[30] Given the latent divergence between local interests and central power, it was inevitable that efforts by the center to exert its power more effectively would provoke resistance from local authorities.[31]

While the central leaders continued to urge workers to defeat the power of the bourgeoisie, they gradually began to emphasize more pointedly that nationalization must keep pace with the capacity of the center to supply enterprises with resources. In January 1918 the Council of Commissars directed that all acts of nationalization be approved by the Supreme Economic Council, and in February it decreed that only the SEC and the Council of Commissars were empowered to declare an enterprise nationalized.[32]

In January, Lenin still defended the local takeovers. At the Third Soviet Congress, commenting on the ease of the seizures of banks and factories, he stated that he repeatedly advised workers who sought his advice on the disposition of seized property to take all they needed but to keep production going: " 'You'll make mistakes but you'll learn.' "[33] In March, however, after the factory committee movement had been dissolved, Bolshevik leaders took a new tack. Lenin announced that management must catch up with conquest; now socialism required labor discipline, accountancy, and centralized control more than it needed new expropriations.[34] Miliutin proposed a system of labor conscription to discipline and organize workers. Reporting on government policy at a plenary meeting of the Economic Council of the Northern Region in May, Molotov stated that small-scale production units, although predominant in Russia, ill suited socialism. He followed Lenin's lead in stressing state capitalism, Taylor methods, piece rates, and the employment of specialists. In April the SEC reminded the localities that any improperly nationalized enterprise would cease to receive appropriations.[35]

Since the attempt by the leadership to brake the process of local nationalization has often been understood as a broad shift in policy, it is important to clarify two points. First, what Lenin termed the suspension of the early "Red Guard attack on capital" was much more a matter of restraining local control over industry and of asserting central power than it was of compromising with the bourgeoisie. Second, the common impression of a slowdown in the pace of nationalization reflected only the center's lack of knowledge about local events.[36]

The 1918 industrial survey indicates that of 3338 enterprises surveyed, 2502 had been nationalized after March, and only 836 before it (see table 2). These figures show that the number of later acts of nationalization was not increased by the decree of 28 June, which extended the state's formal authority over about eleven hundred previously unnationalized large firms. Since the decree did not by itself change the management of these firms, they did not appear in the survey as nationalized unless the government had also sent out new administrators.[37] The figures do show, however, a substantial increase in the proportion of nationalization acts by the center (i.e., the Council of Commissars or the SEC): from 4.6 percent in November–December and 5.7 percent in January–March to 29.3 percent in April–July.

The formation of the Supreme Economic Council did not improve the leaders' ability to direct production. It was founded with the same casual but ambitious spirit that accompanied so many undertakings of the period. As we saw in the preceding chapter, several days after the October uprising Lenin asked Osinskii, Savel'ev, and V. Smirnov to organize a Supreme Economic Conference, the general outlines of which were familiar from the antecedent organizations of the Provisional Government and the German practice. The first proposal envisioned placing the new body under the Ministry of Industry and incorporating into it existing public and state boards for particular branches of industry.[38] Lenin insisted, however, that the new organ be made independent of and superior to its predecessors and that it be charged with organizing general economic and financial administration for the state. The final decree creating the Supreme Economic Council charged it with working out general production plans for the economy and coordinating the work of local and central or-

Table 2
Expropriations, 1917–1918

Expropriating institution	Nov–Dec 1917		Jan–Mar 1918		Apr–July 1918		July–Aug 1918	
	No.	%	No.	%	No.	%	No.	%
Council of Commissars	10	3.4	18	3.3	250	20.5	178	14.0
SEC	4	1.3	13	2.4	108	8.8	167	13.0
Local soviet	208	69.8	300	55.8	422	34.5	295	23.0
Local sovnarkhoz	24	8.1	66	12.3	308	25.2	463	36.2
Trade union	9	3.0	33	6.1	60	4.9	39	3.0
Other	43	14.4	108	20.1	74	6.1	138	10.8
Total	298	100.0	538	100.0	1222	100.0	1280	100.0

Source: V. Z. Drobizhev, *Glavnyi shtab sotsialisticheskoi promyshlennosti: Ocherki istorii VSNKh, 1917–1932 gg.* (Moscow: Izdatel'stvo Mysl', 1966), p. 100, table 14.

Note: Includes acts of nationalization, sequestration, confiscation, municipalization, and socialization.

gans. On the first of December 1917 the Central Executive Committee of the Soviet approved the draft and on the fifth it was published.[39]

The dilemma that the SEC faced from the start was typical of many nominally supreme Soviet organs. Its comprehensive powers could only be used "on the margin," that is, where other sources of authority had not preempted it. Organizations with independent claims to power frequently ignored it. It was deluged with work of an ad hoc character and devised its structure by trial and error. Demands for fuel and supplies piled up. Factories demanded instructions on demobilization and conversion. Its presidium, Osinskii recalled, scarcely knew what its tasks were, other than to direct the nationalization of industry. Control over nationalization was hard to obtain, however. Although the SEC intended to plan branch-wide nationalizations, it found it was overwhelmed with requests to order the nationalization of individual enterprises.[40] Generally it resorted to the method, for want of a better one, of appointing a commissar to carry out each act of nationalization. These commissars, who worked closely with the Cheka, had almost unlimited powers over both workers and owners, and acted largely on their own discretion. Friction between the SEC and the Cheka about control over the commissars led Osinskii to seek closer liaison with the Commissariat for Internal Affairs in directing spot nationalizations.[41] Thus instead of making policy on general matters, the SEC quickly found that the work it did adapted to the circumstances, consisting primarily of responses to the stream of individual cases that came to it for rulings.[42]

Not all the work of the SEC consisted of decisions about particular cases. Larin headed a department called the Economic Policy Committee. Citing its authority, he personally ruled on numerous major issues. For example, he permitted authorities in the Urals and in Turkestan to issue their own currency, but denied them the right to manage local industry and over their protests forced them to accept bourgeois specialists onto their boards. He personally undertook the organization of planning for several large development projects. Such decision-making led to an inevitable reaction: Osinskii was replaced by the older Rykov as chairman of the SEC in April 1918 and at the same time the SEC issued an order (in effect to Larin) that all decrees published in its name must first be cleared with the SEC presidium. The Economic Policy Committee itself, its wings clipped further by an order of 7 May 1918, survived until finally dissolved on 1 November 1918.[43]

Repeatedly the Council of Commissars urged the SEC to get down to the work of regulating industry. The continuing lack of coordination in economic policy became a recurrent topic at Council of Commissar meetings as the SEC made little progress in overcoming its difficulties. Finally, over the unanimous dissent of the SEC's leaders, the Council of Commissars revised the SEC's mandate in the summer of 1918. In effect, it rendered the SEC's legal status congruent with its actual role by declaring it the equivalent of a commissariat for industry.[44]

There was now no central organ for economic planning and administration.

2 : Glavki *and Local Power*

Contemporary participants and observers frequently blamed much of the disorder in economic administration on a conflict between the two lines of authority running through the SEC apparatus: one organized industry under central boards for each branch or group of products, while the other placed the economy of each territorial jurisdiction under a local economic council (called *sovnarkhoz*) which was overseen both by the corresponding local soviet and by the SEC at the center. Rykov himself, at the September 1918 plenum of the SEC, noted that these two principles of organization were in competition and observed that the First Congress of Regional Economic Councils, meeting the previous spring, had decided that local offices of the branch boards were to be placed under the authority of local economic councils. In practice, however, as Rykov pointed out, the SEC ignored this by sending out specialists to organize management at newly nationalized enterprises.[45] Indeed, through 1918 and 1919 the effective policy of the regime was to grant the branch administrations autonomy with respect to local soviets or economic councils. The branch boards succeeded in expanding their power at the expense of and over the protests of the economic councils in towns and provinces.

The formal creation of the *sovnarkhozy* slightly preceded that of the *glavki,* or chief branch boards for particular industries. In late December 1917, the SEC adopted a decree establishing regional councils for the large areas surrounding the principal industrial centers.[46] These regions included the Urals, the North (around Petrograd), the West (surrounding Smolensk and Minsk), and the Central Industrial Region (around Moscow).[47] These regional councils were to be subordinate both to the policy-setting authority of the SEC and the administrative oversight (*kontrol'*) of their corresponding soviets. They were

empowered to "decide matters of fundamental and general concern for the entire region." Furthermore, on the initiative of
provincial (*guberniia*) soviets, provincial economic councils could
be formed on the same pattern. The decree described that pattern in close detail. Each regional council would be divided into
fourteen branch sections; others could be added according to
local circumstances. Each section was to have four main functional departments. Their subsections were listed. The fourteen
parallel departments would create joint commissions, which
would create permanent executive bureaus.[48] As would often be
the case thereafter, the regime's ability to lay out a theoretically
satisfying organizational blueprint considerably surpassed its
ability to institute working organizations.

By May 1918 there were seven regional (*oblast'*), thirty-eight
provincial (*guberniia*), and sixty-nine district (*uezd*) *sovnarkhozy*.[49]
The powers of these local councils were ill defined. As bodies
under the supervision of the soviets, they were expected to
serve local interests. Formally the soviets were autonomous in
local matters. The Congress of *Sovnarkhozy* in May–June 1918
attempted to straighten out the problem of overlapping jurisdictions between the regional and provincial councils by reaf-
firming the power of regional councils to direct their regional
economies. On the other hand, the congress declared that all
the *sovnarkhozy* were "auxiliary and executive organs of the SEC
in the localities."[50]

Initially the regional councils—particularly the Regional
Council of the North—exercised a considerable degree of discretion to run the regional economy, primarily thanks to the
inability of the center to enforce its will over great distances.
With time, however, the regional councils ceased to be the center
of gravity in economic administration, losing their powers to the
glavki, on the one hand, and to provincial and urban *sovnarkhozy,*
on the other. White Guard successes in the civil war left some
regional councils with little or no territory; in other cases they
were too weak to maintain a grip over their regions. By the time
the second of the *sovnarkhoz* congresses took place, in December

1918, the Southern and Urals councils had ceased to function, and the Volga and Urals organizations were ineffective. The congress decided to dissolve all of these. Two months previously, in late October, the SEC had already disbanded the Moscow Regional Council, on the grounds that it was redundant: the SEC itself had essentially taken over its sphere of decision-making.[51] From the end of 1918 to the end of 1919 the general principle of administrative centralization was pursued to the utmost degree. At the December *sovnarkhoz* congress, Larin declared that regional councils were merely transitional bodies enjoying provisional powers until full centralization was attained.[52] The intense pressure of civil war further strengthened the *glavki* at the expense of the territorial councils.

One reason for the relative weakness of resistance to centralization under the *glavki* lay in the conflict among the *sovnarkhozy* themselves. The provincial councils attacked the regional councils for ignoring provincial needs. Similarly, district councils protested the inadequate interest shown in them at the provincial level. Lower-level organs were required to supply the resources on which the superior organs depended, but in turn had to seek subventions from above to keep their local enterprises open. This problem was especially acute at the district (*uezd*) level.

Frequently district *sovnarkhozy* became general economic departments for their soviets, taking over responsibility for revenue-generating functions. In Viazma, for example, the *sovnarkhoz* not only ran match-producing, leather, flour, butter, and other enterprises, but it also tended the baths in the army barracks, plumbing in houses, and the vegetable garden of the local soviet executive committee; it repaired bridges, inspected school cleanliness, and drew up budget estimates for local repair projects. Others handled the local postal service, housing, labor regulation, and the sale of spirits. Another fiscal technique was the illegal taxation of nationalized enterprises. Judging by the efforts the SEC made to stop this practice, it must have been widespread. The SEC also found it necessary to forbid the taxation of goods over which the state held a monopoly. Since nearly every essential commodity was in short supply and hence subject to a state monopoly, these restrictions seriously hampered the local councils in their search for new taxes.[53] The general shortage of qualified administrative personnel and of material resources made each local council a potential rival to its superordinate councils and to the center.

Often the local councils, in fact, welcomed centralization to the extent that it brought them relief from the demands of higher-standing territorial councils. However, as the center increased its own demands on the localities, tension between center and locality rose. In August 1918 the Commissariat of Internal Affairs reported that "the period of spontaneity and arbitrary self-rule [by the local soviets] of the provinces, districts, and counties [*volosti*] has by now passed. . . . Now the opposite process has begun."[54] The "opposite process" brought with it conflict between the *glavki* and the local councils. During the autumn of 1918 the center repeatedly ordered local organs to refrain from interfering in the management of enterprises under *glavk* jurisdiction. One such order initially complained of "constant interference" by local authorities, wording Lenin tactfully amended to "several cases of interference." Another directive, this one from the Commissariat of Internal Affairs, tartly observed that "the time when it was necessary to control [i.e., referring to the principle of 'workers' control'] the activity of factory enterprises has passed." To force the local councils to submit, the center threatened to cut off critical supplies, such as fuel, financial subsidies, and personnel.[55]

The tensions provoked by the loss of local authority to the *glavki* were exacerbated by the inefficiency of the *glavk* system itself. The proliferation of *glavki* led to overlapping responsibilities, creating conflicts and delays in administration, and often caused them to make conflicting demands on local enterprises and *sovnarkhozy*. Ideally the SEC was to coordinate the activity of these boards, but as their numbers grew, the SEC lost effective control over them. As criticism of the *glavki* mounted, among the public as well as among many leaders both at the center and in the localities, this disorganized system came to be called, derisively, "glavkism" or even "glavkocracy."

In general, *glavki* were formed whenever the center sought complete control over the production and distribution of a particular product or material. Some were created specifically to manage state firms, often on the basis of groups, or *kusty,* which were clusters of parallel enterprises, usually located in the same vicinity. Others were intended to exercise broader supervision over an entire branch, regulating state and private firms alike. Regardless of their initial form, however, their functions were essentially the same. These were extremely broad in scope, encompassing general policy, management, finance, labor regulation, supply, distribution, intrabranch organization, and planning.[56]

The *glavk* form, and some individual *glavki,* was taken over from the industrial boards and committees that had been created before and during the world war. When branch boards were reorganized as *glavki,* the principal change was to allow trade unions the opportunity to add workers to the *glavk* collegium. Such was the case, for example, with the leather board, which was simply the old National Leather Committee, a public regulatory body, on which some representatives of the leather workers' union joined the industrialists who oversaw the industry. Lenin approved of this pattern and singled out the leather industry, along with the textile and sugar industries, as a model of the cooperation between the bourgeoisie and working class that he envisioned under the principle of state capitalism.[57]

One of the standard criticisms of the *glavki,* in fact, touched on this practice of proportional representation by former owners, trade-union leaders, and specialists on the boards. It was often asserted that the *glavki* gave insufficient scope for the working class to assume administrative positions and created too many opportunities for the bourgeoisie to retain power. Although this line of criticism usually originated in local *sov-*

narkhozy, it is evident that the leadership regarded the *glavki* more as a means of centralizing government control over industry than as a means of ensuring workers a majority position in industrial management. In the twenty *glavki* for which figures on social composition as of December 1918 are available, scarcely more than one-third of the staff consisted of workers, while representatives of former state offices comprised 38 percent. Over half of the personnel were drawn from bureaucratic, technical, and entrepreneurial strata. One year later, proportions were roughly similar. Of 232 members of 53 *glavki,* 36 percent were workers, 34 percent were engineers, and 20 percent were former clerks.[58]

Besides being vulnerable to criticism about heavy nonproletarian representation, the *glavki* also came under attack for inefficiency. The textile *glavk,* for example, was unable to distribute the stocks of textiles that had accumulated before the revolution, leaving the trade union to sell off inventory as best it could by opening a retail outlet at a warehouse.[59] The timber industry was run by three individuals who lacked any experience in the field. When the industry was nationalized, merchants sold off their stocks on the black market without paying back the debts to the state that they had incurred before nationalizaton.[60] Resentment of the *glavki* was strongest where local authorities had attained a high level of competence in coordinating local production. They were understandably distressed when orders from central organs disrupted local production plans. Probably the *sovnarkhoz* where such sentiments ran strongest was the Economic Council of the Northern Region. This council had formed directly, as we saw, from the city-wide organization of factory committees and had begun to draw up production programs for Petrograd industry immediately upon its foundation. Control by the party center was assured by the appointment of Viacheslav Molotov, even then the nonpareil apparatchik, as chairman. Yet even Molotov attacked the *glavki* at the Second *Sovnarkhoz* Congress in December 1918 on the grounds that they were less than half proletarian in composition.[61] Nevertheless, throughout 1919, as the economic crisis grew worse and the war emergency sharper, the leadership strengthened the powers of the *glavki* in the interests of centralization.[62]

The SEC presidium created *glavki* with startling informality. A. Gurovich, a "bourgeois specialist" who worked for the SEC in mid-1918, recalled that a *glavk* was created whenever a leader desired it; if someone reported on the need for a particular department, the presidium commissioned that individual to create it and did not inquire to see whether its mandate would conflict with that of another body.[63] By the summer of 1918 the SEC possessed some fifty agencies, of which twenty-six were considered regulatory centers and twenty-four were assorted managerial, functional, and service offices. The actual existence of some of these bodies was doubtful and the lines of responsibility were frequently hazy.[64] As the number of *glavki* and other central organs grew, the problem of coordinating their overlapping activities became insuperable.

The SEC's response was to expand the scope of the power it claimed for its central organs. Not infrequently it drew up plans for developing or reorganizing the economy of a region, either in ignorance, or against the will, of the local authorities. For example, in April 1918 it sponsored a national contest for a plan to reorganize the Urals industries and offered a prize of 100,000 rubles. One interested specialist who sought further details discovered that the SEC had no idea where the needed information might be found: it had no contact with officials in the Urals about the project.[65] As SEC presidium member Lomov put it, the center's plans were "beacons" rather than minutely accurate prescriptions: they would still be valid tomorrow even if they could not be realized today.[66] Most of the rest of the SEC leaders shared his view.

At numerous meetings and in the press the theme of central-local conflict sounded. Representatives of the center complained that local authorities demanded advances but failed to submit accounts of their expenditures, while local spokesmen accused the center of disregarding their needs. Local *sovnar-khozy* were particularly critical of the leather, textile, soap, and paper *glavki,* which were considered the more backward industries. It was no coincidence, critics charged, that these *glavki* were filled with former owners.[67] The issue of center-locality conflict dominated the Second *Sovnarkhoz* Congress, where well over half the delegates attended the sessions of the section on administrative organization. The congress could not resolve the issue, because of the strength of local opposition to the leaders' position on centralism. One may suppose that the deadlock over this issue explains why no *sovnarkhoz* congress was held from December 1918 until early in 1920.[68]

Hypercentralization multiplied the lines of command and accountability, which ultimately reduced central control. A small condensed milk plant, for example, which employed fewer than fifteen workers, became the object of a months-long competition among six organizations: the SEC, the *Sovnarkhoz* of the Northern Region, the Vologda *Sovnarkhoz,* the Petrograd Food Commissariat, the Vologda Food Commissariat and the central *glavk* for milk.[69] This case, which was by no means untypical, demonstrates that authority was dissipated in both "horizontal" conflict among agencies of equivalent rank and "vertical" conflict among nominally superior and subordinate bodies. From the standpoint of such unyielding advocates of centralism as Larin, the resulting disorder was caused by parochialism on the part of local organs, bureaucratic work styles, or bourgeois sabotage. To attacks on "glavkism," he responded adamantly: "We cannot turn back from socialist organization to fragmentation."[70]

Against the centralist mainstream, however, some in the party's upper ranks began as early as mid-1918 to reconceptualize the relationship between central and local interests. One group, taking for its motto the Leninist ideal of "democratic centralism," began to modify the centralist orthodoxy. A principal spokesman for this group was Osinskii, who, after he was replaced by Rykov as chairman of the SEC in April 1918, left

Moscow to organize a *sovnarkhoz* in Khar'kov. At the First *Sovnarkhoz* Congress (May–June 1918), he reported that his six weeks in the provinces had taught him that the center must rely on strong regional and provincial councils, since they were more capable than was the center of managing the nationalized sector.[71] Moscow became a stronghold of the localist viewpoint. T. V. Sapronov, chairman of the Moscow Soviet and a member of the Democratic Centralist group, presided over meetings of the Moscow Soviet and party organizations in late December 1918 which adopted resolutions condemning excessive interference by central organs in their everyday affairs.[72] The following month, at a conference of the Moscow City Party Committee, Osinskii and Sapronov attempted to win support for a decentralizing amendment to the new constitution, but failed to carry the motion.[73]

The Democratic Centralists continued their campaign at the Eighth Party Congress in March 1919. Sapronov stated that it was incorrect to call the system as constituted "centralized" since the parallel hierarchies of branch administrations and *sovnarkhozy* overlapped and conflicted.[74] In December 1919, at the Seventh Soviet Congress, Osinskii reported on his past seven months of work in the localities. Seen from their perspective, he observed, the center was bureaucratized, isolated, ignorant of local needs, and filled with bourgeois specialists. Osinskii groped for a formula to express his image of a better system: "I stand not for a local point of view and not for bureaucratic centralism, but for organized centralism,—I cannot seem to find the actual word just now,—a more balanced centralism."[75] The proposal that Sapronov offered as a solution would have made each *sovnarkhoz* answerable to its corresponding soviet, and the local organs of the *glavki* subordinate to the *sovnarkhozy*. The Eighth Party Conference, held immediately before the Seventh Soviet Congress, adopted such a resolution, excepting only military organs from the control of local soviets.[76]

Perhaps the most interesting theory about center-local relations attempted to justify centralism because it equalized the well-being of different regions; it was a departure from the normal practice of defending the advantages of centralism for rational oversight and planning. It came in a series of articles written in late 1919 in the *Bulletin of the Commissariat of Finance* by the chairman of that commissariat's Taxation Bureau—and the journal's editor—L. Obolenskii.

Obolenskii asserted that to pose the issue as that of the state versus the localities was incorrect. The problem was for the state to balance the needs of each community against those of all the others. He proposed a rule to make a decision in each case. Where the needs of one community exceeded those of all others, they might be satisfied locally, at local expense, but not if to do so would incur cost for the state at large. At the same time, the state was obliged to raise the welfare of each community, step by step, first ensuring that a minimal level of welfare was assured for *all* communities. He recognized that this rule would have to be modified by special local circumstances and in itself offered no immediate program. In another article he pointed out that existing social goods could not be evenly redistributed: some indivisible goods, such as plumbing, brick buildings, hospitals, and schools, were concentrated in some communities but not others. Therefore the best way to eliminate inequalities was to unify all local budgets through the central state budget, so that improvements could be directed where they would alleviate the greatest deprivation. Such unification was only possible if localities ceased to think in the old categories of central *versus* local needs.[77] Interesting as Obolenskii's argument was, there is no evidence that it affected policy in any way. Indeed, it is impressive that the value of interregional equalization counted for so little among the goals of state policy.

The conflict between center and locality grew acute during the latter half of 1918, remained severe through 1919, and then, when the Seventh Soviet Congress at the end of 1919 decided that glavkism had become excessive, began to abate as the powers of the localities were restored. The resolution adopted by the Eighth Party Conference that put the local organs of the *glavki* and other central bodies at the disposal of the local *sovnarkhoz* and made the latter subordinate to the local soviet passed the Seventh Soviet Congress as well.[78] Now the SEC sought to delineate, for the first time, the respective powers of the *glavki* and the *sovnarkhozy*. The approach taken was not to differentiate their functions, but to divide the enterprises themselves into three categories, roughly according to their size and importance. At the Third *Sovnarkhoz* Congress (23–29 January 1920) a proposal to this effect was adopted. The Soviet Central Executive Committee confirmed it in February and the Ninth Party Congress did so again in March.

In the first group were to fall those enterprises whose production bore significance for the entire state; they would continue to be administered directly by the *glavki*. Those in the second category would be managed by the provincial councils but would be obliged to meet organizational and production plans issued by the center. Enterprises in the third group would be considered of purely local significance and would be managed by the *sovnarkhozy* autonomously. When the lists were drawn up, 2370 enterprises entered category one, 3450 category two, and 1084 category three. After the Eighth Soviet Congress, 1829 enterprises (chiefly textile plants) were reassigned from the first to the second and third categories. The figures are slightly misleading in that some of the largest enterprises, such as the Putilov works in Petrograd, did not fall into the first group, thanks to the strength and adroitness of certain local councils.[79]

Throughout 1920 the *glavki* dissolved, and by the end of the year only sixteen remained in existence.[80] As Red victories brought large new territories under Soviet rule, the government established regional authorities to oversee their economies. Trotsky's economic plan, adopted by the Ninth Party Congress in March 1920, called for the creation of new regional centers in the Urals, Siberia, and the Ukraine.[81] In these regions a new unit, called the production bureau, combining branch and regional authority, administered groups of industries concentrated in the given area. In addition, the government attempted to establish provincial stocks of basic resources for use in trade and production, although it placed restrictions on the power of the provincial organs to use them.[82] Unfortunately, virtually no data is available with which to judge the success of these new endeavors. An observer wrote that the new Labor Army-based regional authority failed to take hold in the Urals and that as it declined in influence, the one authority remaining was the party.[83] In any case, these new structures had little time to upset entrenched informal structures before they were themselves overtaken by the New Economic Policy.

3 : Socialist Federalism

The Bolshevik leaders applied the principle of administrative centralism to the question of economic relations among the diverse national regions that were being restored to Russian rule. The standard party position on political reintegration, as expressed in the constitutions of 1918 and 1923, stated that unity through federalism would permit nations to enjoy formal equality within a close-knit proletarian state. What federalism implied for economic ties, however, remained to be spelled out.

The process whereby most of the lands that had been part of the former Russian empire and had been torn from Russian control were rejoined to the Soviet state has been thoroughly discussed by E. H. Carr and Richard Pipes.[84] Rather than summarize this complex tale, I will simply make the point that the ideal of economic union under centralized control was frequently cited by Bolshevik leaders as a reason for the forcible subordination of each new republic to Moscow's rule. Economic centralism was never held to contradict nominal political federalism.

Early on in the revolution, some leaders who believed in economic federalism urged that the Soviet constitution create "a federation of social-economic organizations" rather than "an alliance of territorial governments or states."[85] The idea here was to constitute class, trade-union, and political groups as communes, which would be linked federally with others in province-wide councils; provincial councils would elect regional (*oblast'*) councils, which, in turn, would form the Russian Republic.[86] This rather corporatist concept resembles some features of the current Yugoslav system. Stalin, among others, strongly opposed the proposal for fear that it would weaken the power of the state. As Carr has pointed out, the constitution as adopted formed a nominal federation of the traditional kind, but one which in reality was no federation at all, since no specifically federal organs were created.[87]

Well before the successful campaigns of the Red Army made the issue a real one, Bolsheviks discussed the structure of a socialist economy that would include non-Russian territories. Unity was the note invariably struck. At the First *Sovnarkhoz* Congress, Karl Radek looked ahead to the future of economic relationships among the parts of the old empire that were severed at present. Asserting that the empire had been an economically integrated whole (a united economic organism, in his words), he called upon the Soviet revolution to restore that unity. In a similar vein, Lomov claimed that under the old regime Russia and the Ukraine had "gravitated" toward one another and would therefore form a single entity in the Soviet economy as well.[88] Undoubtedly the leaders' preoccupation with the "natural unity" between Russia and the Ukraine gained force from their recognition that German troops were at that moment themselves gravitating rapidly toward the Ukraine's coal and food reserves.

So long as Germany could prop up the anti-Bolshevik Ukrainian government, these speculations about the future remained academic, although useful as indicators of the Bolshevik approach to economic federalism. After the fall of the German government and the collapse of the Ukrainian Directory, local and Russian Soviet forces quickly moved to establish a Ukrainian Soviet Republic and to link it politically, militarily, and economically with Soviet Russia. Bertram Wolfe argued, on the basis of documents in the Trotsky archive, that military considerations were the primary motivation in this union.[89] Certainly this point is hard to refute. But it is also possible to see in this union, which did serve (as Wolfe noted) as a prototype of the later unions between Russia and other republics, the realizaton of the Bolshevik model of a command economy spanning all the regions ruled by Soviet governments. Among Bolshevik leaders no alternative to such a model had been articulated. Economic considerations were entirely compatible with the aim of military subordination of all Soviet regions in the federal union.

The conviction among most party leaders that socialism had to possess a centrally planned and administered economy helps to explain their indifference toward making any pretence that the nations in the union were equal in power. The Ukraine was to be considered the equivalent of a province (*oblast'*) in the federation; the same formula was hastily reproduced in Belorussia, Latvia, and Lithuania. As pragmatists, the leaders were conscious of the weakness of the political forces in the borderlands separating Bolshevik Russia from Germany and the hostile Allied powers; they knew how vulnerable those areas were to outside pressure and how stark the choice of political alignments was for them. As utopians, the Bolsheviks assumed that the socialist future could only extend the scale of centralized integration. Socialism, as Artur Kaktyn' put it, was the day "when there are no more classes or state, but only one common mankind with a general centralized and maximally simplified regulation of the society's economic processes."[90] Even the democratic wing of the party's Left did not warn against the restoration of Russian national domination through the new Soviet economy. As Lenin recognized shortly before his death, it was easy under such circumstances for socialist doctrine to conceal imperialist aspirations. A writer in the journal published by the Commissariat of Nationalities hinted at this when he claimed that the center viewed federal union through "economic eyes."[91] Zinoviev may scarcely have grasped the implications of his statement in September 1920: "We cannot do without the petroleum of Azerbaijan or the cotton of Turkestan. We take these products which are necessary for us, not as the former exploiters, but as older brothers bearing the torch of civilization."[92]

The decree issued by the Central Executive Committee on 1 June 1919, calling for the creation of a single economic center for the Russian, Belorussian, Latvian, and Lithuanian republics fully corresponded to the longer-range vision of socialism that the leaders possessed, although its immediate rationale was military. Once foreign and White insurgents in these territories succeeded in overturning Soviet rule, the decree was a dead letter. However, the treaty signed between Russia and Azerbaijan in September 1920, which Stalin (as Commissar of Nationalities, the principal architect of Russian domination) considered the model for peacetime relations between Russia and other republics, again provided for Azerbaijan's direct economic subordination to the Russian SEC and commissariats. Subsequent treaties with the Ukraine, Belorussia, and the Autonomous Region of Bashkiria followed the same outlines. The economies of all these areas would be directed by the central plan in respect to production, finance, pricing, and the distribution of goods.[93] In turn these agreements formed the model for the inclusion of other regions into the Soviet Russian Republic and, after 1923, the Soviet Union.

Thus although the leadership had grown aware that there were limits to effective central control and had moved to moderate the excesses of glavkism at the end of 1919, it did not apply the same lessons to relations between the Russian center and the reunited borderlands. Rather, the economy of the socialist state was conceived as a unitary whole, in which the autonomy of any of its parts was, first, restricted to matters of purely local significance, and, second, granted at the pleasure of the central authorities. Far from being federal in structure, power in the new state was delegated hierarchically from the center.

[CHAPTER FOUR]

The Mobilization of Labor

THE TWO PRECEDING CHAPTERS have outlined the formation of organizations with a distinctive and exclusive claim to state power. Much of the authority they posssessed had been generated by the activity of workers organized in factory committees and associated bodies. The incorporation of these institutions into the state's apparatus eliminated the threat that the state might have to compete with society for authority.

Nonetheless, the rules governing the relationship of labor to the new regime remained to be elaborated. On what terms would the trade unions meet the state when the state was the principal employer of the working class? What were the unions' powers to be—could they bargain autonomously on behalf of workers, or were they to be regarded as subordinates in the state hierarchy? The urgency of restoring industrial production went far to blunt the edge of the issue, at least in the immediate term. It did not erupt in full force until the end of the period when the very existence of the trade unions seemed threatened.

In the early months of the revolution, a variety of forms of labor-management relations existed. Some firms, particularly those still owned and run privately, operated on the basis of collective agreements negotiated between the owner and the trade union representing the workers of the enterprise. Such agreements had become common during the period between February and October 1917 and remained in use after the Bolsheviks took power. On 29 June 1918, the Council of Commissars laid down rules governing contracts between workers and employers, whether these were state or private. The trade union would negotiate the agreement on behalf of the workers, but would submit it for the approval of the Commissariat of Labor as well.[1] However, through 1918 collective bargaining fell into desuetude because workers increasingly turned to the Commissariat of Labor directly for help in drawing up their contracts. In other cases, the Commissariat of Labor intervened to restrain the workers' wage demands, particularly when they affected nationalized enterprises. Gradually the commissariat replaced the trade unions in setting wages. This placed the trade unions in the position of assisting the state in enforcing compliance with the terms of the agreement.[2]

By far the most important feature of the emergent system of labor relations was not the loss of collective bargaining but rather the growth of compulsion. By a variety of methods, the regime placed workers on a military footing, depriving them of the right to choose their place of work or to leave their jobs. The significance of labor mobilization lies in the fact that it put each individual worker under the unmediated power of the central authorities. The organizations formed directly by the workers lost, for the most part, their capacity to protect workers from the arbitrary use of power. As a result, the trade unions took over auxiliary functions on behalf of the state, charged with disciplining the workers and distributing social benefits among them. The loss of their autonomy allowed the state to allocate labor as it allocated other resources needed for social development. Had the regime been willing, and had the war emergency been less acute, trade unions might have been allowed broader powers to set wages and conditions of work. However, we must bear in mind that the practice of labor mobilization did not develop solely in response to the civil war, nor did the leadership conceive of it as a measure needed only in the immediate crisis. Although the emergency conditions created by war and economic breakdown provided the immediate impetus for the adoption of labor mobilization, the regime was prone to regard it as a means of building socialism.

Two years after the October uprising Bukharin elaborated the theoretical defense of labor mobilization in his *Economics of the Transition Period:* "But socialism too [i.e., not only capitalism], which grows up out of the ruins, must inevitably begin with the *mobilization of living productive power.* This labor mobilization constitutes the basic moment of socialist primitive accumulation." Bukharin considered labor mobilization the means by which the regime would make a decisive breakthrough to a higher level of technological development in the economy.[3] It was assumed among the Bolshevik leaders that labor conscription, once universalized, democratized, and rationalized, would lay the foundations of the socialist economy.

After 1921, the harshness of the War Communism period tempted many of its architects to claim that the needs of war, not the illusions of socialism, had determined the practices of social regimentation. Some wrote off the dreams of a shortcut to socialism as a feverish afterthought or as the self-deception of the brash younger generation of revolutionaries. To be sure, a good case can be made for explaining many of the more violent practices of the period—and above all the policy of forcible grain requisitions from the peasantry—by the absence of practicable alternatives. Nonetheless, if it had been the war and the international situation alone which had dictated the regime's acts, periods when a subsidence in hostilities brought a measure of relief and allowed the leaders to turn their attention to the needs of long-term reconstruction might be expected to have led them to reconsider social mobilization as a means of building the state. But this did not happen. The justification for mobilization merely shifted from immediate war needs to the ideals of class leveling and economic rationalization.

"The social system in these years was later called 'War Communism'," Victor Serge recalled later. "At the time it was called simply 'Communism,' and any who, like myself, went so far as to consider it purely temporary was looked upon with disdain."[4] Trotsky made the same point.

Military communism was, in essence, the systematic regimentation of consumption in a besieged fortress. It is necessary to acknowledge, however, that in its original conception it pursued broader aims. The Soviet government hoped and strove to develop these methods of regimentation directly into a system of planned economy in distribution as well as producton. In other words, from 'military communism' it hoped gradually, but without destroying the system, to arrive at genuine communism.[5]

In fact, it appears that the war actually spared the regime from suffering some of the consequences of its zeal to mobilize by enabling it to demand further sacrifices from the workers. Frequently, workers' protests against the regime were quieted after a resurgence of White activity by giving the state's agitators compelling arguments for peace on the labor front. Instead of provoking increased coercion and repression, therefore, the war sometimes replaced the overt socialist goals of mobilization with appeals to the workers' patriotism. Moreover, as we shall see in chapter six, the war forced the government to suspend its principles to the extent of acknowledging the superior efficiency of crafts and small industries, when its previous policy had demanded the unification of petty production units under central administration. Again, the war partly hid the consequences of social mobilization as a technique of state-building.[6]

In this chapter I consider three related aspects of labor mobilization. The first is labor conscription; the second, the status of the trade unions; and the third, the suppression of working-class protest. Through mobilization the regime generated an exclusive sphere for state power in which the party leadership possessed a political monopoly. As a means of balancing order with transformation in building socialism, however, mobilization ultimately exhausted the reserves of information, initiative, and support outside the state on which the regime's power depended.

1 : Labor Conscription

Marx had envisioned the victorious proletariat replacing the nominal freedom of the laborer and the idleness of the wealthy with a common obligation of all to work. During the war, the Russian autocracy repeatedly proposed instituting a system of labor conscription, but with little result; after two years of discussions, during which the German system was studied as a model, the Special Conference on Defense won the right to "requisition" labor, but this proved ineffectual.[7]

The Bolsheviks also looked to Germany. Shortly after October, Larin prepared, at Lenin's request, a report on Germany's use of labor conscription which was to guide the Soviet regime in instituting a similar system.[8] Labor conscription, indeed, had been proclaimed a goal of the proletarian revolution by the Sixth Party Congress, in July–August 1917.[9] However, it turned out to be far simpler to proclaim the principle of labor duty than to put a system of conscription in force.

The Bolsheviks embodied a general call for a universal labor duty in the Declaration of the Rights of the Laboring and Exploited People adopted by the Third Soviet Congress in January 1918. The declaration proposed labor conscription in connection with two goals: one, the "destruction of the parasitical strata of society," and the other, the "organization of the economy." The principle obtained constitutional sanction when the Soviet constitution of July 1918 described labor as the obligation of all citizens, warning that "he who laboreth not shall not eat."[10]

Labor conscription was always given a double justification: the principle combined the punitive goal of forcing the propertied classes to labor with the positive aim of economic reconstruction. The slipperiness about the purpose of conscription made it less compelling for the regime to lay out the limits of its use. Only slight adjustment was required to turn conscription into an instrument of political repression. Coerced labor as a punishment for various kinds of offenses eventually became widespread. At the outset, however, the regime intended conscription to level class differences by imposing on all a common duty to perform labor.

Such was the one manifest aim of Lenin's proposal in December 1917 to require the wealthy to carry labor books.[11] His draft of the decree listed the various social and occupational categories to which the obligation applied: all property owners, brokers, corporation officers, notaries, monks and clergy, members of the free professions, teachers, engineers, artists, military officers and cadets, school pupils, and policemen. But when the decree was published, this list was replaced by a provision requiring the labor book of anyone between the ages of eighteen and forty-five not already subject to service in the Red Army; in effect, since military service was required of all young men from the laboring classes, labor conscription covered all others. Still later, in early October 1918, the government required that anyone not performing socially useful work carry a labor book which was to be stamped once a month by his local soviet to certify fulfillment of assigned tasks.[12]

More commonly labor was mobilized for economic purposes. The government called up citizens of all classes both for particular emergencies and for open-ended needs. In December 1917, for example, Petrograd's entire population was called out to help clear streets and railroad tracks of snow.[13] The following April the government announced a general call-up: all workers were required to work, to carry labor books, and to obey labor discipline.[14] This decree did not set in motion any full-fledged system for enforcing conscription, so that we should probably regard it as another urgent appeal for labor discipline characteristic of the "breathing-pause" after the Brest-Litovsk treaty. This phase, March–April 1918, was one in which Lenin took an active hand in attempting to restore order in production and was strongly emphasizing the necessity of iron labor discipline.[15]

Two changes over the course of 1918 put teeth into the calls for conscription. One was the growing shortage of labor in the latter half of the year. Unemployment had been a serious problem as war industries demobilized, but the more that workers fled to the countryside in search of jobs and food and were called up into the Red Army, the more unemployment was replaced with shortages of labor in many branches. The flood of out-migration from the cities left Petrograd with a million fewer inhabitants, Moscow a half million, although this was compensated to some extent by the large number of factory closings.[16] Accordingly, conscription came to be used widely as a normal means of recruiting and binding workers to particularly vital occupations. The second change was the declining availability of food. As food supplies dwindled, the ration card entitling a worker to a set share of food each month became a necessity. In turn it enabled the regime to control the labor force by cutting off the rations of those who violated labor discipline or opposed the regime.

As large-scale unemployment disappeared, the regime turned the labor exchanges, which had helped workers to find jobs, into agencies that located and assigned workers to places of work. In early September 1918 the Council of Commissars prohibited any unemployed person from refusing a job offered by a labor exchange. In November 1918 the exchanges were renamed Departments of the Distribution of the Labor Force, or simply labor departments, and they were placed under centralized control. In Janury 1919 their authority was extended to all workers, whether already employed or not. Soon they became agencies charged with preventing workers from leaving their jobs. The exchanges helped to locate workers trained in particularly valuable specialities, ferreting them out of the villages and reassigning them to new jobs. When the countryside needed extra hands to help bring in the harvest, the labor departments sent out detachments of workers from the cities.[17]

I have argued that the practice of mobilization served two ultimately incompatible ends. One was to place the talents, interests, and organizations of civil society at the disposal of the state. The other was to form out of these resources a new state machinery. The conscription of labor counterposes these two purposes dramatically. Individually, workers with a capacity for leadership were needed to serve as cadres; but in their mass, they were needed as a reliable labor force. When the regime needed trustworthy proletarians to organize contested regions of the front, it called on the diminishing core of brave workers still loyal to the regime, as when, in April 1919, the Petrograd Soviet mobilized three thousand workers to carry out organizational work on the Don. In May several hundred workers were sent to district soviets for administrative work. In July 1919, after she had completed a trip through eastern regions of the country on an agitation steamer, Lenin's wife, Krupskaia, wrote with satisfaction of what she had observed: "Workers from Petrograd, who generally appear to be the most effective exponents of the principles of Soviet rule, are scattered everywhere throughout the soviets."[18]

But the principal use of mobilization was to put workers, as a source of labor power, on a footing of direct and martial subordination to the will of the central authorities. Workers were either conscripted to critical jobs or bound to their places of work. Throughout 1919 the latter form of conscription, called militarization, was extended to widening categories of labor. In March 1919 workers at all naval and marine enterprises were placed on military status. In April 1919 the government prohibited coal miners from leaving their jobs. In July all workers and clerks handling fuel procurement, and later those working specifically in the forestry, coal, peat, oil, paper, and river transportation industries, were similarly militarized.[19] Militarization subjected the workers to a discipline equivalent to that of the Red Army, complementing the forced allocation of workers by means of conscription.

The expansion of militarization reached a peak at the end of 1919, when the State Council on Defense declared that any state institution could be placed on military status: under such circumstances leaving one's job would be treated as desertion.[20] Then, as mobilization of labor reached its apogee, when indeed

the economy resembled a vast military camp, significant improvements in the military outlook permitted the leaders to
turn their attention again to the long-term needs of reconstruction. During this brief phase, which came to be called the "second breathing-pause" by analogy with the lull after the Brest-
Litovsk treaty, the dominant figure was Trotsky. It was he who
tirelessly appealed for continued mobilization, and it was his
program for rebuilding the economy that the Ninth Party Congress adopted in March 1920. Anticipating Stalin's five year
plans, the program outlined four sequential stages of reconstruction and development that would be integrated into a
single master plan. First, transportation had to be restored and
food and other raw materials accumulated. Second, the production of machines for expanding transportation and the ex-
tractive industries would be emphasized. Next would come an
emphasis on machine-building for consumer goods industries,
and finally consumer goods production itself would be stressed.
The program also insisted upon the conscription and militarization of workers and specialists alike. Later, Stalinist historians
blamed him for a reckless ardor in defending militarism, but,
in fact, the party produced no noteworthy alternatives to his
program. Although it clearly made some leaders (such as Rykov) uneasy, Trotsky's program was no more than the logical
elaboration of the same principles of social mobilization that
the regime had pursued from the beginning.[21]

The renewal of concern with matters of civil administration
and social reconstruction brought several simmering issues to
the surface. One was that of "single-person" as opposed to
"collegial" management. In the great majority of state firms,
boards comprising workers, state officials, and technical or
managerial specialists bore collective responsibility for administration. Lenin and Trotsky redoubled their attack on this practice, arguing vigorously for the placement of one person in
charge of each office, possibly being advised by a managerial
board with purely consultative rights. Although Lenin and
Trotsky had advocated single-person management since 1918

(Lenin arguing in December 1918 that responsibility must be clear so that the government knew whom to arrest in case of malfeasance), they now linked it with the other measures they believed necessary to prevent total economic collapse, such as the militarization of labor and the formation of labor armies.[22] Within the party there was substantial opposition to single-person mangement, although those who opposed it, such as the Democratic Centralists and some trade-union leaders, sought less to reject it out of hand than to effect some compromise between the two practices.

The dispute raised the ghosts of older issues. The proper role of the "bourgeois specialists"—often simply called *spetsy*, with a derogatory accent on the second syllable—was one such underlying question. When the journalist Arthur Ransome visited Iaroslavl' with Larin and Radek in March 1920 for a party conference held in preparation for the party congress to be held later that month, he found that the workers at the meeting generally accepted the practices of labor conscription and militarization, on the grounds of clear economic necessity. But they strongly objected to single-person management, since it was understood that the single person would be a bourgeois specialist.[23]

The dispute also brought up the controversies over the rights of workers under workers' control and the role of the trade unions. Some trade-union leaders feared that the end of collegiality would reduce the ability of trade unions to name workers to the administration.[24] The larger context of the issue, therefore, was the whole set of unresolved questions about the political rights of workers in the workers' state.

At the Ninth Party Congress Bukharin dealt with the issue on a theoretical plane. Once one agreed that the Soviet state was a proletarian dictatorship, he argued, there could be no defense of collegiality per se, since there were no antagonistic class interests to be mediated through collegial representation. Lenin spoke in a similar vein, claiming that to defend collegiality on the grounds that it preserved "democracy" was to inflate its virtues ludicrously. Both Lenin and Kamenev sought to dismiss the issue by making it appear trivial when set against the economic crisis at hand.

Such points placed the trade unionists and party leaders who favored the preservation of collegiality at a disadvantage. So long as they were compelled to demonstrate their loyalty to the regime they could not claim any intrinsic theoretical value for collegiality, any more than Bolsheviks two years before could argue that "workers' control" meant decentralized and syndicalist forms of organization. The defense of collegiality drew its support from a widespread if unstated belief that it was legitimate to grant the working class a proportional share of responsibility in running industry. Like the practice of naming roughly equal numbers of workers, specialists, and officials to the *glavk* boards, collegial management expressed an implicit compromise between the priority of the state's claims of authority in industry and the continuing assumption that class democracy demanded some form of institutionalized participation in management by the working class. By reducing the matter to the purely practical level, the Leninist center left the supporters of collegiality no choice but to give in. By December 1920 the number of plants run without collective management rose to 2183 out of 2483, according to offical estimates. At all levels the average size of boards gradually fell.[25]

The main focus of policy in this second breathing-pause was on a new round of large-scale labor mobilization. Civilians were placed under a general conscription authority while several units of the Red Army were given labor assignments and renamed "labor armies." Simultaneous decrees in early February 1920 declared a general mobilization of all citizens and of all inventory "living and dead," and provided that a general census be taken to ascertain exactly what the stock of available resources was. During the remainder of the year the work of counting and conscripting workers, horses, and carts proceeded.[26] Each town, according to Arthur Ransome, had its executive committee for labor conscription, composed of one representative each from the War Commissariat, the Labor Department (i.e., the former labor exchanges), and the local soviet. Each factory had a commission to oversee and protect conscripted labor, comprising representatives of management and the trade union. Ransome found that in the spring of 1920 the state of conscription varied widely from region to region and that various stages of its evolution could be noted.[27]

At the same time the region began to convert standing units of the army, those not immediately engaged in combat, into labor armies. Trotsky was the principal advocate of this measure. The aim was to place these large bodies of disciplined if largely unskilled laborers at work on projects in the civil economy instead of demobilizing them. Soviet writers treat the labor army movement skittishly because of its association with Trotsky, so that it is hard to judge its effectiveness. Critics observed that the armies' productivity was extremely low, while defenders claimed that the work was largely free of cost to the state.[28]

Yet other ways of mobilizing labor were found besides conscription and the formation of labor armies. A method relying, in principle, on the voluntary donation of labor to the common good was the *subbotnik:* the Saturday (and later the Sunday, or *voskresnik*) given over to unpaid labor. This had begun in the spring of 1919 as a movement among party members. By April 1920, 13,000 party members and 16,000 nonmembers took part throughout Russia. May Day 1920 was declared an all-Russian *subbotnik,* and virtually the entire population was called out. The figures for May 1920 reflect this massive new effort: 88,680 party members and a million nonmembers were recorded as participating. By the latter half of the year, *subbotniki* became a regular occurrence. They were sponsored as part of campaigns against epidemics, to repair schools, to harvest crops; special *subbotniki* for women and children were held.[29] One may imagine, without cynicism, how great a loss of revolutionary zeal the routinization of self-sacrifice must have incurred. One must also remember the wild inaccuracy of the statistics which in that day and others were reported to the center.

Frequently, particular acts of mobilization represented attempts by the regime to compensate for the limits on the information and control available to it. As in the first breathing-pause, the range of the center's effective control and knowledge fell far short of that to which it laid claim. The center continued to issue conflicting and overlapping directives that it could not enforce. In January 1920 a report on the activity of the Petrograd labor departments revealed that as many as 20 percent of the unemployed subject to conscription had escaped by fleeing to the villages or by finding jobs in the bureaucracy.[30] Frustrated at its inability to round up sufficient numbers of workers in vital fields, the center issued repeated orders of militarization. After the general mobilization of February 1920, the central authorities continued to issue new and more specialized mobilization decrees: for agricultural workers, water transport workers, construction workers, coal miners, domestic servants, women to sew underwear for the Red Army, tailors and shoemakers who had worked in Great Britain and the United States, and so on.[31] Each more specialized call-up undercut earlier, broader swaths, much as the movement through 1919 to expand the scope of militarization overtook each act with a broader one. The marginal impact of each such act was correspondingly diminished. In March 1920 Rykov, speaking at a congress of water transport workers, observed that absentee rates were reaching unprecedented heights of 30 and 40 percent, levels five times those of prerevolutionary times. Mobilization scarcely kept up with the attrition of the work force. Between September 1919 and August 1920 some 35,000 workers left their jobs at thirty-five defense plans; the state was able to mobilize 38,500 new workers.[32]

In fact, the very measurements of disorder that the center gathered must be doubted, due to a severe shortage of information. In August 1919 *Narodnoe khoziaistvo* (The national economy, the journal published by the SEC) reported that the SEC sent out a questionnaire to all local councils to determine their ability to collect and process statistical information. Sixty percent of the councils failed to reply. Of those that responded, only one in six had any sort of section or department for statistics.[33] At the Third Trade Union Congress, in January 1920, Commissar of Labor Shmidt reported that a call for 45,000 workers had been met with a mobilization netting 39,000. After these workers had been sent out, it was discovered that they could not be used; and that turned out to be just as well, because owing to the breakdown in transportation, they were unable to reach their destination.[34]

Political factors also inhibited minor officials from reporting accurately about the state of the system. Emma Goldman offered a vivid example. In 1920 she talked with an engineer who had just visited the Donets basin. While *Pravda* had been publishing encouraging reports about coal production there, in reality the mines were in an extreme state of disrepair. Miners were regimented and starving and were forced to work in ankle-deep water. Very little coal was being mined, but fear of the Cheka kept the managers from sending truthful reports about the situation to the center.[35] The accuracy of the engineer's assessment, and the falsehood of the press reports, were wholly borne out in February 1920, when the worst fuel crisis of the entire three years suddenly came to light. The relatively optimistic projections about fuel availability had kept the regime from making adequate preparations for the winter; an early freeze and particularly severe weather contributed to the breakdown of fuel and food supplies, directly leading to the wave of strikes and protests which brought down the War Communism system (see below, pp. 173–75).

I have emphasized the use of labor conscription in the periods when the regime could shift its attention to long-range policy. Then the great issues of economic organization were again debated, and decisions made, that concerned the relationship between civil society and the state during the transition to socialism. My point has been that for the leadership, the principle of maximum centralization of authority served more than expediency. It consistently resurfaced as the image of a peacetime political system as well: unity, for the Bolsheviks, could only be achieved through the utmost concentration of political power in the hands of the central authorities. There were currents of thought within the party that questioned this assumption, but none that found a suitable alternative. Moreover, and more importantly, civil society was called upon to dedicate every ounce of its energy, its loyalty, and its authority to the rebuilding of the state. The Bolsheviks took pains to prevent any possibility that civil society might refuse. Not only did mobilization put labor at the direct disposal of the central authorities, but it also became a tool for suppressing any political opposition to the Soviet regime.

2 : *The Role of the Trade Unions*

Throughout 1917–1921 the place of the trade unions in the workers' state was unsettled. While they were declared to be the principal organization representing the workers' interests, the Bolsheviks made them an instrument for mobilizing the workers and severely restricted their political and economic powers on the grounds that the state, as a proletarian dictatorship, could not allow any social organization to intervene between it and the working class.

In part the ambiguous position of the trade unions arose out of their slightly disreputable family history. Until the October Revolution, most of the national union organizations had been Menshevik, at least at the higher ranks of their membership.[36] When the Bolsheviks took power, the Central Trade Union Council split, preventing its executive committee from meeting for several weeks. Thus paralyzed, the unions played a relatively minor role in shaping the workers' control decree or the SEC. While hostile to the claims of "workers' control," the unions lacked a clear definition of their own function in a proletarian state, and the hortatory role the new regime assigned to them—that they "must actually concentrate in their hands the management of the whole system of public economy"—was as vague as it was sweeping.[37]

In order to avoid the damning label of Menshevism, union leaders were at pains to demonstrate their loyalty to the regime. The slogan of "independence" for the trade unions was considered a Menshvik deviation that revealed a reluctance to regard the Bolshevik regime as entirely proletarian. (Debates on this issue ran through both the first and second trade-union congresses.) Still, for all their continually expressed loyalty to the Soviet regime, most trade unionists did not seek to merge the unions into the state. Most leaders in the unions and in the state assumed that "statification," or the merger of the unions with the state, would occur sometime in the distant future as the workers themselves grew more politically conscious.[38] For the interim, the unions and the government observed a tacit agreement giving the unions authority to discipline and mobilize workers and to carry out certain welfare functions in return for a small amount of power to represent the workers' material interests. Lenin himself acknowledged the legitimacy of this role in the great trade-union controversy of 1920–1921, when he declared that it was premature to seek to dissolve the unions since they still were needed to protect the workers against the state (see below).

The leadership constantly appealed to the trade unions to help raise worker productivity and to oversee discipline. Bolsheviks on the democratic Left might protest that a more democratic system of administration would raise productivity more effectively than compulsion, but the Central Trade Union Council could not afford to agree. In early April 1918 the council resolved that higher labor productivity was required to end the economic crisis and approved the principle of linking pay norms to output rather than to hours worked.[39] In late 1918 the council took upon itself the duty of enforcing discipline, declaring that if fraternal persuasion failed to correct an offender, he would be expelled from his trade union, "with all the attendant consequences," that is, deprivation of the ration card.[40] The trade union helped to assign workers to different plants as the state closed smaller and less efficient ones. They cooperated closely with the Commissariat of Labor in drawing up mobilization plans. In early 1919, when the Central Council of Trade Unions determined that voluntary appeals to workers were insufficient to move workers to the places of greatest need, it took upon itself the responsibility of assigning workers by force.[41]

The trade unions also exercised some administrative functions. They looked after health insurance, workplace safety, and the distribution of work clothes; beyond this, in the summer of 1920, the unions even began to form general managerial organs called Economic Departments which were parallel to existing state bodies. By the fall of 1920 these had not found a distinctive role and evidently clashed with the organs of the SEC. The Central Trade Union Council found it necessary to remind the branch unions and the regional union councils that the overlap between these Economic Departments and the state's own managerial bodies was harming the common cause; local union officials must remember, its memorandum observed, that the unions existed to recruit the masses to the state administration in order to "reeducate them psychologically."[42]

Probably even more important than their administrative functions was the unions' role in advancing workers to responsible positions in the state bureaucracy. By serving as a pool of loyal, experienced, working-class leaders, the unions strengthened the state at the expense of their own organizational coherence. Normally these individuals were not considered representatives of the trade unions in a strict sense, although occasionally they reported back to their home organizations two, three, or four times a year to face reelection.[43] In general, however, there was no standing requirement of accountability.

As the SEC and its network of branch and territorial organs expanded, the trade unions contributed a rising share of their personnel. Thirty of the first sixty-nine members of the SEC were brought in from the unions and many of the rest, recruited from the local councils, had been trade unionists as well. The unions had nominated over a third of the SEC's staff by the summer of 1919, and over half by the end of 1920.[44] However, the unions lost workers to the state apparatus more quickly than they could replace them. Accordingly, the size of the unions fell sharply. Many workers escaped the cities or joined the army; those with organizational talent entered the party and government bureaucracies. New workers entering industry often did not join the unions. Membership in the Petrograd Metalworkers' Union, the great buttress of Bolshevik support in the October Revolution, fell from 193,000 at the time of October to 57,000 in early 1920. As a consequence of the weakening of the union organizations, in some industries the state and the union merged *de facto*, with administrators serving simultaneously as both state and trade-union officials.[45]

The right of the unions to name members to the state's administrative bodies seems to have been recognized, at least tacitly, during most of the period. The practice of naming relatively constant proportions of workers, officials, and specialists continued even after it was formally abandoned as a principle in early 1919. Studies of the social composition of the boards managing factories and those running the *glavki* reveal that workers usually made up 50 to 60 percent of the members; if one includes junior levels of clerical employees in the "worker" category, the proportion rises to around 70 percent.[46] A survey of industry as of 1 August 1919 showed that a rough proportionality had been achieved in the appointments to the collegia of the *glavki*. Just over one-third had been appointed by the SEC and just under one-third by the trade unions. Slightly fewer than 10 percent were appointed by the factory committees; 8 percent were appointed by various congresses and conferences. The class composition of these bodies bears out the presumption of a tacit norm of class balance. However, over three-quarters of the members were classified as specialists; 23.3 percent were workers; 22.6 percent were from middle-level managerial or technical positions; 29.6 percent were from higher administrative or technical positions; 24.5 percent came from professional or clerical backgrounds, such as university faculties or the ranks of *zemstvo* and cooperative employees.[47] In the spring of 1921 an observer estimated that about one-third of the members of managerial bodies were trade-union representatives (generally workers). Another third were drawn from the enterprises directly, and the rest were specialists appointed by the center.[48]

If the trade unions advanced workers, for the most part, the SEC often recruited former owners, managers, engineers, or bureaucrats.[49] The higher the level of the hierarchy, the greater the concentration of nonproletarian elements. By 1920 the SEC employed approximately 15,000 persons classified as specialists. (A specialist could be anyone whose experience or expertise distinguished him from a manual laborer or clerk.) The total number of people emloyed in the SEC's organs as of December 1920 was 24,000. Thus specialists composed nearly three-quarters of the personnel.[50] The relatively low proportion of workers in the state's administrative bodies becomes more striking if we look at higher levels. Of the senior 200 members of the central boards under the SEC in December 1920, only one-fourth had been workers before the revolution. Over one-third were drawn from upper-level managerial, commercial, and industrial classes. The rest were middle- and lower-level technical, executive, or clerical employees by background. Of the 900-odd executive-level employees, only 8 percent were workers. Among the heads of departments and subdepartments the disproportion is yet greater: only 4 percent were former workers, suggesting that operational authority in the SEC was exercised almost entirely by members of the former upper classes and that workers occupied conspicuous but less significant posts. In departments not directly overseeing production, those concerned with functions such as bookkeeping, finance, and control, less than 1 percent of the heads of departments were workers.[51]

Thus the unions were the principal channel through which workers were recruited to administrative positions in industry and through which they defended their claims against a largely

nonproletarian bureaucracy. They became the principal representatives of the working class's interests since the state occupied itself with the interests of the "whole" society, becoming,
as we shall see, "neutral" with respect to class. In this role the
unions were subject to contradictory pressures. They continued
to be needed to represent the workers and did so in the limited
political space open to them. At the same time they were partly
absorbed into the state as their leaders were drawn into the
bureaucracy and as they became part of the apparatus that
mobilized workers.

The consolidation of the unions by industry reinforced the
tendency for unions to become submerged into the state. Beginning in the spring of 1918, the unions were amalgamated
on what was called the "production" principle (as opposed to
that of "consumption"). The reorganization swallowed crafts
unions into larger branch-wide unions. The result was a
smaller number of national unions. By October 1918, for example, Petrograd had only twenty unions rather than fifty. By
early 1919, there were only about twenty-five national unions,
as opposed to the seventy-odd that existed in October 1917.[52]
Consolidation eased the regime's task of penetrating and controlling the unions, although it increased the felt distance between the union leaders and the rank and file, a problem that
workers complained about bitterly in 1920–1921.[53]

The great trade-union controversy that erupted in this period is familiar. What had for long been a latent source of
tension became *the* focal issue of politics in late 1920 when
Trotsky threatened to upset the delicate division of powers
between state and trade unions by "shaking up" the unions in
order to achieve fuller centralization of power.[54] The ensuing
fight finally exposed to open debate the implicit contradiction
between the state's use of public organizations to mobilize labor
and the unwritten rights to defend workers which the unions
claimed. Trotsky's attempt to impose logical closure on the issue was, impressions created by western accounts to the contrary, only the most inflammatory of a series of efforts to re-

solve the ambiguity of the unions' situation. In the fall of 1920 there were two major differences from previous such attempts. As at other times when the external threat was reduced and worker unrest revived, the cessation of hostilities with Poland and the defeat of General Wrangel' renewed trade-union resistance to the trend toward absorption into the state. Second, the serious state of disintegration of the economy impelled the regime to apply unprecendented levels of coercion to maintain order. Trotsky's dictatorial methods of reorganization in the transportation industry warned of the course ahead.

The issue of the "statification" of the unions itself was not new. It had been discussed since the First All-Russian Trade Union Congress in January 1918.[55] Another significant airing of the question occurred in early December 1918, when the metalworkers met and discussed trade-union–state relations. At this meeting, A. Z. Gol'tsman presented the Left position favoring the merger of the unions with the state. The current situation, he argued, was unsatisfactory, for inasmuch as the state and the unions mistrusted each other, the unions continued to pose economic demands and to approach the state as it might have approached private employers, seeking better contracts. The alternative position, offered by V. Kossior, held that the unions still filled, however poorly, an essential role, that of educating the workers and of articulating their interests. It was appropriate for the unions and state to divide their functions; the unions expressing the workers' needs and teaching them the skills of management; the state regulating and coordinating the economy as a whole.[56] Gol'tsman's argument followed the abstract logic of of the theory of proletarian dictatorship, while Kossior took the realist's approach, recognizing the state's claim to a supraclass mediating role and accepting the vital if subordinate position that left for the unions.

Essentially the same positions are restated at the Second *Sovnarkhoz* Congress the same month, where representatives of the *sovnarkhozy* tended to view the statification of the unions as a process already underway, and trade-union representatives

argued in favor of a role outside the state.[57] The most prominent proponent of statification in the SEC was its chairman,
Rykov. At the December congress, Rykov criticized the unions
for harboring an excessive concern for the welfare of their
members. The unions ought not to busy themselves with looking after the workers, he admonished them, because that was
the state's duty. Rather, they should find ways of raising labor
productivity.[58] By the end of 1918, the issue of the trade
unions' relationship to the state had replaced workers' control
as the dominant topic discussed in the economic press.[59]

The dispute continued in 1919. The metalworkers began to
withdraw their formerly unqualified support for "statification"
and to seek autonomous powers for the unions. In mid-1919,
they presented the government with a request that it turn over
to their union a defined portion of administrative responsibility.
Discussions were sharp. The government accused the metalworkers of attempting to create a "workers' aristocracy," as if by
asserting the right to the one form of direct political participation Leninist doctrine recognized—that by class—they en-
dangered the state's monopoly on power. When after heated
disagreement the Bolshevik party fraction in the Central Trade
Union Council rejected the metalworkers' demands, the issue of
trade-union subordination, as a practical matter, was settled.[60]

Nonetheless the votive rhetoric of doctrine continued to
point the other way. The party program adopted in the spring
of 1919, for example, assigned the trade unions responsibility
for the "administration of the whole economic life of the country."[61] A few months later, in the *ABC of Communism*, Bukharin
and Preobrazhenskii explicated this formula: "It is essential
that the trade unions should take an increasing share in the
administration of industry, until the day when the whole of
economic life, from the bottom to the top, shall constitute a
unity which is effectively controlled by the industrial (productive) unions.[62] Explaining such anomalous language in the face
of consistent state subordination of the unions, Isaac Deutscher
could only call it a "syndicalist slip" prompted by the party's

"gratitude" to the unions for their services.[63] It is unlikely that the Bolsheviks slipped in a matter of such acute sensitivity. This was rather the delicate language needed to express two contradictory sets of signals: the manifest position granting the trade unions a vague supremacy as against the latent contextual hints that the trade unions enjoyed certain limited powers at the price of accepting the state's autonomy. In short, it was the gingerly wording of compromise.[64]

When the issue of the unions' powers again became a matter of public dispute in late 1920, the Left and realist positions were revived. The Left—represented at its uncompromising extreme by Trotsky and his supporters, more moderately in Bukharin's group, and in a hazy democratic form by the Workers' Opposition—found the bureaucratization of society an evil caused by the rivalry of too many organs for too few resources. Only if the interests of the working class were not divided into a state sphere and a trade-union sphere could they be placed beyond the reach of inefficiency, particularism, and abuse. With Lenin's support, the realists responded that the state could not and would not serve all the workers' interests, including their education and their protection against the state.[65] In response to the radical critique made by the Workers' Opposition, they acknowledged that isolated cases of misused state power existed, but refused on that account to grant the unions any fixed share of governing power; and they questioned the loyalty of the more searching critics. To the "statists" on the Left, that is, the Trotsky group, Lenin suggested a more tactful approach: Trotsky's call for the full "coalescence" of the trade unions with the state, Lenin said, was: "bureaucratic, unsoviet, unsocialist, incorrect, and politically harmful. . . . The best thing to do about 'coalescence' right now is to keep quiet. Speech is silver, but silence is golden. Why so? It is because we have got down to coalescing in practice." As Richard Day has noted, "Lenin hoped to maintain many of the stringent features of Trotsky's programme but to do so surreptitiously."[66]

The compromise reached at the Tenth Party Congress was the

same that had been expressed over and over, with minor variations, throughout 1917–1921. It concealed the powerlessness of the unions, their lack of any political rights except for those derived from the practical functions the regime allowed them to perform. It glossed over the contradiction between this role and the nominal supremacy the ideology assigned them. Moreover, the regime did not perceive that the return to a market economy with the NEP would restore the *economic* bargaining power of the unions. Although the party congress decided to end grain requisitions and to adopt the New Economic Policy, its resolutions on the trade-union crisis did not anticipate the new role to be played by the unions. The inevitable pressure of the NEP to free the market for labor, thus demobilizing labor and placing the unions in a position analogous to that under capitalism, was not reflected in legislation for a year.[67] So far as anyone knew, building socialism in the industrial sector would continue to require the mobilization of labor.

3 : Protest and Repression

Workers were torn between resentment at the political regimentation of labor and loyalty to the cause of proletarian dictatorship. At various times groups of workers rebelled against Bolshevik rule. But for the most part, forced to choose between "their" regime and the unknown horrors of a White dictatorship, most willingly defended the Bolshevik cause.[68] The effect of this dilemma may be seen in the periodic swings in the workers' political temper. When Soviet rule stood in peril, the war stimulated a spirit of solidarity and spared the regime the defection of its proletarian base. During lulls in the fighting, strikes and demonstrations broke out.

This cyclical alternation began as early as January 1918; a movement protesting the dissolution of the Constituent Assembly quieted down in February when the Germans resumed their offensive against Russia. During that wave of protest in January, workers at a general meeting of the Siemens and

Schuckert works in Petrograd demanded the recall of their comrades from the Red Guard. As the Red Guard occupied more and more factories, 5000 workers of the Neva shipbuilding works turned out to protest the use of workers as police and the practice of turning "comrade peasants" against the workers. Many plants sought to dissociate themselves from the Red Guard altogether. After the violent suppression of a demonstration protesting the forcible dissolution of the Constituent Assembly, a group of workers and Menshevik party leaders met and formed a League to Defend the Constituent Assembly, an organization which spread rapidly to other cities.[69]

Although the January protests subsided during the call to arms in February, the onerous terms of the Brest-Litovsk treaty prompted further outbursts. One of the most interesting organized opposition groups of the period, the workers' delegate movement, grew out of the earlier Menshevik-inspired protests against dissolving the Constituent Assembly. The workers' delegate movement articulated a wide range of grievances, as these excerpts from the instructions given by the Petrograd branch to its representatives to the first national meeting in Moscow, held in mid-March, attest:

We, Petersburg Workers, charge our delegates to tell the workers of Moscow the following:
. . . In our names half of Russia has been given over to the enemy. In our names Ukrainians, Letts, Lithuanians, Finns, Caucasians have been betrayed. In our names the entire land has been flooded with blood. In our names all these criminal acts have been carried out. Thus has our name been surrendered to scorn and covered with curses. . . . [Our government] promised us socialism and destroyed our economy with its senseless experiments. What sort of a socialism could they have brought a backward agrarian country, where there is no technology and no culture, and where war has raged so long?

Instead of socialism—empty factories, ovens grown cold, thousands of unemployed, poverty. . . .

Our organizations are destroyed. After they had been reduced to hapless tools of the regime in our "socialist" fatherland, they ceased to defend us. We are driven one from another, disarmed and beaten

down. Without associations, without the right to strike, without freedom of the press, we are weaker and more weaponless in the face of
our own and German capitalists, as well as state capitalism supported
by hand and machine instruments, than we were under tsarism.

The unhappy thought of turning workers into owners has made
them slaves.

. . . We call upon you to struggle:

For the reinstitution of popular power, for the Constituent Assembly, for democratic institutions.

For the restoration of the economy, against the experiments of Soviet socialism, for our independent workers' organization.

For the end of civil war and the reestablishment of all freedoms.

For a general arming of the people.

For the end of the Brest treaty and against the alliance with Germany.

> Extraordinary Assembly of the
> Delegates of Factories and
> Enterprises[70]

Besides indignation at the degrading terms of the Brest peace,
the document reveals resentment at the evisceration of the
workers' organizations. At the Moscow meeting, the delegates
continued to accuse the regime of turning the unions into weapons against the workers.[71]

The railroad workers were another source of opposition in
early 1918. Under the banner of workers' control, the workers
on each line had taken control over the line's operations and
were reluctant to surrender their power to the center. Although the Bolsheviks replaced the Menshevik leaders of the
railroad workers' union with politically reliable individuals, the
regime did not gain political control over the railroads until the
end of the spring. Even at the *Sovnarkhoz* congress in May–
June 1918, there was still opposition from railroad workers to
the Bolshevik appeals for higher productivity.[72]

Opposition was not confined to those unions where support
for the Mensheviks was entrenched. Throughout the spring,
workers at the giant Putilov and Obukhov plants of Petrograd
grew increasingly sympathetic to Menshevik and Social Revolu-

tionary programs. At Putilov, workers debated the slogans they wished to proclaim on May Day. One they proposed was the demand: "Give us bread and work, and down with Brest-Litovsk!" Even more popular was the suggestion that they boycott May Day celebrations. On the eighth of May, a general meeting of the Putilov workers passed an anti-Bolshevik resolution. The next day, Red Guards present, the Bolsheviks won support for a pro-Bolshevik resolution. The following day some ten thousand of the fourteen thousand workers still employed held another general meeting and passed a resolution protesting the previous day's coerced resolution.[73]

These early protests illustrate what became a common pattern. Demands that were initially economic in nature broadened into political attacks on the regime. The government made acceptance of all its decisions into a test of loyalty, and there were no mechanisms outside the state for resolving economic *or* political disputes. The danger that economic demands by workers might develop into an attack on Bolshevik rule itself therefore remained close. This point was illustrated bluntly in an exchange between the railroad workers and the commissar of railroads early in 1918. At a meeting to discuss recent strikes on the lines, some workers demanded the restoration of the Constituent Assembly. A worker took the floor to explain that the real motivation for the strikes was economic; it was the Mensheviks, he explained, who were trying to make them political. For their part, he said, the workers asked only one thing: give us bread and there will be no political strike.[74] As time went on, the regime was increasingly hard pressed to provide bread.

Through the spring of 1918, unable to voice their demands through the Bolshevik party or the trade unions, many workers left the party or voted against it in elections to local soviets. A circular from the Tula party committee to its rank-and-file members ordered that party work be strengthened in order to stem the mass departure of members from the party. In Ivanovo-Voznesensk, party membership fell from 7200 to

700, and in numerous town soviets, even in Kronstadt, the Bolsheviks lost their majority. It was at this precarious moment that David Riazanov acerbically quipped to a Menshevik party leader that the situation was now directly opposite to that of the preceding fall: then the Bolsheviks had held the soviets and the Mensheviks the government; now their positions were reversed.[75]

Compulsory labor became a means not only of constructing a new economic order, but also of suppressing political opposition. Soviet leaders often claimed that proletarian discipline, unlike military discipline, was self-imposed, democratic, and voluntary, but they willingly blurred the distinction between labor drafted for economic or egalitarian purposes and penal labor.[76] A case in point is the introduction of piece rates in place of hourly wages. In July 1918, when Molotov reported on the need for piece rates in Petrograd, he emphasized the punitive aims of the reform. Other members of the Bureau of the *Sovnarkhoz* of the Northern Region objected to his program, particularly to the point that the state reserved the right to close factories and redistribute their inventories in cases of work stoppages. One speaker complained that an attitude of mistrust for the workers pervaded the entire program. Molotov insisted that the goal of the decree was simply to raise productivity and that severe measures were needed to deal with strikes. The proposal was adopted.[77]

In cities located father from the centers of working-class organization and communications, the government resorted to harsher forms of repression. In June 1918 workers in Tula protested a cut in rations by boycotting the local soviet. The regime declared martial law and arrested the protesters. Strikes followed and were suppressed by violence. In Sormovo, when a Menshevik–Social Revolutionary newspaper was closed, 5000 workers went out on strike.[78] Again firearms were used to break the strike. In Petrograd, however, where the workers were better organized and more numerous, less sanguinary methods were employed.

Perhaps the most serious concentration of opposition in Petrograd was in the Putilov works, which were too large and too important to close permanently. There workers and government clashed continuously through the spring and summer of 1918. Appeals to the Putilov workers to raise productivity failed to achieve noticeable improvements. The planned output of locomotives was not even met by half: between January and August, Putilov expended two million *pudy* of fuel and 100 million rubles. Instead of the targeted seven locomotives, however, only three were produced. The Petrograd Soviet held a special meeting and decided to issue a warning to the Putilov workers that the waste of fuel and raw materials was intolerable to the working masses of Petrograd, and to grant the *sovnarkhoz* and the commissariat broad powers of discipline.[79]

The waste of scarce resources at Putilov was indeed serious, but not only political unrest had caused it. The general shortage of fuel and materials in the city took its greatest toll on the largest enterprises, whose overhead expenditures for heating the plant and firing the furnaces were proportionately greater than those for smaller enterprises. This point—explained by the relatively constant proportions among needed inputs to producers at any given point in time—only was recognized later. Not until 1919 were the regime's leaders prepared to acknowledge that small enterprises, under the conditions of the time, might be more efficient in using resources; and not until 1921 did a few Bolshevik theorists grasp the economic reasons for this apparent violation of their standing assumption that larger units were inherently more productive. Thus not only were the workers accused of politically motivated resistance, but the regime blamed them for the effects of circumstances over which the workers had no control (see chapter six).

In July 1918 the government closed Putilov for two weeks. Its reopening brought no improvement in productivity. In mid-August Molotov, as chairman of the Northern *Sovnarkhoz,* addressed an open letter to the Putilov workers. Observing that the factory was in chaos, that the country's scarce resources were being squandered, and that meetings, petitions, and delegations were spreading demoralization to other factores, he threatened the workers with a lock out.[80] There is no evidence that Molotov's threats overcame the difficulties, but the summer brought a new military crisis which quieted worker unrest.

One of the workers' primary complaints had concerned the sharp increases in unemployment that followed demobilization in late 1917 and early 1918; by summer, remobilization for civil war effectively solved the problem. Moreover, the perception of mortal danger from without and within, coupled with the anti-Bolshevik uprisings in Moscow, Iaroslavl', and other cities, gave the regime far more effective grounds for demanding worker discipline than the promises of long-term socialist construction. If productivity at Putilov did not rise significantly— the July–October plan called for building eleven new locomotives and making capital repairs on twenty more, but only four were produced and two repaired—at least strikes and demonstrations were averted for the time being.[81]

At other plants in Petrograd the government commonly resorted to the lock out as a means of punishing and purging the work force. At the end of June, a strike at the Obukhov works was met with a lock out and "reorganization" which involved numerous lay offs, new rules of discipline, purges of workers' organizations, and new appointments to the factory administration for matters of personnel, discipline, and wages. Over half the work force was discharged. Reportedly these measures succeeded in raising productivity.[82] Similar measures were employed at the Rechkin carriage factory in Petrograd, which was closed for the entire month of July. Half the workers were fired and piece rates were introduced. When the plant reopened, the government claimed that production increased sixfold. Several other factories were similarly closed and purged. By the summer of 1918, the combined effects of purges, lock outs, and resource shortages left fewer than half of the Petrograd enterprises running.[83]

Workers had few ideological weapons at their disposal with

which to protest the government's identification with the proletarian cause. Syndicalism had a certain following among the railroad and water transport workers, but the widespread acceptance of the need for working-class solidarity weakened its appeal for most workers. The workers' delegate movement was caught between the liberal positions of its Menshevik party sponsors and its revolutionary program; it never went so far even as to demand workers' control. The movement had no radical social program to set against that of the Bolsheviks.[84] To many workers, exhausted and vacillating between support for the regime and opposition, the workers' delegate movement seemed to presage a surrender to the White Guards. The movement never succeeded in attracting a majority of workers in any city, although it developed a strong national organization. The general political strike which it called for 2 July ended in failure as loyal workers and Red Guards prevented more than a few limited work stoppages from taking place. The mass arrests which followed effectively ended the movement.[85]

For the regime the key to establishing centralized rule in industry lay in winning control of factory-level mangement and the trade unions. As we know, this process required that the factory committees lose their political independence and become part of the apparatus of trade unions, and that the trade unions themselves become instruments for enforcing economic discipline.[86] Workers' representatives had to be replaced by appointed managers, who were willing to call on the government for support in denying workers' demands for pay raises or permission to leave the factory. The combination of state-appointed manager, loyal trade-union committee, and party organization, which to the present day remains the visible structure of power in the enterprise, had been assembled in most plants by late 1918. Violations of discipline could be punished by the Cheka, the regular courts, or by "comradely courts" organized in the enterprises. Depending on the severity of the offense, violators could be penalized by censure, deprivation of rations, assignment to mandatory labor, or incarceration in a concentration camp.[87] Still, as the strike waves show, the regime's sanctions were not sufficient to prevent all anti-Bolshevik political action. The Soviet regime's power still rested on the support it enjoyed among the workers, and here the immediate threat of White victories was more effective in strengthening its hand than the abstract promise of a remote socialist future.

To what extent protest was deferred by war is suggested again by the new outbreak of strikes in March 1919 after the collapse of Germany and the Bolshevik reconquest of most of the Ukraine. The pattern of repression was also repeated. A strike at a galosh factory in early 1919 was followed by the closing of the factory, the firing of a number of workers, and the supervised reelection of its factory committee.[88] The Soviet garrison at Astrakhan mutinied after its bread ration was cut. A strike among the city's workers followed in support. A meeting of 10,000 Astrakhan workers was suddenly surrounded by loyal troops, who fired on the crowd with machine guns and hand grenades, killing 2000. Another 2000, taken prisoner, were subsequently executed. In Tula, when strikes at the defense factories stopped production for five days, the government responded by distributing more grain and arresting the strike organizers; party work was strengthened and a massive party recruitment drive ensued.[89]

In the same interval strikes at Putilov again broke out, at first related to the food crisis. The workers demanded that the regime assign the task of food distribution to specialists, permit free imports of grain from the countryside into the cities, and raise wages and rations.[90] The government treated the strike as an act of counterrevolution and responded with a substantial political purge and reorganization. An official investigation of the problems at Putilov concluded that many of the shop committees were led by Social Revolutionaries, who were unwilling to submit to the factory committee. These committees were abolished and management representatives were appointed in their stead. An agitation department for the factory was formed to explain state policy. Perhaps the most interesting findings concerned the deficiencies of the factory management. The investigating commission judged the management incompetent; it suffered from "an inability to approach the worker as a teacher to a pupil, and where necessary, as an administrator to a subordinate. [In short, the factory lacked] a competent dictatorial organ, which, being neutral and independent of the masses, should carry out the necessary measures both among the technical personnel and in the labor force, even using coercive measures, corresponding to the indicated needs, for the regulation of production and the raising of plant productivity to the necessary level."[91]

The reorganization undertaken by the commission succeeded in raising productivity, not by using the broad purges such as had been applied the previous year, but by more selective means. Most arrested workers were reexamined and given the opportunity to recant their views. Eight or ten workers were sent to labor camps; about seventy were deprived of rations. The follow-up report noted with satisfaction that once more "revolutionary order reigns." However, trouble reappeared when in the summer the workers threatened to strike again.[92]

Just as labor conscription and piece rates could be used to enforce political discipline in addition to economic discipline, so too the labor book, governing rations, came to serve the ends of political control. Although the SEC, as we saw, had agreed to introduce a labor book system in April 1918, it was apparently not instituted for workers until late June 1919.[93] Ostensibly the labor book was to serve as an identity document and to certify that the bearer was engaged in productive labor so as to entitle him to receive food coupons and social benefits. However, it could readily be converted to a method of surveillance. When Emma Goldman visited Moscow and Petrograd in 1920, she found that the labor book "was a record of every step one made, and without it no step could be made. It bound its holder to his job, to the city he lived in, and to the room he occupied. It recorded one's political faith and party adherence, and the number of times he was arrested."[94] Both in official practice and in the minds of many workers the distinction between labor and punishment was disappearing. The labor departments worked with the Cheka in locating and rounding up skilled workers from the villages and criminals such as speculators; those collected were sent out under the same quotas: the Donets Basin coal mines for the stronger, labor camps for the weaker.[95] The revolution had never come so close to erasing the difference between the armed camp and the concentration camp.

By 1921 Russia had suffered unspeakable devastation. Economic discontent was spilling over to political unrest. The threat that the regime, unable to provide bread, would face a general political strike nearly materialized. Grossly inadequate fuel stores with which to meet an unusually hard and early winter diminished the regime's ability to distribute food rations. On 22 January the government announced a reduction by one-third in the bread ration for the cities. In mid-February workers in Moscow struck for the end of militarization in the name of free labor and for the end of grain requisitioning. A massive city-wide protest spread through Petrograd immediately afterward. Initial resolutions passed by workers' mass meetings at the factories called for the end of grain requisitions and the removal of food blockades from the roads leading into the city. Strikes and demonstrations spread. The regime responded as it had done in the past, with lock outs, mass arrests, heavy shows of force—and concessions, but not before an economic movement with political implications had become a political countermobilization. On all sides demands were made to withdraw Red Army units from the factories and to restore political rights. Menshevik and Social Revolutionary appeals again found a ready audience.[96]

In the past the government had combined concessions with severe repression to restore order, but on this occasion the crisis was so grave that the government's concessions amounted to the first steps in dismantling the very system of War Communism. Not only were the food blockades removed, so that workers were free to bring food into the city, but Zinoviev revealed that the government intended to replace food requisitioning with a new system of in-kind taxation. Freeing the grain trade was so radical a change that it rapidly dispersed the protest movement in Petrograd. It came too late, however, to avert the horror of Kronstadt.[97]

CHAPTER FIVE

Scientific Rationalism in Bolshevik Ideology

1 : Politics, Markets, and Order

BOLSHEVIKS UNIFORMLY REGARDED the capitalist market-place as a cruel and capricious regulator of social relations, susceptible to manipulation by greedy speculators, an arbitrary state, and exploiting owners, and as irrational in its workings as it was harsh. A pamphlet describing the first industrial production plan in Soviet Russia, issued in Petrograd in 1918, illustrates the standard view.

For until now the worker did not know what he was doing, how long he would be doing it, and why he was doing it. The capitalist also was little interested in this question. For him it was much more important to know what percentage profit he would receive. Today his plant is engaged in turning out buttons, tomorrow spoons, the day after to-morrow munitions. One thing only interested him: how to stuff his greedy pocket as full and tight as he could. Therefore he adapted his enterprise to whatever the market prized most dearly at the moment. No matter if no one needed the buttons made by his plant because enough had been made to last for years: if the "market" for some reason (skillful speculation, for example) valued them highly, the capitalist would keep turning out buttons! And, on the other hand, no matter if the peasant sits without plow, without nails, the worker without a spoon, without a shirt, without the most vital necessities; if manufacturing shells swells the capitalist's pocket, he will force the worker to turn out shells! The market, the blind play of chance and profit, the sordid little deals of speculators and the thirsty columns of the capitalist's account-books—this is what directed production, this is what forced the workers to do one thing or another, throwing goods in heaps onto the market![1]

Markets fared no better in more theoretical writings. Before NEP suggested new uses for the marketplace, the Bolsheviks dwelt exclusively on the irrationality, the "blind anarchy," of markets.[2]

Bolshevik theories of social organization, although inchoate at the time of October, always presupposed that commodity exchange would be replaced by an administrative authority guided by intelligent reason. The new state would dedicate itself to developing the great natural resources of Russia that the ancien regime, in its folly and incompetence, had failed to exploit. As we shall see in this chapter, the enthusiasm for planned industrialization attracted a diverse group to cooperate with the Bolsheviks in developmental planning, including scholars such as Grinevetskii, hostile to the Bolsheviks but eager to discuss central planning with them; inactive Bolsheviks such as Krasin and Krzhizhanovskii who possessed engineering and managerial skills; Mensheviks such as Larin, who had joined the Bolshevik party, and V. G. Groman, who did not; with old Bolsheviks such as Lenin and Rykov, who were strongly committed to technological progress.[3]

Only on the margins of Bolshevism were there any willing to voice fears that the concentration of full political and economic power in a state bureaucracy could create a mutant form of dictatorship. While it was an American who in 1919 coined the term *technocracy*, in Russia at the same time A. A. Bogdanov (Malinovskii) worried about the possible emergence of a new technico-administrative class.[4] In the 1922 edition of his prescient book, *Tektologiia*, he referred to two hypothetical forms of socialism that would create new elites to rule over the proletariat: one generated a scientific and technical intelligentsia, the other a modernizing bureaucracy. Shortly thereafter, Bukharin wrote of the possibility that the proletarian dictatorship might degenerate into a "new ruling class."[5] Bolsheviks rarely articulated such fears, however. More commonly they criticized the material forms of inequality resulting from the high compensation of specialists and the use of piece rates, Taylor methods, and shock sectors.[6]

For the most part, Bolshevik doctrine conceived the centralized state to be not only compatible with mass democracy, but even essential to it. Through a proletarian dictatorship, class inequality could be destroyed and opportunities opened for workers to participate in governing the state. At the Seventh Party Congress in early March 1918, Lenin spoke of the need "to recruit every last laborer to manage the state." Later in the spring, when he began to emphasize worker discipline and higher productivity, he still counterposed the need for mass participation to the need for the sternest coercive measures for maintaining productivity. In his article, "The Immediate Tasks of the Soviet Regime," he insisted that specialists direct production, and that single-person management, strict accountancy and control, and stringent discipline ensure unity of will. Yet he asserted that Soviet democracy differed from all preceding systems in its effort to involve the entire working population in governing the state.[7]

At the same time, Lenin eagerly embraced the hope for a scientifically planned transformation of society. In late April 1918 he suggested that the Academy of Sciences begin to devise a general plan for the "reorganization of industry and the economic uplifting of Russia." He actively guided Larin's efforts to organize a Council of Experts composed of leading Petrograd specialists. He encouraged the formation of the Committee on State Works. He demanded that Russia rebuild using the latest mechanical technology available. Larin recalled that Lenin grew more excited than anyone else at the plans for the electric plow, the development of a better seed strain, the production of the first domestic boot tacks. Lenin's American admirer, Albert Rhys Williams, wrote that Lenin frequently stressed the importance of recruiting prominent experts and giving them a free hand in exploiting Russia's vast resources.[8]

Lenin was not alone among the Bolsheviks in celebrating the prospects for technical rationalization at the same time that he stressed the importance of popular participation in government. The program of the Left Communists also advanced both themes. Particularly after the Brest-Litovsk treaty had been signed, this coalition of party leaders who had opposed the humiliating peace worried that the pace of revolution at home was slowing. The Petrograd daily which had served as their mouthpiece reappeared as a Moscow weekly under the same name, *Kommunist*. In the theses published in the latter's first issue (21 April 1918), and the articles in it and the three subsequent issues, both lines of argument are evident: state authority must be democratized; social organization must be rationalized. We can summarize the Left's position in six points. (1) Soviet policy must rely exclusively on proletarian class interests; no compromise with the bourgeoisie is tolerable; workers must take part in all areas of economic administration. (2) Some autonomy should be granted regional authorities in overseeing their local economies. (3) The hierarchical and authoritarian character of the capitalist state must be replaced with nonbureaucratic, noncoercive structures. Where coercion is necessary, it should be self-imposed. Piece rates, comrades' courts, and Taylor methods are suspect. (4) Nonetheless, control over industry must be centralized. For Bukharin, the "administration of things" would be fully centralized, while the "administration of people" would become superfluous. (5) The scale of organization must be as large as possible. Bukharin distinguished the Bolsheviks from the anarchists on the grounds that the latter were "economically reactionary" for denying the advantages of "centralized and systematically organized large-scale production throughout the entire world." (6) Finally, society must develop its productive resources.[9]

In the months following, the Left Opposition tended to divide into two wings, which reflected a larger divergence of democratic and technocratic inclinations in the party. The first tendency, drawing on the first three of the above points, upheld the ideal of a class-oriented and participatory state apparatus, avoiding overcentralization and the excessive delegation of power to neutral experts. The second, stressing the latter three points, sought to keep state power free of commitments to class or local interests so that it could develop Russia as efficiently as possible. Only in the first, fluid months of the revolution were these two orientations joined in a single opposition movement. Subsequently, the technocratic principles of developmentalism and planning became essential elements of the emerging ideological synthesis of the new state, while the progressive centralization of power provoked those concerned with democratic values to form and reform into a series of opposition movements: the Democratic Centralists, the Military Opposition, and the Workers' Opposition.

2 : The Mobilization of Science

Intent on applying the state's power to the task of developing Russia, the Bolsheviks called for the "mobilization of science." Once science was in harness, imagination joined with knowledge would yield the power to "escape the kingdom of blind necessity."[10] Accordingly, from the inception of Soviet rule, the leadership sought to attach scientific and technical expertise to the state's planning bodies.

The terms of the alliance between Soviet power and the scientific-technical intelligentsia emerged rapidly after October, drawing on the rationalistic and developmental perspectives shared by the revolutionary movement and many scientists and technical specialists trained under the old regime. Three strands in particular of the new ideological synthesis may be isolated. The first is rationalism. Like the French revolutionaries of 1789, the Bolsheviks considered October to be as much an act of historical reason as of moral justice, but no revolution has ever laid so much stress on the ability of science to reorder society. Among the scientific intelligentsia, it was not only the young and radical who envisioned a planned

society. So also did many older figures, such as the elderly
professor described to Lenin, who "with tears in his eyes said
with inspiration that he had always dreamed of the perspectives now opening before us, that with gladness he is ready to
devote all the years remaining to him to the new work, the
new construction."[11] Effusive hopes that science might become
the force leading the new age sounded on all sides. Party
publications called science "one of the most important productive forces, determining the fruitfulness and tempo of development both of material and spiritual elements of culture."
Not only would science help plan the reorganization of social
relations, but it would shape socialist ideology and culture as
well.[12]

Heartened by repeated assertions from the party that science
and technology would enjoy a privileged place in socialist construction, ever larger numbers of scientists and technicians (unlike the cultural intelligentsia) agreed to cooperate with the
regime; by mid-1918, according to some sources, the bulk of
them had been won over. Many hoped that the new regime
would finally accord science the respect denied it under the
tsars.[13] One member of the Academy of Sciences recorded in
his diary in October 1918: "I am no optimist and no infatuated
youth, but nonetheless I have begun to think and do think that
we have truly begun to "renounce the old world," not only in
words, that figures of science and education are receiving their
due recognition from the new rulers, that the end has come for
the mockery they received from the former tsarist government."[14] In the prewar decades, many among the scientific
intelligentsia had protested the low level of state support for
science and the illiberal obscurantism of official policy. Their
broad if amorphous faith in a "union of science and democracy" reflected a belief, comparable to the lessons John Dewey
taught in China and elsewhere, that the greater the participation of science in policymaking, the greater the general benefit
to society.[15]

Not all scientists and technicians were attracted by the visionary side of state policy. Some, in fact, considered the regime foolish for pursuing schemes for which it lacked the organizational and material prerequisites. The chemist Ipatieff, for example, found the regime's habit "of starting with big projects and ending in complete chaos . . . too firmly fixed to be altered." The Menshevik Nikolai Valentinov later recalled "the world of phantoms, illusions, revolutionary ecstasy, passionate expectation of a miracle on a world scale, in which communists and Russian people lived from 1917 to 1920."[16]

Nevertheless, many experts considered it a matter of duty to their country to participate in the new order, and the regime was entirely willing to recruit them on nationalistic grounds.[17] Lenin, for example, defended the Brest treaty by asserting that Russia (and he used the ancient term *Rus*) must take advantage of the breathing-pause provided by the treaty to assemble its resources in order to build a mighty and bountiful state. Thus Russian nationalism was the second normative element of this cooperation. Often it joined with utopian dreams of progress, but it also motivated many sober-minded specialists to work for the state even when they harbored strong doubts about the practicality of the regime's objectives. Many of the projects initiated by the regime, such as the KEPS study or electrification, embodied purely national purposes carried over from earlier years.

The third element of the new ideological synthesis was an understanding that only centralized state power could accomplish national development. Ipatieff, for example, strongly urged the regime to retain and reform the centralized administration of the nation's chemical industry, which, as he put it, "we had created during the war."[18] In his book *Postwar Perspectives of Russian Industry,* V. I. Grinevetskii, writing in early 1918, sharply criticized the Bolsheviks' socialist fantasies, but, because of Grinevetskii's eminence and because the essence of the book was a call for planned industrial development, the book was published in 1919, circulated widely among the Bolsheviks, and came out in a second edition in 1922.[19] His discussion of central planning and the priorities of economic reconstruction gave scholarly support and detailed analysis to ideas much like those being advanced by Bolsheviks such as Krasin, Trotsky, and Larin. The book is said to have also influenced Lenin, to whom Krasin gave a copy.[20]

The ideological view of the state as agent of national development preserved an element of tsarist patrimonialism. Among both the scientific-technical intelligentsia and the Bolsheviks, many assumed that the state possessed a unique outlook on the needs of the whole society, one which was unbiased by the particular interests of classes and regions. The sense of inviolability, of Russian *raison d'état*, is conveyed in a phrase used by the eminent natural scientist V. I. Vernadskii to describe the importance of research into radioactivity, when he termed it "a matter of state interest" (*delom gosudarstvennogo blagorazumiia*).[21] An analogous impression of the state's independent role occurs in a remark by Rykov. Arguing in December 1918 that the trade unions had no right to demand fixed proportions for workers on industrial administrative bodies, he denied that the workers needed to defend their class interests, since "the state looks after this;" they should instead be concerned with raising productivity.[22] In mobilizing scientists and engineers, the regime offered them the opportunity to identify their efforts with the Olympian interests of the state rather than the partisan cause of labor.

The first Soviet organization designed to recruit scientists, called the Science Department, formed in November 1917 under the Education Commissariat. Like many other organs of the time, the Science Department's ambitions far outran its organizational capacity. Its two young chairman, L. G. Shapiro and V. T. Ter-Oganesov, seem to have spent much of their time drafting a grand scheme for organizing science in the service of "state construction." Little organizational work was accomplished. For the most part, the department evidently engaged in negotiation with the Academy of Sciences over new research projects: with cautious dignity the academy acknowledged that "a significant portion of the tasks are set by life itself, and the Academy is always ready to [respond] to the demands of life and the state."[23]

Inasmuch as the Science Department did not appear to be making headway in solving the economic crisis, the presidium of the Supreme Economic Council welcomed a report from the old Bolshevik L. B. Krasin, in early January 1918, on the need for an economically oriented technical committee. In mid-February the SEC formed a Central Council of Experts in the hopes of unifying science and technology for the purpose of giving "aid in the resolution of the economic tasks on the agenda." Since most of those recruited to this body had worked together before the revolution, it inherited a certain degree of organizational coherence. However, its administrative responsibilities were not defined, with the result that despite its considerable autonomy, it exercised little effective power.[24]

By spring the government still lacked an effective instrument for tying scientific expertise to economic policymaking and planning. In June 1918 a young Bolshevik engineer, N. P. Gorbunov, who was the secretary of the Council of Commissars, persuaded the council that neither the Science Department nor the Council of Experts was successfully integrating science with state needs, and he offered to create such a body. The Council of Commissars approved his proposal for a Scientific-Technical Department (Nauchno-tekhnicheski otdel, hereafter referred to as the NTO) which would be responsible for planning and coordinating scientific research. Gorbunov, then twenty-six years old, was given the chairmanship.

Gorbunov conceived of the NTO as a comprehensive center of planning and direction for the nation's scientific and technical resources, capable of linking applied research and experimentation with the lines of basic research conducted in institutes, universities, and laboratories. Like its immediate predecessors, the Science Department and the Council of Experts, the NTO expected to move beyond the organization of research to the actual planning of scientific solutions to prob-

lems of social and economic organization, particularly the
planning of economic development. Such tasks greatly exceeded the abilities of such inexperienced bodies. Although
the NTO enjoyed substantial formal power and could assign
projects to any research institutes in the country, its actual
achievements, like those of its predecessors, were slight.[25]

Despite these three attempts to concentrate expertise in governmental hands, the dream of applying planned research to
industrial development remained divorced from the existing
system of economic planning and administration. At most,
these new organs succeeded in sponsoring the establishment of
new research institutes—some forty were created between 1918
and 1921—but they fell short of drafting a comprehensive plan
for research. Rather quickly the NTO came to function as a
commissariat of science. Indeed, at first it was to have been the
commissariat of science, but Gorbunov had managed to place it
under the SEC so as to focus its attention on production.[26]
There it operated as an administrative home for the inherited
scientific-technical establishment. As in the case of many other
early Soviet efforts to create not merely new organs but new
types of organs, the result was to reproduce structures inherited
from before the revolution but to blur the division of responsibility among them.

On the other hand, the NTO was not stillborn, as were many
other organizations of the period. Probably this was due to its
institutional continuity with older bodies. Although young enthusiasts like Gorbunov hoped to reorganize scholarship, they
had to deal with the existing organization of science. At best, the
new Soviet agencies could hope to persuade scientists to support
the projects the government desired to carry out, using a variety
of pressures. Probably scientists obtained government backing
for their own undertakings more frequently than they were recruited to government projects. Mobilization, in the sense of
forced and centrally directed participation, was not the principal
form of the relationship between science and government.

To be sure, the government did not entirely abandon the

model of mobilization in its relations with scientists. At intervals it attempted to place all specialists individually at the disposal of the state. The ideal that all scientific and technical personnel be subject to mandatory call-up to state service was reflected more in the formal registration of experts than in actual conscription. In December 1918 the Council of Commissars decreed that all specialists should be counted and registered for possible mobilization. The following February a bureau was created for "accounting and allocating technical forces."[27] This body was placed under the charge of the NTO rather than under the labor departments or military organs, implying that whatever conscription of scientists and engineers occurred would be directed by specialists rather than by regular administrative authorities.

Enthusiastic about the prospects for concentrating scholarly expertise in a few powerful planning bodies, the regime did not strip existing scientific and technical organizations of their autonomy to the same degree that it did the workers' organizations—the factory committees, cooperatives, soviets, parties, and trade unions. This is particularly evident in the attitude of deference and bluster with which it approached the Academy of Sciences. The academy's power and prestige were immense. Its authority was so great that for the first decade of Soviet rule, it evaded censorship of its publications and the formation of a party cell. While some recent Soviet scholars have stressed the degree of mutual cooperation between the regime and the academy, the American scholar Loren Graham has interpreted the academy's position as defensive if not hostile toward the regime.[28] Whatever the case, until the Stalin revolution, the regime left the academy a certain institutional autonomy.

A project exemplifying the nationalistic and developmental spirit in which the Soviet regime and scientists cooperated was the comprehensive survey of Russia's natural resources conducted under the direction of V. I. Vernadskii (father of the historian). Before the October Revolution, in 1915, Vernadskii, a member of the Academy of Sciences, had organized a commission under academy auspices to study the country's natural wealth in order to gather a base of information for planning future national development. During the war the commission, called KEPS, received only limited support from the autocracy. Vernadskii nonetheless held a grandiose image of the scope of the commission. KEPS would serve as the nucleus of a national network of research institutes, each organized around a particular branch of study. Ultimately the project would guide economic development by directing where new industrial centers should be placed. KEPS continued to labor under the Soviet regime, receiving encouragement from the new science agencies. Despite extraordinarily difficult circumstances, KEPS succeeded in bringing out a six-volume study of the natural resources of Russia. It also issued numerous monographs and collections of materials and actively popularized scientific knowledge in lectures and pamphlets. It created a large number of new research institutes and conducted a number of field studies, concentrating especially on the European North and on Turkestan. The commission viewed Turkestan as a region of enormous potential, which given suitable irrigation could "take large numbers of colonizers."[29]

As Jeremy Azrael has written, the nationalism and vague liberalism of the technical intelligentsia took form in an ethic of "nonpartisan public service or suprapolitical developmental nationalism."[30] These politically neutral loyalties could be transferred to the Bolshevik regime once its leaders had made clear their devotion to scientific progress. After October, therefore, the basis existed for a mutually beneficial relationship between the regime and those members of the scientific-technical intelligentsia who did not oppose the Bolsheviks on political grounds. They looked to the new government to remove the political and economic shackles under which they had formerly suffered and to provide them with the autonomy to carry out their mission. For its part, the new regime turned to the scientific-technical intelligentsia for the types of knowledge that would enable the government to modernize Russia. Science and technology were used to legitimate the new state, for the Bolsheviks believed that the alliance of proletarian power with science would lead to unprecedented breakthroughs in social development. Electrification and the many other projects, some fanciful, some practicable, begun during these years came to define the technologically advanced society of the future.

One cannot but be impressed at the number of projects which sought to overcome the limits of physical nature. Simon Liberman, a former Menshevik and a timber specialist, told of being approached once by a young man who ceremoniously unveiled blueprints for an invention that would store the energy of a falling tree in a machine strapped to a lumberjack's back; he would then be able to fell other trees faster. Liberman grasped that the man had devised yet another variation on the ancient dream of perpetual motion, but instead of turning him down, sent him to another office. Liberman feared to take responsibility for refusing the inventor, since he had the full backing of the Cheka's own Scientific-Technical Department.[31]

Even the fury of the civil war did not prevent work on a number of new inventions in the fields of aeronautics and rocketry. In 1918 alone the Central Aero-Hydrodynamics Institute created a new model of a passenger airplane, an "airsled," a hydrofoil, and an "airmobile." Work on propellers of native design went forward. The Academy of Sciences continued to sponsor research on atomic fission. A scientist named F. A. Tsander worked out a design for a rocket motor capable of escaping earth's gravity.[32] Certainly the Bolsheviks did not initiate the tendency to follow lines of research that tested the limits of the possible. The influence of the nineteenth-century philosopher N. F. Fedorov was felt among scientists and Bolsheviks alike and took the form of seeking the technical means to overcome gravity, entropy, and death. Leonid Krasin himself, whom foreigners invariably considered the most level-headed of the Bolsheviks, publicly stated his belief that science would one day achieve the resurrection of the dead; this had been a favored theme in Fedorov's philosophy.[33]

Desperation played a part as well in the adoption of improbable schemes. In 1919, as fuel supplies grew perilously short, the Chief Fuel Committee directed that a massive effort be launched to collect pine cones for fuel. Invalids and children under ten were to be the main source of labor, since it was hoped that this would be light and healthful work. Tests showed that pine cones possessed one and one-half times the heat capacity of the best firewood and that by pressing cones one could form briquettes. The experiment ran for one year. When trains that started from distant forests loaded with pine cones arrived in Moscow empty, the Cheka suspected sabotage by the bourgeoisie. In fact, the cones, bulky in their unpressed state and fast-burning, were consumed by the trains on their way back to the city.[34]

Projects employing electrical energy enjoyed especial favor. The Commissariat of Agriculture held a contest for the best design of a self-propelling electrical plow and chose two for development. There was some hope that the first models would be operational by the fall of 1920, since the Commissariat supported production with a large appropriation. In one experiment a cable was stretched between two machines situated at opposite ends of a field. A tractor, with a man steering it, moved along the cable; each machine also had an operator. Although it is hard to imagine that such an arrangement can have been more labor-efficient than traditional methods, in early 1921 Lenin nonetheless directed the Commissariat of Agriculture to build twenty such plows, one of which was tested for Lenin in September 1921.[35]

Of course not all of the dreams were fantastic. In many cases they were simply premature. Centralizing information use for comprehensive national planning, for example, would have to await the development of high-speed data processing techniques. Other projects led directly to innovations in mass communications and transportation. In 1920 began experimental runs of an electric train which would eventually link Petrograd and Moscow.[36] Although long-distance rail transport continued to use coal or oil, the *electrichka* has become the main type of commuter train in contemporary Soviet cities.

The formation of the State Works Committee was another attempt to create a central organization for developmental planning. As with other such bodies, its mandate overlapped that of competing organizations. The intention of the SEC in setting up the committee, according to its first chairman, M. P. Pavlovich, was to place planning and administration of all of the state's construction projects in the hands of one organ; by separating construction from utilization, it was hoped, construction plans could be freed of the narrow interests of existing bodies and could thus stimulate the development of new regions and activities. Not surprisingly, the State Works Committee fell prey to the discrepancy between intentions and capacity that beset all Soviet institutions. It was somewhat less well equipped to overcome this than were other organs because it did not inherit any existing organizational machinery.[37] The committee had great difficulty in persuading other commissariats and local governments to allow it to plan the projects which fell within their own jurisdictions, and frequently it found itself unable to carry out even those projects it had initiated or to requisition materials from competing organs.[38]

The State Works Committee succeeded in co-opting many engineers, in part because of the high expectations it stimulated. Rykov boasted that with the creation of the committee "Only Soviet Russia for the first time in Russian history has opened a clear road to the realization of these gigantic projects of state construction."[39] Pavlovich quoted an enthusiastic letter to the Council of Commissars from an engineer working for the committee: "We are on the edge of a new epoch, distinguished by the fact that the construction of Russia in the figurative and literal sense of the word must occupy first place and become the cornerstone of the rebirth of Russia and the industrial life of this country, so vastly rich in materials."[40] But the committee never devised a general plan of operations. It accomplished little besides lending the good offices and resources of the government to the continuation of development projects that were underway well before the October Revolution.

Pavlovich singled out several such projects which had lain on the drafting boards before the revolution without winning governmental approval, among them the Volga-Don Canal, a north Siberian rail trunk line, and the electrification of the Volga cataracts. In later years they all became major projects of the Soviet regime, the first two being showcases of the Stalin era.

The idea of a canal connecting the Volga and the Don dated from the sixteenth century: Peter the Great revived it in the late seventeenth century and construction was begun. For various reasons the project broke down, partly owing to the opposition of the chief inspector, Prince Golitsyn, whose hostility was said to stem from his belief that what God had divided man must not presume to reunite. With the construction of St. Petersburg, the economic significance of the canal declined. According to Pavlovich, all the previous obstacles to the project were now surmountable thanks to the revolution, and he pressed for the resumption of planning. Shortly after the formation of the State Works Committee in June 1918, engineers began working out a five-year plan for construction of the canal.[41]

The second project has been debated in Russia for at least ten years: a rail link between the Ob' River and Murmansk. This would allow the timber of the north and the agriculture of western Siberia to be exploited more fully.[42] However, the starved Russian Republic lacked the capital for so great an investment. Leaders in the State Works Committee and the SEC began in the summer of 1918 to discuss whether to concede to foreign investors the rights to develop the route. The project was called the Great Northern Way. A Norwegian named Hannevig made a proposal to connect the Ob' with Arkhangelsk. With Lomov in the SEC strongly supporting it and against the forebodings of N. N. Sukhnov (remembered today for his excellent memoir of the 1917 revolutions), who had become chairman of the Economic Council of the State Works Committee, the Council of Commissars approved the deal in principle in early February 1919. Just then the Cheka discovered that a number of Hannevig's associates were actually penniless adventurers speculating in Russian timber futures and currency. One hundred people were arrested, all but two of them later released. Despite Lomov's argument that the scandal did not discredit the essential soundness of the project, Pavlovich and others were persuaded that Hannevig had no backing, and the negotiations were dropped.[43]

The third project was the construction of hydroelectric power stations on the Volkhov and other rivers. Electrification was an early preoccupation of the regime. In December 1917 Lenin asked a prominent engineer (and future member of the Academy of Sciences) named Graftio to resume his planning for a hydroelectric station on the Volkhov, which he had begun in 1909–1911. In January 1918 the chairman of the SEC's Electro-Technical Section, P. G. Smidovich, reported to the SEC presidium on the importance of a regional network of power stations using peat and waterfalls. The SEC sponsored planning work for the Volkhov station and began two other projects, one on the Svir' River and another, using peat, at Shatura outside Moscow. Also, in March and April, a series of regional commissions on electrification was formed. In May the Council of Commissars decreed that the State Works Committee should oversee all such construction projects and directed it to form a board overseeing the construction of electric stations. This board began work in June 1918. L. B. Krasin organized an advisory council of experts for the board, called the Central Electro-Technical Council, and persuaded many senior engineers to join. In a decree of March 1919 the Council of Commissars gave the council official status, and its role and personnel remained largely intact through the next eight years. Through the vicissitudes of the civil war, construction proceeded on the local and regional stations that these experts planned. In autumn 1920 a temporary station opened on the

Volkhov to serve the needs of the construction and of several local villages; the station itself was completed in 1926.[44]

As these examples indicate, the State Works Committee could boast of real accomplishments and realistic prospects, although neither were exclusively the achievement of Soviet rule. Where the committee was successful, its success derived from the union of state political and financial support with the plans, dreams, and expertise of the prerevolutionary generation of technical specialists. These specialists were recruited into the state hierarchy by such technically trained and oriented Bolsheviks as Krasin, Pavlovich, Smidovich, and Krzhizhanovskii and were actively welcomed by those party leaders such as Lenin and Rykov who shared with the old technical intelligentsia the dream of rebuilding Russia.

The co-opted experts certainly were not spared the fearful hardships of the time. Many lost their lives to disease, starvation, or terror. Yet the regime did try to ameliorate their lot by exempting them from regular obligations and by granting them special rations. The higher pay to which administrative specialists were entitled (which the famous Dukel'skii letter protested) only begins to suggest their relatively privileged position. Kendall Bailes has recently shown the relative strength which the organized engineers retained throughout the period. Although their union was not allowed to function as a trade union, it did so in fact. It was successful in winning its members both individually and collectively certain exemptions, such as the release of some from arbitrary arrest or the requisitioning of their property or houses.[45] The scientists, too, kept certain corporate privileges. In 1919 members of the Academy of Sciences were placed on a priority ration, and shortly afterward so were all registered scientists (to qualify one must have published notable scientific research—a quite literal application of the publish or perish rule). Other perquisites, such as access to special facilities at health resorts, were also extended to scientists. Perhaps most important were the exemptions scientists enjoyed from the mobilization applied to other groups. At the end of 1919, for example, the Council of Commissars decreed that scientific workers were to be freed of all conscription ("labor, military, etc.") not bearing on their scientific research. This decree was to be distributed to 500 specialists and 50 writers, but not otherwise published.[46]

3 : The Electrification Program

During the pause between the bitter campaigns of late 1919 and the resumption of hostilities in the spring of 1920, the Soviet government renewed its efforts to gather scientific expertise into a single, central planning agency. In the preceding chapter I discussed this "second breathing-space" as a time of revived labor mobilization and formation of labor armies. It was also notable as an interval when the party debated long-term industrial development as a sequence of stages leading from reconstruction to the ultimate triumph of socialism. The discussions culminated in the program adopted at the Ninth Party Congress in March 1920. Along with the measures envisioning labor mobilization, the program called for a central economic plan under which all specialists would participate in organizing production. It also specified priorities in reconstruction: first, transportation and the extraction of raw materials; second, heavy industry; third, the machinery needed to produce consumer goods; and finally, consumer goods themselves.[47] The program stipulated that the "technical side of matters" depended on the extensive use of electric power.

These plans were moot virtually from the moment of their adoption. Although they laid the intellectual foundation for the Left program of the next decade, they remained divorced from operational plans. To the extent that they laid out general political priorities and claimed precedence for certain infrastructural and producers' goods industries, they can be said to have prepared the way for the actual efforts at national economic planning that began, haltingly, in 1920 and continued through the adoption of the First Five-Year Plan in 1928. Otherwise the program gave recognition to commitments and commonsense ideas that were already prevalent. Among these was a nod in the direction of electrification. This period saw major efforts as drafting a general electrification plan: the celebrated Goelro commission—the State Commission on Electrification—took form out of the scattered regional and local boards overseeing electrification.

Although Goelro is renowned, largely because of Lenin's boundless support for it, its more modest predecessors have been forgotten. Goelro was not so much the full-grown offspring of Lenin's imagination as it was the gathering together of several separate planning authorities. Since the electrification program manifested the elements of rationalism, nationalism, and centralism in full measure, it is worth devoting some attention to Goelro's foundation.

As mentioned earlier, the earliest electrification plans under Soviet auspices began, at Lenin's behest, virtually on the morrow of October and had taken organizational shape in the spring of 1918, first with a string of regional electrification commissions, and then with the Central Electro-Technical Council that Krasin formed. From the summer of 1918 on, most local *sovnarkhozy* possessed departments for electrification. At least initially, the SEC encouraged planning at the local level, holding competitions for the best plans for construction and use of local power stations. It was particularly pleased with the *sovnarkhoz* of Zadonsk uezd in Voronezh guberniia, which worked out a detailed plan for electrifying local agriculture: electricity was to compensate for scarce labor, and new industries were to be created in ceramics, metals, and paper production, with these to stimulate and in turn be stimulated by mechanized agriculture.[48]

Between 1917 and 1921 some 157 new local power stations were built, an increase of more than 50 percent over 1917. This accounts for the fact that total electric power output in Russia actually rose over the same period despite drops in the output of the Petrograd and Moscow stations. Throughout

1919 and 1920 alone new local power stations built in Russia numbered in the dozens.[49] But as local stations diverted resources from national electrification projects, the center began to discourage and even forbid such local undertakings. Inessa Armand, working in the Moscow provincial government, wrote that local projects were to be permitted only if they proceeded under Moscow's direct "supervision and guidance."[50] At least one town was, in fact, expressly prohibited from finishing a station it had begun until the Moscow provincial *sovnarkhoz* first worked out a full provincial electrification plan.[51]

At the center a lack of coordination in planning electrification still existed as of early 1920. The SEC and the State Works Committee each had bodies for electro-technical development. In addition, the Agriculture Commissariat had formed a bureau in 1919 to study the potential for electrifying agriculture; in 1920 and 1921 it conducted research and experimentation in electric plowing, threshing, and seed selection. The commissariat also sponsored the electrification of experimental farms around Moscow and the electrification of a *sovkhoz* outside Petrograd in 1920.[52]

During the second breathing spell, these disparate offices were assembled into a single agency. Lenin recruited G. M. Krzhizhanovskii to head it. Krzhizhanovskii was an old Bolshevik—his party work went back to the founding of the Petersburg League of Struggle for the Emancipation of the Working Class—who had attended the Petersburg Technological Institute and subsequently managed the electric power station Elektroperedacha. The new commission, Goelro, took shape in February and March 1920 and soon became the leading national body planning an integrated electric power network.[53]

Although Krzhizhanovskii had been inactive in party affairs for some time, he took on the electrification project with enthusiasm. Under his chairmanship, Goelro posed itself an extremely ambitious task. Electrification was to do more than simply extend the "curves" or proportions of economic growth from before the revolution; it was to alter the very structure of the economy through the use of electrical energy. Through electrification, industry and agriculture would advance simultaneously, and promising but backward regions of the country would be developed.[54] Clearly the Bolsheviks were concerned with more than the building and linking of new power stations: they were proposing a general and long-term plan for industrialization.

When the commission completed its labors and presented its plan to the Eighth Soviet Congress in December 1920, the millennial expectations uniting the Bolsheviks and the technical specialists working with them were revealed. Lenin exuberantly referred to the report as "our second party program."[55] The plan envisioned the need for universal labor conscription into the foreseeable future. It separated long-term and short-term requirements, devising a crash program for dealing with the current situation and a long-term program for reconstruction. The long-range possibilities, particularly in the application of electricity to agriculture, excited the experts most. Land reclamation, soil melioration, vast water control projects, farm mechanization, rain and cloud control, and night illumination to speed growing, were but a few ideas. Once the principle of mechanization was accepted, the planners wrote, new applications would suggest themselves. Electric plows would supersede tractors. The old Russian problem of roadlessness could be overcome with a "mighty network" of electric trams stretching across the rural vastnesses.[56] All that was lacking amid the refulgent prospects was a realistic computation of cost.

The commission estimated that 17 billion gold rubles would be needed for the undertaking over its projected ten-year span. Even had a gold ruble then been in general circulation, the absence of legal markets and the disappearance of goods left equally incalculable the value of an hour of labor or the purchasing power of a gold ruble. The paper currency the government issued was almost worthless. Even if the forced labor were considered free of cost to the state, the value of materials needed could only be estimated arbitrarily. The cost breakdowns contained in the plan were nugatory. Some glimmering of this must have occurred to the planners, since, although they assigned electrification per se a total cost of 1.2 billion rubles and the new transportation system a cost of 8 billion rubles, they did not trouble to estimate the cost of electrifying agriculture.[57]

A comprehensive plan of development must employ cost estimates of some sort if it is to compare the value of the resources to be used. If information about scarcity prices is lacking because markets have broken down, other measures are used instead to make the diverse inputs commensurable: hypothetically one could compare the hours of labor needed to produce all the goods used by each project or even the calories expended in producing all the goods. (Soviet theorists made ingenious efforts along these lines in 1920 and 1921.) Or the planners could calculate separately the needs and availability in physical terms of each quantity. Such became the method of the five-year plans. But without indicators of the value of the goods used and the alternatives foregone, the plan is neither economical nor practicable. It points to a destination but fails to provide for a means of conveyance.

In short, until order was restored to the economy, either under central administration or through the marketplace, the regime could not estimate how meaningful its development plans were. At an earlier phase, confronted by criticism that the production plans drawn up by the Petrograd *sovnarkhoz* for the city's metals industry merely wasted scarce fuel since the factories could not meet their targets, the chairman of the metals department had responded that the plan had only "organizational" significance: it could not be expected to measure the true costs of production.[58] The utopianism of such plans led to the waste of scarce resources, but at the same time helped to legitimate the regime by identifying it with the prospect of the technological transformation of Russian society.

For the Bolsheviks, as for Europeans and Americans in the same period, science had a charismatic quality that led the new regime to prize it.[59] Their attitude was strongly influenced by the metaphorical significance of the scientific projects they pursued. In the revolutionary setting of social upheaval and apocalyptic expectation, science and technology became vehicles for unfettered imaginations. But, much as they spoke of a "mobilization of science," the Bolsheviks did not subject scientists and technicians to the regimentation instituted for workers and for political and cultural intellectuals. Rather, the regime co-opted the intelligentsia on the basis of a nationalistic and developmental ideology. In concert with it, the regime laid out the main lines of planned industrial and technological development which, although they seemed utopian in the civil war period, survived as the guiding principles of the "revolution from above" in the Stalin era: rapid growth of producers' goods industries, construction of great infrastructural projects such as canals and railroad lines, and mass electrification.

4 : The Technocratic and Democratic Left

As we have seen, for many of the Bolsheviks, particularly those with technical training, the promise of socialism lay in the conquest of backwardness. L. B. Krasin, who had studied at the St. Petersburg Technological Institute in the 1890s, wrote in his memoirs that as a student there he had led workers' circles, explaining to the workers the latest achievements of science in the West and blaming the autocracy for holding back Russia's own progress.[60] Krzhizhanovskii saw the Goelro plan, which integrated many power stations into a single nationwide grid, as creating a "single harmonious whole" as opposed to the former "anarchy" when Russia had "millions of isolated steam units." Indeed, he contrasted capitalism, as the age of steam, to socialism, the age of hydroelectric and even atomic power.[61] Projects like the electrification program, gigantic in scale and monumental in purpose, symbolized the ambitions of Soviet rule among those whom we have labeled the technocratic Left.

The Bolsheviks were not alone at that time in rhapsodizing over the power of scientific reason to reorder society. Probably the most striking manifestation of the technocratic outlook was the Taylor movement, named for the American proponent of rationalization in production and management, Frederick Taylor. Throughout Europe, "Taylorist" or "Americanist" methods of scientific management exerted a powerful influence; Charles S. Maier has aptly noted that Taylorism was most popular where representative government was held in lowest repute. Italian syndicalists and fascists, for example, were particularly drawn to engineering models of government. Mussolini embodied his fascination with technology in the fascist program ("the state is more than a state, it is a dynamo"), forming local *gruppi di competenza* in the fall of 1921, and after 1924, state-level *consigli tecnici* to help overcome internal social conflict by raising the level of development of the entire nation.[62]

Taylorism was appealing not only for its promise of superseding the political contests of classes and interests, but also because it represented, as Taylor himself saw, a "mental revolution" directed toward increasing the total national wealth and eliminating scarcity.[63] For Taylor, once prejudice was replaced with empiricism in the analysis of society, science might be directly applied to social modernization. In Russia, the rationalistic and developmental bias of the new regime attracted those of both the older and younger generations eager to be rid of reactionary politics based on myopic parochialism (see section 2 above). A new state, impartial, just and informed, would be the neutral arbiter of the quarrels of factions and classes. This distaste for politics, this turn to technical solutions to social dilemmas, had already been reflected in the "suprapolitical" stance of much of the scientific-technical intelligentsia. A similar aversion to the principle of an autonomous politics characterized Lenin, who claimed that the novelty of the Soviet state lay in its devotion to economics instead of politics. As he told Albert Rhys Williams, the Soviet government was an economic authority for an economic age.[64]

Although most of the advocates of Taylor's methods in Russia were engineers, the most active disciple was a factory worker and poet named Alexei Gastev. The son of a schoolteacher, and himself expelled from a teacher's institute, Gastev became known as an early "machine poet" who celebrated the liberating forces of the machine age, much like the futurist artists of the time.[65] Gastev achieved celebrity as the principal Bolshevik "poet of Taylorism." At the First Trade Union Congress, in January 1918, he presented a resolution calling for the adoption of the Taylor system; it passed.[66] At the First Congress of *Sovnarkhozy,* five months later, he again reported on Taylor methods, proposing that consumption be pegged to productivity and pointing out that Germany had already successfully taken this step.

Gastev's proposals met sharp opposition. Lozovskii wondered where Russia would find the model worker whose output would be taken as the norm and asked what would become of the masses of exhausted and starved workers that Russia did have. He went so far as to warn of creating a Russian Asiatic despotism.[67] Yet Gastev persevered. He wanted to create an Institute of Labor which would study the potential for what he called human "magnetizability" and man's "thermal possibilities." The institute would offer a curriculum of study for social engineering, covering such subjects as Taylor's methods and "psycho-technology." Early in 1921 his efforts were rewarded when a group of Taylorists in the Commissariat of Communications sponsored a conference on the scientific organization of labor. Soon after, the Central Council of Trade Unions heard Gastev's report on his proposed institute and accepted it almost without debate.[68] The institute was duly created and Gastev became its first director.[69]

Gastev hoped to transfer to machines all the toil of human creation: "machines," he predicted, "from being managed will become managers." The new society would be "mechanized collectivism." Like many technocratic theories, Gastev's vision subordinated individual volition to the unitary will of the collectivity. Although the technocratic Left generally emphasized the higher rationality made possible by subordinating political interests to efficiency needs, even Kritsman feared to go as far as Gastev. Kritsman found it necessary to insist that the development of productive forces would not make men automatons; it was better technology and better use of machines—in short, better organization—which would allow human creativity to find new ways of increasing productivity.[70]

The technocratic tendency offered a rationale for a national, as opposed to class, identity for the state, a functional basis for status stratification, and a hierarchial political system. In contrast, the democratic Left stressed egalitarianism, fraternity, and mass participation as legitimating values for the state. The democratic wing interpreted social solidarity in terms of corporate harmony, the harmony, for example, of an orchestra or chorus. For the democratic Left the only answer to the growing isolation and autonomy of the bureaucracy lay in bringing the masses into administration, strengthening party and class control over the state apparatus, and abolishing special privileges for the bureaucrats.[71] Bukharin's draft party program, circulated in 1918, contrasted democratic content (seen as "life") to hierarchical form: "From top to bottom a workers' management of industry is gradually created. . . . If the higher boards are not supported by the local ones, then they will hang in the air, become bureaucratized, or, as they say, bureaucratic institutions from which any live revolutionary spirit has fled."[72] Centralization was necessary, he conceded at the session of the Central Executive Committee of 29 April 1918, and during a civil war democracy must be limited. But decentralization to a considerable degree was also essential to expand the opportunity for worker initiative (*samodeiatel'nost'*): "There must be a director's stick, but it must be wielded by the workers themselves."[73]

The democratic Left argued that institutions lacking the active participation of the masses would become isolated and bureaucratized. The masses must be encouraged to take part in making administrative decisions. But the Left failed to specify the powers which rightfully belonged to the masses. It advanced no concept of rights. Given the paramount stress on collective interests, its attention to popular initiative could only refer to the freedom to perform given duties in the state hierarchy more efficiently. A delegate at the Second *Sovnarkhoz* Congress in December 1918 objected to passage of a proposed resolution on precisely these grounds. The resolution observed that the nationalization of industry and the formation of state administrative boards had "created new conditions for the independent initiative of the working class." What could independent initiative (*samodeiatel'nost'*) mean, the delegate wondered? Surely socialism demanded that it refer to the power to oversee the economy, since proletarian dictatorship would be meaningless if there were still an organ outside the working class that "supported" the workers' initiative. The initiative of the workers had to be the very government of the state.[74] His remarks outraged the other delegates. He had, however, raised the fundamental dilemma of socialist construction. If the realm of the state's powers was not the same as that of the working class's political activity, who would govern the state?

Although members of the democratic Left formed opposition groupings in each of the first three years of Soviet rule, they rarely agreed on any particular set of institutional arrangements for checking the power of the bureaucracy. At times they defended workers' control (although they did *not* do so in the 1918 opposition), collective management, and stronger local power. But they never raised the defense of any of these institutions to the plane of principle. As a consequence, their democratic ideals remained detached from any given structure. The only safeguard of democratic solidarity on which the democratic Left insisted was class purity in the composition of the state. Whenever it was disturbed by the undue power of the central state organs, the democratic Left was less likely to look to mutual and binding checks among state bodies to overcome it than to call for the cleansing out of class-alien elements from the bureaucracy.

For both democrats and technocrats, the object of state-building was not, therefore, to establish deliberative and problem-solving procedures by which conflicts of interest might be resolved, but to design so perfect a society that such conflicts would not arise. The problem of *achieving* the harmonious equilibrium of socialism preoccupied Bolshevik theorists on both wings. Many devised theoretical schemes depicting Soviet social development as a sequence of phases.[75] For example, Osinskii presented socialist construction as a three-stage process: first the proletariat seized economic centers and established its dictatorship; then it reconstructed the relations of production; finally it raised productivity through technical and organizational work.[76] Trotsky's four-stage economic plan of 1920 was another such sequence of stages.

The most abstract of these constructs was the Kritsman-Bukharin theory, which was first introduced by Kritsman in *Narodnoe khoziaistvo* in 1918. Kritsman asserted that the revolution passed through four consecutive phases: ideological, political, economic, and technical.[77] Bukharin adopted the idea and presented it in *The Economics of the Transition Period*. The ideological revolution referred to the shift in popular consciousness from patriotism to class awareness. Political revolution meant the destruction and reconstruction of the state. Economic revolution put forth a new model of productive relations after extensive breakdown; Kritsman believed that the Soviet regime was still in the economic stage and urged that socialist reorganization be completed as rapidly as possible through the use of inherited trusts and syndicates. Finally, technological revolution would begin when the new model of productive relations attained equilibrium, enabling technology to increase the productive power of the new society.[78] In the postrevolutionary stage, class struggle was replaced with a social "regulator"—the state. In Bukharin's model politics was replaced by automatic direction provided by the state's statistical bureaus.[79] The image was prophetic: not that of a machine guided by a political reason, but that of a servo-mechanism or cybernetic system automatically adjusting itself to new conditions.

After Kritsman had presented the scheme again in his long 1924 essay, "The Heroic Period of the Great October Revolution," a Bolshevik reviewer pointed out that the political and economic revolutions were in actuality different aspects of the same process. He found Bukharin's presentation of the same scheme in *Economics of the Transition Period* more successful because Bukharin recognized the intertwined character of these processes. In short, as the reviewer perceived, the Kritsman-Bukharin "stages" were no more than analytically segregated aspects of a single historical event.[80]

It was necessary, nonetheless, for the Bolsheviks to devise step-theories of the transition period in order to demonstrate that socialism would be the outcome of the revolution. Step-theories supplied a temporal sequence connecting the two orders of time in which the Bolsheviks moved, the revolutionary present and the socialist future. These theories relied upon figurative images of socialism which tended to remove it to the conceptual plane of Utopia. Bukharin foresaw, as the end of the revolutionary process, "a new, higher, golden age."[81] No more venerable image of Utopia exists than that of the "golden age": Plato draws it from earlier Greek myth in order to create a new myth for the *Republic;* Dostoevskii presents dreams of a golden age in three novels; even Chernyshevskii allows Vera Pavlovna to dream of a golden age in *What Is to Be Done?* The golden age is a poetic device for an order *out of time,* an age lost before history but recoverable at the end of time.[82] The step-theories imposed analytical order on the chaos of the revolutionary period, dissolving the problem of the transition period into poetic imagery.

Among the technocratic Left, the democrats' preoccupation with the achievement of social harmony only generated impatience. A striking expression of this position appeared in an article by Ia. Gol'tsman, a member of the Central Committee of the Metalworkers' Union, in 1918. Scoffing at the "utopianism" of the democratic Left, Bukharin, in particular, Gol'tsman called for industrial progress in order to liberate society. Attractive pictures of stateless communism offered no practical answers, and arguments about "state capitalism" were useless exercises in scholasticism. To realize technological progress, power must be centralized: Bukharin's "Central African revolutionariness" would not fool the workers.[83]

Gol'tsman's practical-mindedness and stress on technological progress led him to embrace Lenin's program of centralization and to dismiss "workers' control." Impatient with theories of statelessness, committed to modernization, his attitude typified a current of working-class sentiment which created a base of support for Soviet dictatorship among those proletarian activists whom the revolution had thrust into prominence, such as Gol'tsman, Chubar', and Veinberg. Among the Bolshevik intelligentsia this attitude defined the technocratic Left. Reinterpreting Marxist doctrine, its members held that surplus labor survived under socialism so as to be reinvested in social development. Indeed, the extraction of surplus labor became the *goal* of socialism, because, according to one author, "the development of the communist revolution is the development of the productive forces."[84]

Both the technocrats and democrats had to face the problem that the social solidarity upon which the socialist state's power rested had not yet been attained. In response, Bolsheviks commonly stressed the importance of education in raising the consciousness of the mass of workers and peasants. Krzhizhanovskii, for example, aware that the "new internal loan" from the workers that would be demanded in order to electrify Russia would arouse resistance, called for thorough popular education to explain its importance.[85] The problem of power tended to be reduced to that of education: many leaders were prone to beg the question of democratic choice by describing Soviet institutions as "schools of communism." The metaphor became so widespread, and so equivocal, that Kollontai was tempted to attack it as cant:

When one begins to turn over the pages of the stenographic minutes and speeches made by our prominent leaders, one is astonished by the unexpected manifestation of their pedagogic proclivities. Every author of theses proposes the most perfect system of bringing up the masses, but all these systems of "education" lack provisions for freedom of experiment, for training and expressing creative abilities by those who are to be taught; in this respect our pedagogues are also behind the times.[86]

But even Kollontai does not escape the educational bind, as she demands greater "freedom for experiment" when the problem she poses is the powerlessness of the masses.

Lacking a structural theory with which to criticize the Soviet state, the democratic Left, even in its most radical incarnation as the Workers' Opposition, could not advance much beyond trenchant insights into the bureaucracy's loss of class purity. At the Tenth Party Congress, the Workers' Opposition protested their concern for party unity. They claimed that not they, but alien elements in the party and state, were the true obstacles to unity. Their solution was to rid the party of impurities. They did, to be sure, suggest some procedural controls, such as greater openness of decision-making and greater accountability, through elections, of leaders to masses. The call for elections was tempered, though, by the demand for "workers' centralism." They alluded to the extinct ideal of workers' control in calling upon workers' committees to run enterprises; but the degree of autonomy the committees might possess was limited, in the Workers' Opposition program, by the equal stress on maximum concentration and centralization of control over all productive resources, with national development to be guided by a comprehensive plan.[87]

In responding to the attacks by the democratic Left, Lenin went some distance to concede the severity of the problem of bureaucratization and repeatedly demanded the infusion of proletarian forces into the state apparatus. He also stressed education and the gradual raising of the cultural level of the general population. Never did he accept any of the structural prescriptions of the democratic Left, however. Party policy consistently subordinated democratic ideals to the demand for centralized power.

Yet the weakness of the democratic wing was its strength as well. An idealized conception of social solidarity, with its potentially antiauthoritarian implications, remained embedded in Soviet culture together with the companion ideals of collective service and egalitarianism. In later periods, these ideas would become the basis for serious critiques and reforms during the "Cultural Revolution" of 1928–1932 and again in the Khrushchev period. But their abstract quality also helped to ensure that the "golden age" on the other side of Soviet history would forever remain a Utopia.

[[CHAPTER SIX]]

The Cudgel and the Machine

In mid-1919, Alexander Shliapnikov, who a year later became a leader of the Workers' Opposition, analyzed the difficulties the Bolsheviks were experiencing in their efforts to construct a centralized administrative apparatus. He contrasted two styles of organization, which he likened to familiar objects: that of the *dubinushka* or cudgel, signifying brute force; and that of the *mashinushka* or little machine. Shliapnikov complained that the government's customary response to disorder was to use the cudgel to smash through the obstacles to its will. The results of this method, he argued, were to increase the haphazardness of results, to personalize authority, and to run the state in a *kustarno,* that is, a homemade or handicrafted, way. For the Bolsheviks, *kustarnye* methods had to be overcome, because they corresponded to the old world of crude petty-bourgeois individualism. Needed instead, Shliapnikov wrote, was the machinelike approach to organization pioneered by the Ford Motor Company, where each worker performed a specialized function in the collective effort.[1]

With this simile Shliapnikov conveyed the self-defeating character of the Bolsheviks' mobilizing methods. The use of the coercive cudgel to build a state generated the phenomena that Shliapnikov deplored—disorganization, random behavior, and arbitrary power. But although posing cudgel and machine as problem and solution, Shliapnikov identified the antinomian quality of Bolshevik socialism, which sought to reconcile the principle of national mobilization with that of an imper-

sonal, harmonious technocracy. The use of the cudgel to mobilize resources for the construction of so highly organized a
state created the dilemma for which the cudgel was the only
solution. In this chapter I will analyze three interrelated aspects of this vicious circle, which lasted until the Bolsheviks
retreated to the NEP. First, I examine the dispersion of administrative authority in the state, caused by the severe insufficiency of information at the disposal of the center and its
inability to coordinate the competing bureaucracies which
were nominally subordinate to it. Second, I consider the
center's efforts to reconcentrate the power to command resources through the use of "shock methods" and similar
attempts to narrow the scope of its control to a few high
priority sectors. Finally, I discuss the proposition that the fragmentation of social organization to which the regime was
forced to bow in the end was itself a product of the repeated
blows of the cudgel.

1 : The Weakness of Central Control

In the third chapter, I called attention to the friction between
the *glavki* (and other "vertical" bureaucracies) and the *sovnarkhozy* that attempted to oversee local industries. Through most
of 1918 and 1919, it will be recalled, the *glavki* succeeded in
aggrandizing power at the expense of the localities. At the
same time their numbers multiplied. As a growing number of
expanding agencies competed for dwindling resources, effective central control, as Rykov pointed out, became more difficult, not less. State bodies claimed monopolies over the goods
they produced, impeding those organs responsible for supply
and distribution. As a result, continuous bureaucratic conflict
interfered with the center's decisions about the allocation of
resources.[2]
An observer of the *glavki* noted that one reason they worked
so poorly was that they often gave instructions without knowing
whether they would be obeyed. Neither they nor the local *sov-*

narkhozy with which they clashed could plan effectively owing to uncertainty over their powers and resources. The *glavki* were often attacked for interfering in day-to-day management of enterprises. At the end of 1918, V. Kossior warned that central economic organs would do better to confine their efforts to the general regulation of the economy, rather than attempting to manage all the enterprises; overextension only led to chaotic, *kustarnye* results. One of the strongest critics of the "glavkomania," Artur Kaktyn' of the Northern Economic Council, contended that the *glavki* simply ignored the physical obstacles to central control, such as distance and poor communications between the center and the localities.[3]

As each agency accumulated what control it could over the resources it needed, overlapping claims inevitably conflicted. A common solution was the creation of interagency organizations to handle questions cutting across departmental lines. However, as these multiplied, they added to the confusion over lines of responsibility. Larin, initially the strongest advocate of *glavki,* made some incisive comments in a pamphlet of 1920. He observed that the government tended to create a special bureaucracy for every need; for the procurement and distribution of felt boots and bast sandals, Chekvalap was created, the All-Russian Extraordinary Commission for *Valenki* and *Lapti,* an interagency commission which proceeded to cover Russia with regional Chekvalaps and even to send its own representatives to yet other interdepartmental commissions. One *mot* of the time concerned an apocryphal interagency body made up of representatives of the Food Commissariat, the Agriculture Commissariat, and the *glavk* for the Air Force, created for the purpose of resolving the question of obtaining bird's milk.[4]

The problem of bureaucratization was commonly lamented. One line of explanation of the problems of the bureaucracy proceeded by analyzing the structural conditions in which bureaucrats worked. An article in *Novyi put'* in early 1919 reviewing current press reports noted that the issue currently dominating the press was the effect of bureaucratization in stifling initiative (*samodeiatel'nost'*). Bureaucrats and public alike, according to the article, recognized that bureaucracy was growing prodigiously, but that explanations for the phenomenon varied. Noting that clerks labored constantly under the suspicion of sabotage, received niggardly salaries, and suffered all the scarcities of the time, the article's author concluded that low productivity was to be expected from them. Early in 1921, the Hungarian expatriate economist Evgenii Varga renewed this argument, pointing out that bureaucratism, not the bureaucrats, should be blamed. Bureaucratism, a condition occurring when "means became their own ends," was fostered by the fact that clerical pay was too low, leading to moonlighting and corruption.[5]

More often, however, poor performance was attributed to the social and political composition of the bureaucracy rather than to its setting. Most critics taking this tack emphasized either or both of two points. One was the fact that the state depended on old clerks and specialists who returned to their former indolence once in Soviet employ. Lenin, for example, responding to attacks on bureaucratism and glavikism at the Seventh Soviet Congress in December 1919, argued that simple reorganization would not solve the problem, since the same old bourgeois specialists would still be needed to run industry. Lenin's solution was to infuse more workers and establish better supervision in the bureaucracy.[6]

The other, and more verifiable, explanation lay with the low levels of experience and education of those entering the bureaucracy. Many clerks were barely literate or were teenagers not yet out of school. Visitors to state offices in this period attested to the youthfulness, inexperience, and indifference of the employees.[7] A common jibe of the time concerning the SEC was that it was a nest of women or that it being run by *sovetskie baryshni* (fine young Soviet ladies).[8]

Zinoviev summed up these various arguments at the Eighth Soviet Congress (December 1920), distinguishing between the "objective" and "subjective" causes of bureaucratism. Under the first heading he placed the necessity of allocating scarce resources; under the second the low quality of personnel in the state apparatus. Their carelessness and lack of culture made far more difficult the task of administering industry, difficulties that the Bolsheviks, he conceded, had at first seriously under-estimated.[9] Lenin himself came to appreciate the problem of culture as opposed to class as he searched for remedies to over-bureaucratization in 1922. The course of his disillusionment has been detailed by Moshe Lewin and Adam Ulam and is revealed in his articles on the Worker-Peasant Inspectorate. Lenin did not turn to legalism, liberalism, or decentralization as the answer to the problem. Indeed he seems to have discarded the answer he formerly gave, that of injecting more workers into an ailing apparatus: the workers, he wrote, "would like to build a better apparatus for us, but they do not know how. . . . They have not yet developed the culture required for this." Instead his solution was strictly educational: "In order to reno-vate our state apparatus we must at all costs set out, first, to learn, secondly, to learn, and thirdly, to learn."[10]

Over the short run the regime could not raise the general level of culture sufficiently to make the bureaucracy a reliable instrument of central control. Rather, it turned to bureaucra-cies standing outside the regular administration to check abuses of power. These included the party, the Cheka, and the organs of state and workers' control. None was wholly satisfactory. Rykov put the best face on matters in an interview with Arthur Ransome when he noted that the newer members of the party had no knowledge of the class struggle, or of Marx, but had joined the party in order to participate in the construction of the new order.[11] The party's personnel were stretched thin. In November 1920 Rykov observed that one reason for the isola-tion of the upper levels of the party hierarchy from the lower was the excessive demands placed on party members, so that many factories were left without a communist cell, or even without any communists at all.[12] A report from September 1920 revealed that no more than 2 percent of the entire staff of the SEC departments and *glavki* were party members; many organs had none.[13] Maintaining the party's quality contradicted the need for rapid expansion to meet the need for leadership and administrative skill. Recruitment to the party had a boom-and-bust quality. After the purges and mobilizations in the summer of 1919, party membership was substantially lower than its October 1917 level; thus the immense swelling of the ranks caused by the recruitment drives of late 1919 and 1920 weakened controls over the quality of recruits. The control the party could exercise over the state bureaucracy became problematical; the party shared many of the same "subjective" defects, as is evident from the fact that during the purge of 1921, a quarter of the members were dropped from party rolls.[14]

The same "objective" and "subjective" factors prevented the political police, the Cheka, from serving as a check on bureaucratic abuses. It possessed substantial power to investigate and punish crimes by state employees and created special institutions to expose sabotage in economic administration. However, the eyewitness and memoir literature agree that the Cheka was ineffective in eliminating corruption, ignorance, and inefficiency in the bureaucracy, very largely because it possessed many of the same defects. It attracted individuals hungry for power and revenge, whose inability to distinguish real from imagined sabotage was commonly criticized by leaders and citizens alike.[15] Although it often subjected officials and specialists to harassment, degradation, and arrests, it did not rationalize the structure of power.[16]

The organs in which the leaders invested their hopes for general financial and administrative oversight belonged to the Commissariat for State Control and its corresponding workers' organs formed by the trade unions. Elsewhere I have pointed out that the regime did not manage to merge these bodies into a single and comprehensive hierarchy and that the State Commissariat was roundly attacked for claiming far greater power than it could effectively wield. It was commonly criticized for displaying attitudes of bureaucratic arrogance. To reform it, the central leadership periodically attempted to restructure it, to merge it with workers' organizations, and to give it broader powers, but it remained unable to satisfy the demand for a general accounting and supervisory body. Through its inspections, it did occasionally correct abuses by other bodies (for example, it arranged the release of some who had been wrongfully arrested by the Cheka). On balance, though, State Control probably hindered the work of central and local agencies more than it helped them, because it was incapable of reviewing all receipts and expenditures for all official organizations, as it claimed the right to do, and it could not serve as the fund of managerial expertise that the leaders hoped it would be.[17]

The conventional explanations for the bureaucracy's "objective" and "subjective" faults failed for the most part to examine the underlying causes for the fact that central control declined as the state swelled. The most fundamental cause was the state's inability to replace the "fingers" of market-based coordination in the economy with the "thumbs" (or cudgels) of state power. More immediately, there were three proximate factors which undermined centralization. The first was the erosion of ideological constraints. Nearly all non-Bolshevik observers stressed that corruption pervaded the state. Although in discussing this point one is restricted to impressionistic or anecdotal material, the literature is rich in evidence. General Ipatieff, whom we encountered in the last chapter, found graft common to all business transactions of the period, honesty impossible for anyone. Alcohol, which in potable forms was under a prohibition which lasted until 1923, became a vital medium of illegal exchange. Working in the Commissariat of Health, Fedor Dan noted that bribery and "gifts" had become a "universal custom," not merely in dealings among individuals, but in the agreements among government bodies as well.[18] Even when Soviet officials were honest, their ignorance of the matters they oversaw allowed subordinates ample opportunities for the pursuit of private gain.[19] The terrible shortage of food and consumer goods forced citizens onto the black market to meet subsistence needs and led government agencies to buy and sell goods and services outside official channels. As we shall see shortly in greater detail, corruption was simply a border zone between the state-run sector of the economy and the vast marketplace of private trade.

The blurring of the line between showcase projects and outright deception occurred early in the regime's existence. The Commissariat of Education maintained favored schools, with access to any resources they needed, while most schools suffered neglect. Visitors to the Soviet Republic were not simply shown the revolution's finest accomplishments; they were often isolated and pampered, as if to shield them from the realities of Russian life. Visiting in the spring of 1920, a British trade-union delegation was served sandwiches by white-frocked servants at a hotel where the floor on which the reception was held had been completely redecorated. Victor Serge recalled that when the delegates to the First Congress of the Communist International arrived in early 1919, they were "shepherded from museums to model nurseries" without coming into contact with "the real, living Moscow, with its starvation-rations, its arrests, its sordid prison-episodes, its backstage racketeering." Nor was it true, Alexandra Kollontai wrote in 1920, that the civil war made it impossible to improve the squalid living conditions of the workers. When any Soviet agency demanded a renovated building for its own use, all the necessary building materials and labor could be found.[20]

Beyond the pervasive corruption of the socialist and egalitarian ideals of the revolution, two other factors weakened central control. The first was the rapid growth in the size of the state bureaucracy, which matched the decline in the number of productive workers. In early November 1920 Larin claimed that the state employed nearly one million clerks.[21] Even by the end of 1919 over half of the SEC's budget was consumed by personnel costs. The ratio of clerical to productive workers grew. In 1918 it stood at 1 : 9.1. By 1920 it had become 1 : 5.4. At the ten metal plants comprising the GOMZa combine, the corresponding figures were: 1916, 1 : 10; 1920, 1 : 4.[22] Since September 1918 the SEC's apparatus had grown fourfold, from 6000 as of September 1918, to 24,000 by the end of 1920. By the end of January 1921, 26,000 employees were registered.[23] Taking local economic councils into account, the entire SEC system numbered 234,000.[24] Aside from the enormous burden this bureaucratic expansion placed on the economy, it clearly increased the center's inability to manage industry.

Above all, the center lacked basic information about the performance of the economy. It had little idea of the size of the state sector, the number of officials and workers in its domain, or how they were distributed. It lacked the knowledge on which to judge the costs or effects of the policies it proposed. Confronted by one crisis after another, the center relied on the cudgel to command results and resolve uncertainty. Elementary information about the state of production could not be gathered; reports, when they came in, contained widely divergent figures about the same branches.[25] Most state organs kept only rudimentary books, and only in 1920 did most start submitting accounts to the center regularly.[26] Lacking information about the availability of fuel, raw materials, and labor and about the state of repair of equipment, the *glavki* issued blind production orders. Through the entire period, there was virtually no meaningful planning of production. Occasionally local *sovnarkhozy* drew up plans, and interbranch supply and distribution plans did exist for some products. For the most part, however, plans bore little operational significance, and there was no general or systematic planning.

As Lenin put it in his address to the Tenth Party Congress, during this period the regime lacked a point of reference for perceiving the excesses of its policies. The government simply did not have the experience necessary to observe moderation.[27] Lacking knowledge, the regime was susceptible to the appeal of fantasy. We have already discussed such examples as the famous pine-cone campaign and the cost-free electrification program. Wits, in fact, quickly dubbed the Goelro plan "electrifiction."[28] However, as the broad-gauge effort at total national centralization failed to bring the economy under its control, the regime narrowed its field of action to a few "shock" sectors. Here it intended to swing its cudgel as precisely as possible and for maximum effect.

2 : Bottlenecks and Breakthroughs

For most of the period, the leaders sought to overcome the erosion of their power by making new efforts to concentrate power at the center. We have seen that this process often took the form of creating new bureaucracies, such as *glavki* or inter-agency committees, each charged with responsibility for some specific function or resource. Rykov called attention to this pattern as early as December 1918, when he noted that the state still lacked a unified and efficient apparatus and responded to needs simply by creating hierarchies on top of each other. His solution was to eliminate superfluous middle levels of power.[29] The notion that intervening layers of authority which cut off the center from the enterprises and localities must be "smashed" was a common one: it was propounded at virtually every conference and in nearly every article. Even the Workers' Opposition took this tack, although joining it with demands for democratization, when it called for a true "workers' centralism" to replace the plethora of competing, corrupt, and unproletarian bureaucracies choking the state. But the creation of such intervening layers was not accidental. It was the unavoidable result of the manner in which the Bolsheviks constructed the state. Only in late 1920 and early 1921 did an alternative theoretical position emerge in Bolshevik discussions of administration.

Although the drive for full centralism was relaxed, as we saw, at the end of 1919, the center continued to claim direct control over the most vital sectors of production and allocation. The renewal of labor mobilization in 1920 accompanied the rise of a new use of the cudgel's power, called "shock methods." Shock methods narrowed the focus of activity by singling out specific enterprises, projects, and categories of workers and providing them with special rations, closer support, and more personnel. In general, shock methods were not successful. Two principal reasons existed for this. The first was that as soon as a small group of exceptionally well favored enterprises was set aside, uncontrollable political pressures led to the addition of new enterprises to the list, which reduced the stock of resources available to each. The result was that soon none was supplied adequately, and a new and yet higher priority category of enterprises would have to be established.

The other reason had to do with the secondary effects of shock methods. Shock methods made sense in a system in which they produced usable resources, the value of which was greater than the losses incurred in producing them. This might occur if morale could be stimulated that otherwise would not have been available, or if reserves of raw materials or human energy could be tapped that would be wasted under normal circumstances. But in a system with absolutely no reserves, no goods or human energies to spare (the convertibility of resources having long since been exhausted), each swing of the cudgel intended to divert supplies to a shock sector reduced the net availability of supplies for the entire system. As a consequence, shock methods yielded one-time, short-term benefits at the cost of longer-term losses. Obviously they could not long be sustained.

In the broad sense of the term, shock methods began in late 1918, when 250 defense plants, employing a quarter million workers, were placed on military rations.[30] After 1919 the system was extended, apparently, to nondefense plants as well. By the spring of 1920, over one million workers were receiving special rations. By October, 1.4 million workers and employees were on such rations; by December, 2.7 million. Rations were going to well over half of all workers in productive branches: all those in the paper industry, nearly all in mining, around three-quarters of those in metalworking, textiles, and railroad transport. One might imagine, therefore, that shock rations would have come to mean little more than ordinary rations.

And, indeed, the norms of the special rations were rarely met. The average proportion of fulfillment was between one-quarter and one-fifth; on the other hand, ordinary rations were fulfilled even less.[31]

A similar devaluation of the shock concept can be seen in the expansion of the number of plants put on shock status. As the number of shock enterprises increased, the effectiveness of the category decreased. Between June and December 1920 the number of metals plants on shock status rose from 20 to 240; by December there were thought to be 1716 shock enterprises altogether. A different system was tried, called "model factories." In August the presidium of the SEC named a group of model factories, at first 20 in number, and later 27.[32] These existed side-by-side with the various categories of shock plants. The problem was that the relative priority of the different categories of enterprises so identified was not firmly fixed or consistently applied. For example, one issue of *Novyi put'* (October 1920) contradicted itself on the question of whether the Putilov workers were on shock status. One article claimed that Putilov was one of 6 metal factories in Petrograd on shock rations. The following article asserted that Putilov and others had been removed from the top priority list when Moscow decided that they were too hard to supply. It had been decided to reopen one factory and place it alone on shock status. However, at the same time, a list of factories of second priority was created, which included Putilov and 20 other plants.[33]

In October 1920, a survey of fifty-five metalworking factories showed that in some respects, those on full shock status were operating in worse conditions than those assigned lower priority. Certainly these figures (shown in table 3) should be treated with great caution, but they do indicate wide disparities in the ability of shock methods to ensure fulfillment of plan targets or to supply enterprises more effectively, particularly with labor, then they could be supplied through other channels.

Shock methods were a response born in desperation. At best, their successes were costly to other enterprises dependent on

Table 3

State of the Metalworking Industry, October 1920 (percentage of input requirements or output targets met)

	Full Shock	Conditionally Shock	"Especially important"	Others
Adequacy of fuel supply	100%	70%	73%	100%
Adequacy of labor supply	25	72	66	91
Adequacy of materials supply	100	80	85	80
Fulfillment of program	33	102	104	95

Source: Novyi put', no. 11 (1920), p. 15.

state supply channels. Where they failed, they could not be justified at all. An attempt to stem the fuel crisis by building a rail link between the Caspian Sea and the Urals connecting the towns of Emba, Aleksandrov-Gai, and Krasnyi Kut, called the Algembra project, was placed on military footing. In March 1920 its scope was expanded by the plan of building an oil pipeline starting from the opposite end. The two lines were to meet in June 1921. Immense quantities of rails and timber were sent to the sites. By mid-May 1920 the project employed 15,000 workers. Efforts to send 20,000 more were side-tracked by the beginning of the Polish war. The 1920 harvest, construction projects in the west, and other needs prevented more shipments. Although the government continued to expend resources on the project, it ultimately was abandoned.[34]

Shock methods, by strengthening individual factories, checked the persistent pressures to reduce wage differentials among workers. Solomon Schwartz concluded that although the differentials among categories of labor *within* factories showed a marked leveling trend during the period, differences *among* factories reached ratios as high as 1 : 10. Since wages were hinged to output, more successful factories could pass the cumulative benefits along to their workers.[35] In fact, wage differentials were too low to suit the leaders, who acted repeatedly to reward the efficient and penalize the slack. Ruble bonuses lost all meaning, however, with the devaluation of Soviet currency, and pressures toward equalization resumed. The government sought to use in-kind bonuses, but their effect was hampered by the frequent problem of late receipt (delays of three or four months were common).[36] However, as workers came increasingly to depend on in-kind rations, the government could more easily link output to reward. In October 1920 the Council of Commissars decreed a new system of bonuses. Enterprises that reached 200 percent of their target in a given month would receive 100 percent of a given food bonus; 100 percent fulfillment would be rewarded with 40 percent of the bonus. Lower levels of fulfillment would not be rewarded. Technical and administrative personnel would receive one and one-half times the individual bonuses given to workers. For model enterprises the standards were set higher.[37] But this was only one of many such attempts to devise differentials.

At the end of 1919, the Seventh Soviet Congress resolved that inequalities in pay were too great and that a uniform food ration for labor should be instituted. Various proposals accordingly circulated. The Council of Commissars embodied a decision to reduce differentials in a decree adopted on 30 April 1920, but decided to delay implementing it until September.[38] More important than decrees in determining the structure of workers' pay, however, were two factors. Actual rations were determined in any given enterprise by the state's ability to reward productivity or support high-priority sectors, and this was always problematic. Second, any formal attempt to legislate differential incentives ran up against the equalizing forces inherent in the workers' dependence upon the state for bare subsistence goods—food, clothing, communal services—which were less amenable to differential distribution than money wages. By 1920 over 90 percent of all wages were paid in kind, but the rations actually received often fell below 50 percent of the norm.[39]

Still, the various efforts to create favored sectors and categories had some effect in countering equalization, particularly in the cumulative advantage of successful factories. The differentials provoked protest from the workers. At the Tenth Party Congress, Lozovskii complained that aside from the privileges enjoyed by the top administrative stratum, at least thirteen rationing categories had been established: extra-shock, shock, half-shock, and so on. He reported that at workers' meetings and conferences, the workers repeatedly demanded that the state equalize wages and that party members live like workers.[40]

The failure of shock methods prompted a variety of explanations. Kamenev pointed to one problem at the Ninth Party Congress in March 1920, when he observed that each Soviet leader demanded extra resources for some sector in which he took an especial interest.[41] Lack of coordination at the top set the system at cross-purposes. Other commentators began to see shock methods as essentially self-defeating. An American socialist visiting Russia noted that each application of shock methods produced results up to a point, at which time it would be discovered that other sectors were in similarly bad straits. For example, when a few locomotives had been repaired, fuel to run them would be unavailable.[42] While the sequential exposure of bottlenecks in a system is a crude form of self-regulation, it gradually became apparent to the Bolsheviks that shock methods were on balance reducing their capacity for systemic planning.[43]

This point came to be made explicitly in the course of a discussion, in late 1920, of the failure of shock methods. By the time a congress of representatives of shock factories met in early 1921, it was scarcely surprising that the delegates vociferously complained that the center had given too many factories shock status without being able to supply them and then held local authorities responsible for seeing that they met production targets. As early as September 1920 press articles began to criticize the shock approach for failing to bring about the coordination required by true centralism.

At first the commentaries fell back on the old truisms—central power must break through the power of the intervening, conflicting organs and provide all organs with direct and explicit goals.[44] Soon, however, the discussion took a turn toward the identification of the conditions of true central planning. (Elsewhere I have discussed the transformation of this new awareness of the harm shock methods caused to the whole system into a concern with the internal dynamics of an economic system.) Out of this discussion came a theoretical understanding of the laws that applied to a planned economy. The foundations of "material balances" planning were laid at this time, although Soviet planners found it difficult in succeeding years to apply the abstract criteria identified by the theorists to the attempt to draw up national balance sheets of materials flow. The discussion of shock methods taught a crucial lesson to those inclined to analyze them empirically: the economy had to be treated as a complex system, not as an army, and its self-regulating tendency had to be respected as a principle of planning. At the end of 1918, for example, the Northern Economic Council had boasted that all resources in the local economy had a designated use, even if the plans could not be fulfilled. Overall, their targets were met by no more than 50 percent, with light industry meeting its targets by 75 percent, transport by 30 percent, agricultural implements by 10–15 percent. Bolshevik theorists now grasped that contrary to their earlier belief (that plans are beacons, will still be valid tomorrow, have symbolic but not organizational significance, and so forth), target planning of this kind was worse than no planning. It only compounded bottlenecks by concentrating resources in the least efficient enterprises.[45]

The real breakthrough, then, in smashing the bottlenecks of the system was not achieved through the use of shock methods. It was instead a significant theoretical advance in Bolshevik thinking about economic systems. Shock methods corresponded to the martial spirit of the mobilization system, in which the center employs its cudgel to break the barriers to its control. In war, as in Trotsky's heroic defense of Petrograd in the fall of 1919, such methods produced dramatic results. But the Bolsheviks mistook the economic dilemmas they faced in the rear in imagining them to be soluble by the same means. The problems were entirely different. In war, the "multiplier effect" of one side's success was reflected in the surge of its morale and the collapse of that of the enemy. Over and over in the Russian civil war, a successful attack by one side so dismayed the other that its forces melted away or even defected to the winning side. In fact, like many civil and guerrilla struggles, the war more often took the form of the cyclical disintegration and reforming of each side's forces than that of a series of well-defined advances and retreats. A forceful offensive might demoralize and rout the enemy until it stretched too thin and in turn succumbed to a counterattack. This phenomenon undoubtedly owed much to the general weakness of morale on both sides and the breakdown of society on most fronts, particularly in rural areas where the allegiances of the peasant masses were fluid.

But society, even in its ruin, had still been formed by the development of a national system of production and exchange. Although terribly reduced in capacity, the institutions it had shaped continued to support the state, which was unable to place them entirely on a collectively administered basis. The relationship of the state economy to the black, gray, and peasant marketplaces outside its walls still retained the characteristics of a system, tending toward a point of equilibrium between demand and supply. Mobilizing methods such as the shock system centralized control over resources but led to larger losses of control and information, yielding negative overall returns. In his memoir of the period, Viktor Shklovskii commented that the system had tried to get ahead by stealing from itself.[46] In war, success was available at the expense of the other side. In the economy there was no other side.

3 : Public Authority and Private Markets

We might summarize the argument so far as follows. Through mobilization, including labor conscription, repression, and shock methods, the Soviet regime attempted to reassemble a revolutionary society into a centralized state. Organizations and initiative formerly outside the state, particularly those belonging to economic enterprise, would now be joined to and guided by the state. The anarchy of markets would be replaced with a planned order.

We have also seen that the state actually constructed was a sprawling and ramshackle edifice, the product of no architect's design. The coordination of its bureaucracies occurred less through the leaders' decrees than through the bargains struck within and across agency lines. As Charles Lindblom puts it, under such circumstances bureaucracies become rough approximations to markets. Similarly, Anthony Downs refers to the problem of "leakage" in bureaucratic organizations.[47] In the Bolshevik state, not only goods, but also information, leaked from the leaders' grasp. As we saw, the Bolsheviks themselves were troubled and confused by the bureaucratization of their system, which impeded central control and rational policy, and they discussed its "subjective" and "objective" causes without entirely grasping the effects of their attempt to centralize power beyond the capacity of their central decision-making bodies to use it. We noted that their normal response to the problem was to pound at it with the cudgel: mobilizing larger or smaller categories of workers or goods; nationalizing more enterprises; setting aside priority sectors for favored treatment. I have argued that the net effect of continued mobilization was to reduce the center's actual power while generating a great number of formally official bureaucracies.

In this section I wish to fill in the final term of the argument. Earlier I mentioned that corruption in the state apparatus was a kind of border zone; it combined an internal with an external function, depending on whether one considers it from the perspective of the leaders' power or that of the larger society of which the state is a part. Within the state, corruption helped preserve the regime by providing a means of compensation for the problem of missing or misallocated goods. Leakage of any form converted state power into private power and thus was directly antithetical to mobilization. But from the standpoint of society, corruption was merely one of the numerous forms of localized markets and private initiative, of varying degrees of legality, which established a provisional equilibrium between needs and resources in the broader system made up of the regime *in* society.

Private markets included bribery and the ubiquitous black market, but there were markets of other colors as well, since officials frequently found it necessary to recognize, temporarily, various side-arrangements with private contractors, suppliers, and agents.[48] There was a vast and largely unsuppressed peasant market. Citizens made private purchases from artisans, craftsmen, and repairmen, some operating individually and some in cooperatives. The state itself had recourse to market transactions with such craftsmen at times. Looking at the matter more broadly still, the rage for collectivism had the paradoxical effect in Russia of stimulating the cultural innovations of brilliant modernists in painting, music, theater, dance, poetry, architecture, sculpture, social theory, economics, politics, and natural science. Rarely in history have so many individual geniuses flourished in so brief a time.

To say, therefore, that the mobilization of society produced its own antithesis, the fragmentation of society into a new age of petty-bourgeois individualism, is to hasten to an incomplete judgment. Small-scale production, trade, and initiative were indeed stimulated by the inability of the cudgel's blows to achieve a harmonious order. They did indeed sustain the state through the desperate standing crisis of the civil war. But most important, state-building through mobilization and the domain of small-scale markets, however irreconcilable at the level of principles, were inextricably connected. They both grew out of the revolutionary convulsion of a society in which few strong civil institutions had developed and where, instead, only state power was capable of serving as an adequate organizing principle for preserving society.[49] Through mobilization, the Soviet regime did reduce the organized power of social institutions outside the state. It did not at the same time convert these to a centralized order.

In this period it was commonplace not only for private citizens to barter and buy on the black market to meet their subsistence needs, but also for state agencies and nationalized enterprises to deal through middlemen to obtain necessary goods.[50] Enterprises sometimes hoarded in order to have merchandise to trade. One match factory, for example, had stockpiled 31 million boxes of matches. Shadowy intermediaries and speculators sprang up to facilitate supply. Frustrated by the fact that the state could not devise operational plans of allocation while speculation was thriving, Rykov at one point in 1918 called on factories to advertise their stocks in newspapers. Nevertheless the practice of sending out agents to buy what could not be commandeered continued. In December 1919 Rykov broke down the sources of the state's supply of firewood: one-third of provincial procurements came through private contractors.[51] The State Works Committee, discussed in the preceding chapter, frequently hired private contractors to perform construction and repair work, even in Moscow.[52] In November 1920 Larin wrote that these agents and contractors were the last remnants of capitalism in the state. They received millions of rubles in advances from the government, risking nothing. If they returned the advance after a time without finishing the job, they lost nothing, the money having become even more worthless in the interval. Their own valuables were well hidden. But the state lost time and money.[53]

Another form of the state's dependence on private markets was the practice of paying workers with the products of their own factories. Apparently this was widespread, especially in 1918. At one textile plant in Moscow, workers received the equivalent of 200 rubles per month in cloth; necessarily, they traded it on the black market. The textile *glavk* (Centrotextile), unhappy with this dispersion of stocks, closed the plant to end the practice. Evidently the decision to pay workers in kind had been made by the factory committee, but in other cases the practice was explicitly sanctioned by the government. For a time (probably in 1920), 10,000 Moscow soap workers each month were paid two dozen bars of soap, which, owing to the extreme scarcity of soap and the epidemic of typhus, was a valuable black market commodity.[54]

The nationalization of commerce resulted in a great many leaks in the dam of state monopoly. Having taken over the consumers' cooperatives and commercial enterprises, the state created new organs for retail distribution. Many were managed by former merchants employed as "specialists," who in some cases used their position to sell off state goods for personal gain. The witticism of the day was that "the nationalization of trade means that the whole nation is trading."[55] At times the food shortages grew so desperate that the state legalized private commerce, called *meshochnichestvo*, or bagging, which meant direct sales of commodities carried from the countryside into the cities, whether by speculators or by peasants. In September 1918, according to Lev Kritsman, bagmen sold over 4½ million *pudy* of grain in Moscow and Petrograd. This was over twice the amount that the Food Commissariat had planned to distribute; however, the Food Commissariat's plan was met by less than one-half. Bagging was legal only for exceptional and temporary intervals, but the purchase of food on the black market was nearly universal for city residents. Kritsman later tried to estimate how much bread flowed through private markets and how much through the state channels of distribution. He estimated that for 1918 and 1919, 40 percent of the total bread supply came through official channels, and 60 percent via free markets.[56]

Officially tolerated markets took quite another form when, for a time in early 1919, large areas of the Ukraine were reunited with Russia. While the planners intended to subordinate the Ukrainian economy to the Russian (see chapter three), in actuality the Ukraine was plundered randomly, like a vast treasure chest of food and fuel. No coordinated policy for exploitation was followed. Each railroad line, each enterprise, each state organ sent its own respresentatives south to procure what they could. The Russians were often blocked, however, by their lack of goods to exchange, by the failure of their ideological appeals, and by the hostility of many Ukrainian peasants who believed that the Soviet government was run by Jews. Bidding against each other, the Russians paid any price they could get, causing food prices to multiply out of hand: food prices in Kiev rose by four and five times. The Food Commissariat, dismayed at this costly free-for-all, ruled that only sixteen Russian organizations were entitled to make independent purchases. In any case this interlude was soon interrupted by the Grigoriev uprising and the successes of the Denikin campaign, which sealed the Ukraine off from Russia from June until November.[57]

Not only the Ukraine was treated as an open market. Thousands of Soviet enterprises and agencies regularly sent representatives into the grain-producing provinces around Moscow and Petrograd to bargain with the peasants for grain, a practice called *otpustnichestvo*. A report in September 1919 stating that over four thousand organizations were thus competing with the Food Commissariat (which formally held a monopoly on food procurement), indicated that in the previous year all these organs combined had obtained as much grain as the Food Commissariat itself. A decree of 5 August 1919 by the Council of Commissars prohibited any organization save the Food Commissariat from making purchases, and later in the month the government again outlawed the practice of bagging.[58]

Certainly the city population depended on the black market for most of its food, and depended on it as well to liquidate its own goods. One estimate put the proportion of urban food consumption satisfied by state rations at 20 to 25 percent; another at 30 to 40 percent; another at 25 to 40 percent in grain-deficient provinces and 35 to 55 percent in grain-surplus provinces.[59] The statistician Strumilin investigated the budgets of Petrograd workers and found that on average their food budgets were higher than their incomes. The difference was made up by black market barter. But Strumilin and other official writers justified the state food monopoly by pointing out that to legalize speculation in grain would inevitably raise food prices beyond the reach of the poorest category of workers. Rationing thus protected the destitute from absolute starvation, but could not provide an adequate diet for anyone. A measure of the suffering of workers is suggested by Strumilin's figures about the disparity between real wages and market prices for bread: between May 1918 and May 1919 wages rose by less than three times while bread prices rose by over five times.[60] The most famous black-market site was the Sukharevka in Moscow. As many times as the police raided it and closed it down, commerce there invariably resumed. It was the indispensable source of subsistance goods for all but the newly privileged. The old upper classes sold off their precious belongings; workers sold cigarette lighters and other gadgets fashioned from scrap materials; peasants sold food. A German visitor to Moscow in 1920 wrote that the city lived largely from the black market, an observation confirmed by all other eyewitnesses.[61]

Private markets also disposed of the production of a large sector which, for the most part, worked outside state plans or administrative authority: cottage industry. Here I mean both urban and rural craftsmen, artisans, and repairmen. Government policy and economic conditions during the first two years of the revolution had contributed to a sharp drop in the number of artisans and craftsmen and of craft enterprises. One writer estimated that before the world war, some 2½ million artisans and craftsmen (*kustari* and *remeslenniki*) had worked in rural areas and another one million in the cities. In ten central Russian provinces, where 900,000 were once active, only 237,000 remained by 1920. In Petrograd and environs, some 30,000 to 35,000 craft industries and shops had existed before the war, but by 1920 all but 800 had closed.[62] Yet this much diminished sector of Russian life proved difficult to penetrate.

One reason for its resilience was that the circumstances of the time, the breakdown of the national market, the absence of materials, the devaluation of money, had tended to reverse the advantages of scale. Smaller enterprises increased their proportional share of employment and output in industry as larger plants closed. Less specialized, less technologically advanced than large firms, they could more readily adapt themselves to the needs of the market.[63] The other major reason was that both central and local organs frequently turned to craft enterprises for the goods they needed. While sometimes they used mobilizing methods to force craftsmen to produce goods, usually they entered into contractual arrangements with them, agreeing to supply them with materials or loans and to pay a certain price for the product. In effect, the form of relationship perpetuated the craftsman's ties to the market. The military authorities were particularly prone to bypass local governments and to deal directly with craftsmen. The shortage of military articles such as cartridges and leggings became so critical by the spring of 1919 that the military organs, in effect, legalized craft enterprises. The effect was immediate. Craft production doubled and the number of new craft cooperatives formed between September 1919 and November 1920 more than doubled. They also began producing such civilian goods as carts, sleds, tools, and utensils, in addition to war materiel.[64]

Local governments also found that in order to compensate for their declining ability to oversee local industry and to satisfy local economic needs exacerbated by the encroachment of the *glavki* onto their territories, they needed to support local craft enterprises as well. By cooperating with craft cooperatives, they frequently were able to reach higher plan targets than could the central authorities.[65] The only way to ensure that the craft enterprises could keep operating, however, was by allowing them access to the free market in supplies and hence by allowing them to sell to the market as well. A study carried out by the Petrograd regional economic council in August 1920 showed that craftsmen bought from and sold to the free market almost exclusively rather than trading through state distribution channels.[66]

Thus although the state formally owned many thousands of tiny enterprises, usually as a result of local acts of nationalization or municipalization (the 1920 census of industry showed that one-seventh of the state's enterprises, over five thousand in all, only employed one worker), such forms of control were ineffectual.

Stimulated by legalization and by the government's growing dependence on its production, cottage industry grew in proportion to the total economy in 1919 and 1920. This made it a more tempting target for nationalization by local and central authorities, particularly after military emergencies declined to the point where they no longer interfered with the Bolshevik preference for centralization. Late in 1920 a new round of efforts at nationalizing the craftsmen was launched at both the central and local levels. In September 1920 craft enterprises were divided into three categories. Into the first fell home enterprises where no labor was hired. Such enterprises could remain private, but were to be brought under state supply and distribution channels as much as possible. The second category consisted of enterprises with up to five employees if a motor were used, ten if not, and these were required to be registered and licensed and were prohibited from selling to the free market. The third category consisted of larger enterprises, and in November they were declared nationalized. Yet the impossibility of regulating craftsmen forced the SEC subsequently to exempt them from the latter decree. In any case the effect of the final act of nationalization was negligible since it was soon overtaken by the NEP.[67]

Local governments also used the general trend toward industrial deconcentration after 1919 to expand their own powers of regulation over cottage industry, but their actions were sometimes overruled by the central authorities, who feared the effects of the loss of craft production. In July 1920, for example, the Petrograd Soviet decided to close down some fifteen hundred craft and cooperative shops and enterprises, but the SEC reversed the action.[68] In effect, local and central authorities were in competition for the power to control the craftsmen. In turn the latter were able to use this collision to their advantage by evading absorption into the state and to maintain their vitality in the free market.

The regime was no more successful in bringing rural markets under administrative control. A study of three central Russian provinces for the months between September 1919 and January 1920 disclosed that of all products acquired by peasants, only 11.1 percent were acquired at fixed prices through state and cooperative outlets; 53.9 percent came through the free market, and 35 percent through in-kind exchange, presumably with state organs. The government accepted, out of necessity, the many weekly peasant bazaars. For the most part, the countryside was drawn into the sphere of state monopoly only as a source of requisitioned grain. Many food products and handicrafts, and most agricultural labor, were allocated almost entirely by forces outside the state's reach. The immensity of the crafts and peasant market economy and the dependence of the state upon it support Varga's comment about the introduction of the NEP, to the effect that the market had been flourishing all along and NEP only gave it formal legality.[69]

In October 1920, a provincial economic exhibition was held in Petrograd. Displaying the proudest achievements of industrial and agricultural production attained under Soviet rule, it must have resembled a humbler version of the VDNKh (*Vystavka dostizhenii narodnogo khoziaistva*) outside Moscow today. Like many of the exhibits at the VDNKh, the objects shown were prototypes rather than currently available goods, and hence symbolized the promise rather than the reality of socialism. In a sense it was a microcosm of the political system. Before the public were the prospects of industrial technology and the products of cottage industry; flocking to view them were throngs of exhausted people.

The first exhibit visitors saw was a model of a peasant's hut, equipped with electric appliances and a telephone, and lit by electric light bulbs. This particular image, the peasant hut illuminated by electric light and connected by wire to modern civilization, was a favorite of Lenin's; in December of that year, he recounted the tale of a visit he paid to a peasant village, where an elder solemnly thanked him for bringing artificial light to the village and enlightening the dark masses.[70] And as we have seen, the electrification of the countryside was also a priority of the State Electrification Commission (Goelro), which at the time of the Petrograd exhibition was in its sixth month of drafting the general electrification plan for Russia.

If the peasant hut represented the ideal of modernizing Russia's rural sector, a working tractor proved one of the most popular exhibits. Tractors had never been built before in Russia, and the model on display had been produced by the Obukhov works in Petrograd as one of three prototypes. The tractor filled the hall with noise and vibration when its motor ran, visibly conveying the potential of native Soviet industry.[71]

The bulk of the exhibition comprised smaller and more practical goods. Visitors admired electric wood choppers, mechanical flour mills, printing presses, and modern household goods such as locks, tin pots, copper fixtures, and water valves. Many of the products on display were the work of craftsmen's cooperatives operating in the province. The hit of this part of the exhibition was a display of the different kinds of coal-tar extracts. Other cooperatives contributed textbooks, briefcases, brushes, saws, saddles, boots, and a large set of scientific instruments. A machine turned out cigarettes at the rate of 5500 per hour. A chemical factory showed artificial fertilizers, mineral paints, and wood-extracted sugar. The agricultural exhibits included the produce of factory gardens, a rapidly expanding institution of the period. There were food items that had been unobtainable for years. As the press report commented, "the public looked at the candy, chocolate, and other products, and very unwillingly left the pavilion."[72]

The exhibition stands as a poignant and curiously apt image of the period. For all the regime's efforts to realize the prospects opened by socialism through centralization and mobilization, it had only succeeded in assembling handmade, almost iconic, representations of the socialist future, themselves of no practical use, such as the model tractors, the Algembra oil and rail lines, central production plans, the electrification plan. Large-scale organization had given way to the realm of the small-scale, petty-bourgeois producer, who had survived war, nationalization, and shortages, and could still turn out ingenious machines and imaginative by-products of native resources. Yet it was precisely the petty-bourgeois mentality that the Bolsheviks well understood to be the greatest enemy of the order they sought to build, because of its prevalence and its antipathy to Bolshevik socialism. Local electric stations, factory gardens, cottage industries, bagging, and the ineradicable Sukharevka market demonstrated the resilience of small-scale enterprise in the face of centralized control. The more the state relied on its cudgel, the more the larger system was propelled by private initiative and informal markets. Unable to control the petty-bourgeois sector, and indeed partly supporting it, the government seized what it could by administrative force and thereby reinforced the leakage of its power.

Perhaps now it is possible to identify the causes of the final collapse of the system. In the fourth chapter I pointed out the recurrent pattern in which war crises alternated with waves of popular protest and hypothesized that the state's legitimacy was contingent on the workers' belief in the need to support the state against White Guard and foreign intervention, but that there was widespread antagonism to the state's claim to represent proletarian interests. The tremendous surge of strikes and protests which swept through the capitals in February 1921 and the Kronstadt uprising immediately following thus had a general background in the workers' withdrawal of support from the regime once the military threat had subsided.

The spark provided by the fuel and food crisis of 1921 was the immediate cause of the collapse. This crisis derived from the mounting breakdown of transportation, which Trotsky's militant reorganization had only partially remedied (and that at the cost of substantial losses in popular support and material resources), the cumulative effects of the exhaustion of fuel stocks, and the terrible administrative disintegration caused by the repetition of shock methods. Moreover, the winter of 1920–1921 proved to be unusually severe, and river navigation had to close early. By early 1921, neither rail nor river deliveries were reaching Petrograd; there was no fuel for transport and no transport for fuel. Local firewood procurements dropped, in part because of the heavy depredations in previous years on nearby woodlands. Industrial production in Petrograd fell sharply and suddenly. Few were prepared for these calamities, although few had been so optimistic as Larin, who wrote in November 1920 that economic prospects in all areas for 1921 were better by far than 1920, and that with the coming elimination of money, cheap and efficient planning would overcome the current anarchy.[73]

That the final crisis had not come sooner was due in part to the prevalence of private markets and in part to the drop in the size of the industrial sector supported by state administration. Workers had fled the cities. By September 1920 Petrograd had less than one hundred thousand workers, less than one-quarter the number at the time of the autocracy's fall. Moscow's working-class population fell by two-thirds in three years. But the productivity of industry fell even more sharply. Worker productivity was about 20 percent of its prewar level. The Putilov works had one-sixth of their prewar work force, but turned out barely one-tenth the production.[74] Strumilin attempted to quantify the relative contribution of various factors to the fall in labor productivity and concluded in eary 1919 that nearly half had to be attributed to the exhaustion of the workers. On the other hand, he later calculated that the drop in the workers' caloric intake was even steeper than the fall in worker productivity.[75]

The workers' ability to labor at all under such conditions testifies to their heroism and endurance, called forth within a wide zone of motivation bounded by revolutionary faith at one end and fear of the concentration camp at the other. Some are tempted to say that the revolutionary and disciplined working class which had brought the Bolsheviks to power had been scattered to the winds by 1921: decimated in the bloodshed of the civil war, dead of overwork and disease, promoted into the party and state bureaucracies. Their places had been taken by peasants. Less committed to the Bolshevik cause, the argument goes, these raw recruits were readier to desert it in the crisis of 1921. Trotsky first made this case about the Kronstadt mutineers. The Soviet historian Gimpel'son echoes it by citing an estimate that by early 1921, nearly 80 percent of the workers at the large plants in Petrograd were of nonproletarian background. Isaac Deutscher built his analysis of the fall of Trotsky around the destruction of the old working class and the exhaustion of Bolshevik revolutionary spirit.[76]

Although the changing social composition of the working class over the early years of revolution is indisputable, how strong a case one can build upon the fact is less evident. The argument advanced here suggests that the system itself (i.e., the state-in-society) had reached the point of collapse. The system was closed to exchange with the outside world because of the Allied embargo and blockade ringing Russia. It could not escape the negative feedback effects delivered by the blows of the mobilizing cudgel on the expanding fragmentation of state power. Each round of mobilization sought to unlock some hidden store of energy but produced an even greater countereffect in the form of bribery, black markets, hoarding, speculation, deception, and small-scale enterprise. Thus mobilization reduced the aggregate quantity of usable resources. Only when the crisis of February 1921 exposed the full depletion of society's reserves, both moral and material, did the Bolsheviks finally put aside the cudgel.

CHAPTER SEVEN

Mobilization and the Evolution of Soviet Politics

1 : Reconstruction

IN THE SUMMER OF 1918 Lenin's old comrade Grigorii Zinoviev gave voice to fears that must have troubled many Bolsheviks. "Sometimes," he confessed, "it seems that this is not it, that perhaps this is an enormous historical misunderstanding, that we are taking something else for socialism."[1] He answered his own challenge with the consoling reflection that if Russia had not been ready for socialism, the workers could not have taken power so easily.

After another three years of war, hunger, and chaos, this assurance no longer held. Metal production was 3 to 5 percent of prewar levels.[2] Large-scale rebellion in the countryside, mass political strikes in the cities, and the defection of the Kronstadt garrison made it apparent to party leaders that persistence in the old course was leading to disaster. But what exactly was the old course? How far could the regime retreat in its policies without losing power? The immediate issue was to determine how extensively private production and trade could be permitted to replace administrative controls. The underlying issue was whether the dismantling of the mobilization regime would re-create political forces independent of and even hostile to the state.

Until NEP the Bolsheviks did not consider that under the duress of civil war they were imposing a relationship between state and society very different from that needed to build socialism. Through the worst moments of the civil war, leaders continued to assure the public that progress toward socialism had not faltered.[3] Political demobilization therefore caught the regime by surprise. The Bolsheviks had identified their state with a social interest which was singular, universalistic, and as yet largely unrealized; the revival of private and public interests therefore threatened the state's ability to dominate society. Ideological readjustment took some months. It was difficult for the Bolsheviks to grasp that by explaining their disastrous initial policies as the unavoidable consequences of intense military pressure, they were free to regard the current retreat as an advance toward socialism by another route.

When Lenin admitted at the Tenth Party Congress that the regime's attempt to socialize the entire economy had gone too far, his position was neither well understood nor fully accepted. Many preferred to think that the errors of the past had been forced upon the party by historical necessity. But the disagreements over the character of that necessity gave the game away. In the early months of NEP, as theorists debated whether the principal architect of Bolshevik socialism had been war or revolution, one senses again a reluctance on the part of the Bolsheviks to accept the burden of political choice. Some, like Karl Radek, agreed with Lenin that War Communism had been the necessary and even successful organization of a war economy. Others, such as V. Smirnov, argued that War Communism resulted from the elimination of private property.[4] The very label Lenin attached to the period—war communism—was nothing if not ambiguous. Could it not mean militant communism? Did it not suggest ironic detachment from outlived illusions?

The party continued to make room for such unrepentant enthusiasts as Larin and Kritsman, who were reluctant to concede that the principles of the early period had been in error at all. Kritsman summed up the experience of the period by asserting, however illogically, that the market as a form of social organization had at last been overcome; only the *anarchy* of markets remained. Larin, in an address to a party club in Moscow in October 1921, called for a "Communist backlash" to prevent the retreat from going too far. The Council of Commissars evidently heeded the warning, for it named both Larin and Kritsman, along with Kurskii, P. Bogdanov, Osinskii, and Shmidt, to an Economic Commission charged with maintaining restraints on the retreat to capitalism.[5]

Lenin's speech at the Tenth Party Congress set the terms of the new consensus, however. He stressed that the party must recognize the limits on its power to achieve socialism in an overwhelmingly peasant country. As he put it, the revolution could hope for ultimate success under either of two conditions: revolution in the west, or compromise with the majority of the Russian peasantry. And the peasants, he insisted, would not tolerate the continuation of the relationship that had been maintained until now. He acknowledged that although necessity had played its part in shaping Bolshevik policy, the party had gone too far in the direction of nationalizing industry and centralizing distribution. Now, to satisfy the middle peasant, it was necessary to permit free trade.[6] The alternatives faced by the regime were stark. The socialist city, having lost its ability to meet minimal peasant needs through socialism, now had to retreat to a petty-bourgeois capitalism. It is hard to fault Lenin's assessment. The full consequences of the state's plundering of the countryside became tragically apparent later in 1921 when a harvest failure along the Volga brought starvation to millions.

Earlier I called mobilization a means of subjecting social resources to state control. As I have shown, the regime failed to mobilize the countryside and succeeded in diverting only some of the peasantry's products and labor to its own needs. The collapse of the mobilization system left in doubt the issue of the relationship between the state and the peasantry. Many in the party had hoped to use force for a one-time accumulation of a "food fund" with which to begin industrialization; such was the program of the Ninth Party Congress. The hopelessness of such prospects now prompted the Bukharinist Right to speculate about the possibility of building socialism on the basis of

uncoerced town-country exchange. Simplifying these alternatives to the utmost, Stalin summarized them as the *smychka*
through metal and the *smychka* through cloth.[7]

The *smychka* (link or alliance) stood for the most fundamental
problem of social integration in Russia: the terms of exchange
between working class and peasantry. Cloth stood for light and
consumer-oriented industry, whose products circulated rapidly
and generated demand for recovering industries and revenues
for the state. Bukharin held that with a high volume of commodity turnover and efficient production in state industry, agriculture could gradually be modernized and socialized. Like those
Bolshevik theorists who had discovered the existence of "system-
ness" in the economy, Bukharin became preoccupied with ways
to maintain social equilibrium so as to spare society the pitched
warfare between peasants and state that war communism provoked. To supplant pure coercion, therefore, a new basis for
social integration was needed in order to mend the "degenera-
tion of the social fabric." Bukharin even called for a kind of
socialist pluralism based on voluntary associations.[8] It was Stalin
who recognized that the security of the socially isolated regime
remained at issue under such a solution. For, as Moshe Lewin
has brilliantly shown, society, save for that primitive and inde-
structible other Russia of folk society, had either been destroyed
or absorbed into the state. The state did indeed "hang in air"—it
had to re-create its own base.[9]

Stalin's solution, of course, was the "*smychka* through metal."
This required the forced expansion of the country's heavy industry and the control of agriculture. The logic was that of war
communism, but the state's penetration of society and its capacity for centralized control were now far greater thanks to the
tremendous expansion and consolidation of party and soviet
power in the 1920s. In the first phase, Stalin conducted, under
the auspices of a purge of the Right, a "cultural revolution"
that destroyed what limited social pluralism then existed. The
cultural revolution invoked all the battle cries of Bolshevik socialism: planning, industrialism, and mobilization; it accommo-

dated both the class-based populism of democratic Bolshevism and rationalist developmentalism. The assault on privilege struck blows against the alliance between the regime and the scientific-technical intelligentsia. The state required a sturdier alliance with an intelligentsia risen out of "its own people."[10] During this period the regime discredited the old engineer corps through staged trials; Stalin even called attention to their semiotic purpose when, in 1931, he called the trials "signals" of the need for a revolutionary attack on backwardness.[11]

2 : *Renewed Mobilization*

Stalin's revolution from above drew directly upon the model of the mobilization regime devised and imperfectly realized in the early period. Not only the tasks of policy in the two periods, but, more importantly, the structure of power in state and society, reveal continuity between the period of Bolshevik socialism and the Stalin revolution.[12] Stalin's Bolshevik fundamentalism refused to absorb the advances in the theory of planning that had been made in 1920–1921 or the possibilities of using markets in parallel with developmental planning discussed in the mid-1920s. The links between the two periods extend to the very showcase projects which the October Revolution had revived with such hope, but which it had failed to complete: the White Sea Canal, rural electrification, the Volga-Don Canal, the development of Turkestan. If Stalin had learned nothing since war communism, he had also forgotten nothing.

Bolshevik socialism in the early period had been defeated by the coincident problems of a backward agriculture and the civil war. Less hampered by the weakness and isolation of the party than was the regime in the early period, and free of the necessity of defeating the White armies, Stalin achieved the quasi-feudal relationship between peasantry and regime through which a massive program of industrialization might be launched. Planned industrial development, so often articulated as a goal during the breathing-pauses in the early period, now became the overriding priority of all policy. As before, it dictated the forms of social mobilization, including the centralization of state power, the absorption of autonomous workers' organizations into the state, and the independence of state policy from class interests. Again, as in the early period, the tension between mobilization and institutionalization resurfaced as a product of the use of mobilization to destroy the independence of social institutions. Again the regime called upon the antibureaucratic zeal of the young and the radical in the party, the Komsomol, the working class, and the intelligentsia. Absorbed into the state, however, these groups faced the same dilemma as the democratic Left of the early period: the contradiction between the egalitarianism of their proletarian values and their privileged status.

After the restoration of social hierarchy in the mid-thirties, even the populist style of proletarian revolution faded. The political elite restored a provisional compromise with the survivors among the scientific-technical intelligentsia,[13] and although educational opportunities for the masses widened tremendously, the resurrection of traditional formality in the classroom mirrored the delineation of power and status in society. Rank returned to all spheres of officialdom, marked by displays of brass and braid in the smart uniforms of the new class. Leaving behind the rough and ready Bolshevik culture, with its air of working-class authenticity, the regime began to associate the state with older national heroes. The public worship of the state turned from a celebration of the proletarian acquisition of power to rituals of elite continuity with a glorious tradition, linking Ivan the Terrible, Peter the Great, Lenin and Stalin in a winding lineage.[14] The renewed acceptance of institutional hierarchy did relax the frenzy of the first phase of mobilization, but also entangled the state in rule-bound rigidity. Some have argued that the permanent purge was the only compensatory means to restore dynamism to state administration; others point out the political motives of the purges, noting that those likeliest to remember the older norms of Leninism were decimated most thoroughly. The Stalin Constitution and the *Short Course* revealed that the original Bolshevik aim of building socialism had been fulfilled.

Stalin's revolution closed the gap between state and society by eradicating civil society, or *obshchestvennost'*. The state revived patrimonial ideals of service by society to state. Between the small normative sphere granted to private domesticity and the vast scope of the state's responsibilities only pockets of traditional culture survived: the peasant world, say, of an Ivan Denisovich; religious faith among Orthodox, Old Believers, dissenting sects, Baltic Catholics, and Central Asian Moslems; and, perhaps most dangerous, an awareness among the old cultural intelligentsia of a transcendent moral obligation to *remember*. Beneficiaries of the post-Stalin demobilization, these subterranean veins of culture gained in strength during the "liberal" years and often contributed to the impulse for reform. As in the early period, when universalizing the obligation to labor was considered a democratic measure that overcame the antagonism between capital and labor, Stalin left no room for organized action outside the state. The logic of Bolshevik socialism culminated with the revelation that socialism referred to the growth of the state's might.

After World War II, which had impelled the renewal of mobilization by reviving powerful traditional loyalties—family, friendship, country, and church—the reestablishment of hierarchical authority required a new normative synthesis, one compatible with industrial expansion and party monopoly. The resulting alliance, as Vera Dunham's book *In Stalin's Time* wonderfully shows, was neither technocratic nor populist, but "middle class." The regime began to deliver on some of its long-standing promises. For the bureaucratic elite, the regime acknowledged the encroachment of instrumental values, such as privatism and consumerism, upon Soviet culture that had begun in the 1930s. The signs of the new embourgeoisement recalled the "high" style of prerevolutionary society, its sweetening embellishments of music lessons and pink lampshades.[15] Again, the intelligentsia was suspect. Excluded from the Big

Deal (Vera Dunham's memorable term for the alliance between Stalinist political authority and the new Soviet middle class), the intelligentsia provided the remembered democratic norms for the reform movements of the thaw period, when social idealists and the "I" poets harked back to the old values of equality, candor, and participation. Pounding on the walls of the de-Stalinizing state, they often sought no more than to be admitted to a Bigger Deal.

3 : Rationalization

Khrushchev resorted to mobilizing campaigns of limited scope as a means of attacking the entrenched Stalinist opposition. He directed public attention to the old ideals of popular participation and intolerance for bureaucratism, and, to overcome opposition in the central ministries, he revived the principle of administrative deconcentration through strong regional councils, the *sovnarkhozy*. His populism was hardly radical. Its instrumental side was frankly acknowledged as the just reward for the common man's long sacrifice. At the same time, through media campaigns and the new party program, he revived the rhetoric of collective sacrifice, as in the virgin lands campaign. He recalled the universalistic and outward-looking commitment to world revolution, and he capitalized on the immense symbolic appeal of Sputnik's triumph over earthly gravity. But for all his identification with the early mobilizing themes, Khrushchev's populism was demotic rather than democratic, stylistic rather than structural; he relied on a folksy Bolshevik bluster to sustain him through his inability to achieve major breakthroughs in the system's performance. Vulnerable because of his growing dependence on personalistic leadership, he was finally unable to forge a strong alliance with any institutional group or to deliver more than symbolic rewards.

As I observed earlier, the success of the mobilizing strategy depends upon the center's penetration of state and civil institutions. In the vastly more complex bureaucratized state of the post-Stalin era, no one leader could accumulate the personal authority over the political system that Stalin had enjoyed. The abolition of mass terror and the encroachment of legalism on political power narrowed Khrushchev's personal decision-making power.[16] However, the personalistic and arbitrary nature of Khrushchev's leadership and the relatively unrestrained competition among bureaucratic interests characteristic of the Khrushchev period reflect the transitional nature of his regime. Apart from the apparent tacit agreement within the central political elite to rule out terror, political power was fluid and unstable.[17] Khrushchev ultimately fell victim to this flux, and his successors sought to stabilize the authority-building and policymaking processes in reaction to his erratic and personalized leadership.[18]

Nonetheless, the faint and ritualistic echoes of mobilization that survive in the form of "campaigns" for particular policy initiatives suggest the relative weakness of the center to implement policy in the face of bureaucratic fragmentation and resistance. Campaigns focus attention, centralize initiative, divert resources to a common goal. The campaigns of the Khrushchev period were an intermediate form between the institutional flux caused by mobilization under Stalin, when the lines of authority constantly shifted in response to new upheavals, and the elaborately formalistic, perfunctory political rituals that campaigns have become since Khrushchev fell. While emphasizing centralism in a context of institutional stability, Khrushchev's successors raised bureaucratic consolidation to its highest point in Soviet history, only to become its victims. Early in the Brezhnev period, both the democratic rhetoric of stateless communism and the decentralizing reforms of Khrushchev's rule were dropped, along with Khrushchev's "voluntaristic" faith that revolutionary zeal could succeed where expertise could not. Aware of the dilemma of information overload in overcentralized systems, contemporary writers on administration have sought, like their predecessors in 1920, some automatic method for simultaneously concentrating vital data at the center while winnowing out distracting detail at lower levels.[19] The rationalization of administration has required new and sophisticated methods of acquiring, processing, and applying information, along with appropriate modifications of ideological doctrine and concern with systematizing the flow of feedback from the public. Under Brezhnev, the "scientific organization of management" replaced Krushchev's tatterdemalion populism as a legitimating theme. Probably the preoccupation of the early Andropov regime with strengthening discipline and social order reflected an adjustment in the ideology of administrative rationalism rather than a reversion to the Bolshevik cudgel.

At the same time, the regime has strongly encouraged popular participation in administration. Formal membership in the committees of popular "control," factory production conferences, task-oriented soviet commissions, and the like is strikingly high.[20] Nearly all intellectuals and officials carry out some public duties (*obshchestvennye porucheniia*), and among workers, the figures range between a third and a half. At the same time, figures on participation can be misleading. A great deal of this public activity is purely nominal; in many cases enrollment figures are inflated. Most people who carry out assignments do at least part of the work during work time. Most workers do not consider that they actually affect management in the enterprises through the workplace-based organizations.[21]

Close studies of civic participation have suggested that participants can be divided into two categories. A group of professional activists, who take on the organizing and propagandizing work under the direction of the party apparatus, leads a larger body of relatively passive citizens in a variety of approved activities.[22] The activists extend the authority of the party into workplaces and residences, encouraging comments and suggestions from the general public to the extent that they concern the application rather than the formation of policy.[23] Thus channeled and directed, social activism has not been permitted to acquire autonomous forms, as began to occur in the heady days of de-Stalinization, or as occurred during the Prague Spring or the Polish renewal. The stability of the system depends upon the party's success in recruiting activists to serve as links between the regime and the masses.[24] The regime offers an array of privileges to the rationalizers, managers, and activists who support it, but their political rights are carefully circumscribed. They may engage in bureaucratic self-aggrandizement, but, as Alexander Shtromas puts it, no one may advance a "second pivot" of authority to compete with the party.[25] To compensate for the fragmentation of administrative power, bureaucratic elites are drawn into a common political class or elite, enjoying common privileges and status, and sharing an outlook of statist patrimonialism.

The subterranean culture of opposition and withdrawal, often categorized in the West as "dissent," reflects but does not sustain the ideology of the political elite.[26] Older traditions, religious, intellectual, and popular, are refracted through the unauthorized media of circles and *samizdat* in new guises. The old democratic norms of communal solidarity and fraternal equality find their way into various philosophical systems propounded by underground currents of Right and Left. In their attraction to absolutism and disdain for political choice, many of these currents mirror the official political culture even in rejecting it. Similarly, the official economy is paralleled by an extensive realm of private and illicit markets, which siphons goods, labor, and services from the state-organized economy. As in the War Communism period, individuals and enterprises operating legally are often dependent on the second economy, which thus sustains the official economy while in the longer term draining it of vitality and predictability. In the present, the regime has come to encourage private subsidiary enterprises of factories and farms, recalling the grudging toleration for petty-bourgeois enterprise that the regime was forced to adopt in 1919 and 1920. In both the cultural and economic dimensions, then, the Soviet regime has failed to create a socialist civil society, a socialist *obshchestvennost';* instead it has reinforced the duality of official culture and economy, and the interstitial realm of the "second economy" and the "second culture" which mediate between state power and private society.[27]

Through the course of Soviet history, the two imperatives of rule, the construction of a state and the construction of a society, have remained at odds. The creation of a state entailed the formation of permanent, hierarchically bounded, and binding institutions to carry out state policy. The transformation of society required the consolidation of values and economic forms which did not depend on state mandates. In each period, the regime has recombined democratic or rationalistic norms with bureaucratic or mobilizing structures to generate political authority. During spells of ambitious socialist construction, the state has employed mobilization to reconcentrate authority, but such periods invariably give way to phases of institutional consolidation. Mobilizing Russian society during the early period, the regime suppressed those independent social institutions which might have become the core of a new socialist society, drawing them instead into the apparatus of state power. Groups remaining outside the state were than regarded askance, as actual or potential enemies. When mobilization led to a weakening of actual central control and required the state to relax its claims and institutionalize its power, demobilization averted crises but created opportunities for new claimants to power. In both the 1920s and 1960s, consolidation led to dangerous levels of social pluralism. Both periods were followed by renewals of centralism which stressed ideological coherence and hierarchical control, but paid for it heavily with immobilism.

New challenges greet Brezhnev's successors. Discussions late in the Brezhnev era identified the principal task on the political agenda to be that of raising the productivity of labor.[28] General Secretary Andropov identified this as a priority of his regime.[29] Whether this problem can be confronted without sacrificing the principle of a unitary social interest, without opening the possibility that social interests may be multiple and competing, remains to be seen. Two alternative strategies for the future suggest themselves from the foregoing analysis. The first is a renewal of mobilization. In the present, however, institutional entrenchment has progressed to the point that only a sweeping campaign of the Stalinist or Maoist variety is likely to alter bureaucratic behavior markedly; Khrushchev-style halfway measures are unlikely to suffice. The other option is a renewal of political control over policy through pluralism. Here the power of the central bureaucracy is reduced by dispersing it more widely to economic and cultural institutions. In the political and market competition such a course would open up, some interests would emerge relatively weaker. The working class could find its position threatened. If such a solution stimulated growth, however, eventually all interests save those served by political decay would benefit.

NOTES

INDEX

Notes

Note: Transliteration in this book follows a modified Library of Congress style except that familiar names, such as Trotsky, are given their usual English spelling. Events that occurred before the changeover to the Gregorian calendar on 1/14 February 1918 are dated by the old calendar, while later events are dated by the new calendar.

1 : The Bolshevik Mobilization Regime

1. Paul Craig Roberts, *Alienation and the Soviet Economy* (Albuquerque: University of New Mexico Press, 1971), esp. ch. 2, " 'War Communism'—Product of Marxian Ideas."

2. E. G. Gimpel'son, *"Voennyi kommunizm": politika, praktika, ideologiia* (Moscow: Mysl', 1973), pp. 221–2.

3. Robert Service, *The Bolshevik Party in Revolution: A Study in Organisational Change, 1917–1923* (New York: Barnes and Noble Books, 1979); T. H. Rigby, *Lenin's Government: Sovnarkom, 1917–1922* (Cambridge: Cambridge University Press, 1979).

4. Peter J. D. Wiles, *The Political Economy of Communism* (Oxford: Basil Blackwell & Mott, Ltd., 1962), pp. 29–30; Gimpel'son, *"Voennyi kommunizm,"* pp. 3, 45.

5. David A. Baevskii, *Ocherki po istorii khoziaistvennogo stroitel'stva perioda grazhdanskoi voiny* (Moscow: Izdatel'stvo akademii nauk SSSR, 1957), pp. 23, 68.

6. I. A. Gladkov, *Ocherki sovetskoi ekonomiki, 1917–1920 gg.* (Moscow: Gosudarstvennoe izdatel'stvo politicheskoi literatury, 1956), pp. 102–7.

7. Laszlo Szamuely, *First Models of the Socialist Economic Systems: Principles and Theories,* trans. Gy. Hajdu; trans. rev. Maurice H. Dobb (Budapest: Akademiai Kiado, 1974), pp. 10–17; Lev Kritsman, "Geroicheskii period Velikoi Russkoi Revoliutsii," *Vestnik kommunisticheskoi akademii* 9 (1924): 1–124.

8. David E. Apter, *The Politics of Modernization* (Chicago: University of Chicago Press, 1967), ch. 10, "The Mobilization System as a Modernization Prototype."

9. Using the terminology suggested by the anthropologist Mary Douglas, one could say that the mobilization system emphasizes the boundaries defining "group" rather than the interior status distinctions which demarcate "grid." Mary Douglas, *Natural Symbols: Explorations in Cosmology* (New York: Pantheon Books, 1970).

10. John Morton Blum, *V Was for Victory: Politics and Culture During World War Two* (New York: Harcourt Brace Jovanovich, 1976).

11. A. Lomov, *Razlozhenie kapitalizma i organizatsiia kommunizma* (Moscow: Redaktsionno-izdatel'skii otdel VSNKh, 1918).

12. *Trudy I-ogo vserossiiskogo s"ezda sovetov narodnogo khoziaistva (26 maia–4 iiunia 1918 g.): Stenograficheskii otchet.* (Moscow: VSNKh, 1918), p. 19. Hereinafter called the first SNKh Congress.

13. *Trudy II-ogo vserossiiskogo s"ezda sovetov narodnogo khoziaistva (19 dekabria–27 dekabria 1918 g.): Stenograficheskii otchet* (Moscow: VSNKh Redaktsionno-izdatel'skii otdel, 1919?), pp. 166–67. Hereafter called the Second SNKh Congress.

14. Stephen F. Cohen, *Bukharin and the Bolshevik Revolution: A Political Biography, 1888–1938* (New York: Alfred A. Knopf, 1973), pp. 89–90, discusses Bukharin's innovative notion of the costs of revolution, which included the disequilibration of society. Only socialism could restore a just social equilibrium.

15. John Keegan, *The Face of Battle: A Study of Agincourt, Waterloo and the Somme* (New York: Vintage Books, 1977), p. 271.

16. John Keegan and Joseph Darracott, *The Nature of War* (New York: Holt, Rinehart and Winston, 1981), p. 68.

17. Harold D. Lasswell, *Propaganda Technique in World War I* (1927; rpt. Cambridge: MIT Press, 1971). Also see Phillip Knightley, *The First Casualty* (New York: Harcourt Brace Jovanovich, 1975), ch. 5, "The Last War."

18. Lasswell, *Propaganda*, ch. 3, "War Guilt and War Aims."

19. Eugen Varga, *Die Wirtschaftspolitischen Probleme der proletarischen Diktatur* (Hamburg: Verlag der kommunistischen Internationale, 1921), p. 18; Kritsman, "Geroicheskii period," p. 68.

20. Cohen, *Bukharin*, pp. 30, 70.

21. Hannah Arendt, *On Revolution* (New York: Viking Press, 1965), pp. 164–65. For "public space," see p. 129.

22. Karl Marx, *Critique of the Gotha Program,* (Peking: Foreign Languages Press, 1972), p. 168.

23. Charles E. Lindblom, *Politics and Markets: The World's Political-Economic Systems* (New York: Basic Books, 1977), p. 171.

24. N. Bukharin and E. Preobrazhensky, *The ABC of Communism* (Baltimore: Penguin Books, 1969), p. 118.

25. V. I. Lenin, *Polnoe sobranie sochinenii*, 5th ed., 55 vols. (Moscow: Izdatel'stvo politicheskoi literatury, 1958–1965), vol. 36, p. 157. Hereafter Lenin's

writings will be referred to as *PSS*, with the appropriate volume and page number.

26. Ibid., 42:237.

27. Moshe Lewin, "The Social Background of Stalinism," in Robert C. Tucker, ed., *Stalinism: Essays in Historical Interpretation* (New York: W. W. Norton & Co., Inc., 1977); idem, "Society, State, and Ideology during the First Five-Year Plan," in Sheila Fitzpatrick, ed., *Cultural Revolution in Russia, 1928–1931* (Bloomington: Indiana University Press, 1978).

28. *Desiatyi s"ezd RKP(b), Mart 1921 g.* (Moscow: Partiinoe izdatel'stvo, 1933), p. 408. Hereafter called the Tenth Party Congress.

2 : *The Factory Committees and Workers' Control*

1. A substantial literature has arisen on the factory committees and workers' control in revolutionary Russia. Citations to many sources will be found in my article, "Institution Building in Bolshevik Russia: The Case of 'State *Kontrol*' " *Slavic Review* 41 (Spring 1982): 91–103.

2. Sharon Zukin, *Beyond Marx and Tito* (Cambridge: Cambridge University Press, 1975), ch. 1–2; Ellen Comisso, *Workers' Control Under Plan and Market* (New Haven: Yale University Press, 1979); Carole Pateman, *Participation and Democratic Theory* (Cambridge: Cambridge University Press, 1970); Paul Blumberg, *Industrial Democracy: The Sociology of Participation* (New York: Schocken Books, 1969).

3. B. N. Gorodetskii, *Rozhdenie sovetskogo gosudarstva, 1917–1918 gg.* (Moscow: Nauka, 1965), pp. 47–48.

4. Falk Döring, *Organisationsprobleme der russischen Wirtschaft in Revolution und Bürgerkrieg (1918–1920): Dargestellt am Volkswirtschaftsrat für den Nordrayon (SNChSR)* (Hannover: Verlag für Literatur und Zeitgeschehen, 1970), p. 37; Richard Lorenz, *Anfänge der bolschewistischen Industriepolitik* (Cologne: Wissenschaft und Politik, 1965), p. 25; *Novyi put'*, no. 3/4, 1917, p. 3; John L. H. Keep, *The Russian Revolution: A Study in Mass Mobilization* (London: Weidenfeld and Nicolson, 1976), pp. 37–38; S. N. Prokopovich, *Voina i narodnoe khoziaistvo*, 2nd ed. (Moscow: Sovet vserossiiskikh kooperativnykh s"ezdov, 1918), pp. 237–46; S. D. Zagorsky, *State Control of Industry in Russia During the War* (New Haven: Yale University Press, 1928), p. 50.

5. The Soviet statistician Strumilin calculated that workers experienced a drop of 7 to 15 percent in real wages between 1913 and 1917; Gladkov a drop of 50 percent. Keep, *Russian Revolution*, pp. 45–47; Gladkov, *Ocherki*, pp. 14–15; V. I. Selitskii, "Osnovnye itogi bor'by rabochego klassa Rossii za kontrol' nad proizvodstvom i raspredeleniem v period dvoevlastiia," in I. I. Mints et al., *Rabochii klass i rabochee dvizhenie v Rossii v 1917 g.* (Moscow: Nauka, 1964), p.

290; John Reed, *Ten Days That Shook the World* (New York: New American Library, 1967), pp. 34–35.

6. P. N. Amosov, et al., comp., *Oktiabr'skaia revoliutsiia i fabzavkomy: Materialy po istorii fabrichno-zavodskikh komitetov*, 2 vols. (Moscow: Izdatel'stvo VTsSPS, 1927), vol. 1, pp. 15, 27–30; D. A. Kovalenko, "Bor'ba fabrichno-zavadoskikh komitetov Petrograda za rabochii kontrol' nad proizvodstvom (mart–oktiabr' 1917 goda)," *Istoricheskie zapiski* 61 (1957): 69–71.

7. Solomon M. Shvarts [Schwartz], "Fabrichno-zavodskie komitety i profsoiuzy v pervye gody revoliutsii" (manuscript, n.d., Hoover Institution Archives), p. 2; D. Dalin, "Evoliutsiia ekonomicheskoi politiki sovetskoi vlasti," *Vestnik prodovol'stvennykh sluzhashchikh*, no. 10, 1918, pp. 7–9, no. 11, pp. 13–16.

8. Shvarts, "Komitety," p. 8.

9. Ibid., p. 5; *Sed'maia (aprel'skaia) konferentsiia RSDRP (bol'shevikov), Protokoly, 24–29-ogo aprelia 1917 g.* (Moscow: Gosudarstvennoe izdatel'stvo politicheskoi literatury, 1958), pp. 275–6. Hereafter called the April Conference.

10. Lenin, *PSS*, 32: 105–11.

11. N. Osinskii, *Stroitel'stvo sotsializma: Obshchie zadachi: Organizatsiia proizvodstva* (Moscow: Izdatel'stvo Kommunist, 1918), p. 33.

12. Quoted in B. M. Freidlin, *Ocherki istorii rabochego dvizheniia v Rossii v 1917 g.* (Moscow: Izdatel'stvo Nauka, 1967), p. 128.

13. *Shestoi s"ezd RKP(b), 8–16 avgusta (26 iiulia–3 avgusta) 1917 g.* (Moscow: Gosudarstvennoe izdatel'stvo, 1927), pp. 152–54. Hereafter called the Sixth Party Congress.

14. Ibid., pp. 158–60.

15. Ibid., pp. 216–18.

16. Ibid., p. 210; Amosov, *Oktiabr'skaia revoliutsiia i fabzavkomy*, 1:217–19, 2:170.

17. Amosov, *Oktiabr'skaia revoliutsiia i fabzavkomy*, 2:26, 42–43.

18. Ibid., 1:169.

19. Ibid., pp. 171–73.

20. Ibid., pp. 174–86; V. L. Meller and A. M. Pankratova, *Rabochee dvizhenie v 1917 godu* (Moscow: Gosudarstvennoe izdatel'stvo, 1926), pp. 317–19.

21. The full text may be found in I. A. Gladkov, ed., *Natsionalizatsiia promyshlennosti v SSSR: Sbornik dokumentov i materialov* (Moscow: Gosudarstvennoe izdatel'stvo politicheskoi literatury, 1954), pp. 77–79.

22. Lenin's comments did not clarify the issue. At the conference of factory committees and trade unions of the city of Moscow on 27 June 1918, he stressed the importance of organization and discipline. He urged the factory committees to go beyond mere technical and financial concerns and to delve into management, acting as organs of the state. *Protokoly 4-oi konferentsii fabrichno-zavodskikh komitetov i professional'nykh soiuzov g. Moskvy* (Moscow: Izdanie vserossiiskogo tsen-

tral'nogo soveta professional'nykh soiuzov, 1919), pp. 19–20. Hereafter called the Fourth Factory Committee and Trade Union Conference.

23. Gorodetskii, *Rozhdenie*, p. 47.

24. Meller and Pankratova, *Rabochee dvizhenie*, pp. 72–73; Kovalenko, "Bor'ba," p. 77; A. Pankratova, *Fabzavkomy Rossii v bor'be za sotsialisticheskuiu fabriku* (Moscow: Izdatel'stvo Krasnaia Nov', 1923), p. 183.

25. Amosov, *Oktiabr'skaia revoliutsiia i fabzavkomy*, 1:71–72, 75–76.

26. A. M. Pankratova, *Fabzavkomy i profsoiuzy v revoliutsii 1917 g.* (Moscow: Gosizdat, 1927), p. 68.

27. M. L. Itkin, "Nekotorye funktsii rabochego kontrolia v period podgotovki vooruzhennogo vosstaniia (iiul'–oktiabr' 1917 g.)," in Mints, *Rabochii klass*, p. 315.

28. Pankratova, *Fabzavkomy Rossii*, pp. 202, 213–14; Meller and Pankratova, *Rabochee dvizhenie*, pp. 112–14; Ia. Fin, *Fabrichno-zavodskie komitety v Rossii: Kratkii ocherk ikh vozniknoveniia i deiatel'nosti* (Moscow: Izdatel'stvo RIO VTsSPS, 1922), p. 9.

29. Amosov, *Oktiabr'skaia revoliutsiia i fabzavkomy*, 2:48–49.

30. *Novyi put'*, no. 3, 1919, p. 15; Amosov, *Oktiabr'skaia revoliutsiia i fabzavkomy*, 1:43–44; Freidlin, *Ocherki*, p. 158.

31. Amosov, *Oktiabr'skaia revoliutsiia i fabzavkomy*, 1:75.

32. Ibid., pp. 145, 170–73.

33. Ibid., 2:82–85.

34. A. G. Egorova, *Profsoiuzy i fabzavkomy v bor'be za pobedu oktiabria (mart–oktiabr' 1917 goda)* (Moscow: Izdatel'stvo VTsSPS, Profizdat, 1960), p. 134.

35. A. V. Venediktov, *Organizatsiia gosudarstvennoi promyshlennosti v SSSR*, 2 vols., vol. 1, *1917–1920* (Leningrad: Izdatel'stvo leningradskogo universiteta, 1957), p. 100; Gladkov, *Natsionalizatsiia*, pp. 228–34, 236–38.

36. Amosov, *Oktiabr'skaia revoliutsiia i fabzavkomy*, 2:111–13, 193–95; Fin, *Fabrichno-zavodskie komitety*, pp. 19–20.

37. V. Z. Drobizhev, *Glavnyi shtab sotsialisticheskoi promyshlennosti: Ocherki istorii VSNKh, 1917–1932 gg.* (Moscow: Izdatel'stvo Mysl', 1966), pp. 45–48, 58.

38. *Narodnoe khoziaistvo*, no. 11, 1918, pp. 7–9, 23–25; *Novyi put'*, no. 3, 1919, p. 25; *Ekonomicheskaia zhizn'*, no. 95, 1924, p. 3.

39. *Novyi put'*, no. 3, 1919, p. 26.

40. *Ekonomicheskaia zhizn'*, no. 95, 1924, p. 3.

41. G. Tsyperovich, "Vospominaniia o Lenine," *Krasnaia letopis'*, no. 2 (23), 1927, p. 230.

42. *Narodnoe khoziaistvo*, no. 11, 1918, p. 22.

43. See, for example, vol. 1, ch. 12 of William Henry Chamberlin, *The Russian Revolution, 1917–1921*, 2 vols. (New York: Grosset & Dunlap, Universal Library, 1965); S. N. Prokopovitch, *The Economic Condition of Soviet Russia* (London: P. S. King and Son, 1924), pp. 4–5 ff.

44. V. Z. Drobizhev, "Sotsialisticheskoe obobschchestvlenie promyshlennosti v SSSR," *Voprosy istorii*, no. 6, 1964, p. 63.

45. Ekonomicheskaia zhizn', no. 1, 1918, pp. 1–2; *Narodnoe khoziaistvo*, no. 11, 1918, pp. 11–14.

46. *Narodnoe khoziaistvo*, no. 11, 1918, pp. 11–14; *Ekonomicheskaia zhizn'*, no. 1, 1918, pp. 1–2.

47. V. Z. Drobizhev and A. G. Medvedev, *Iz istorii sovnarkhozov (1917–1918 gg.)* (Moscow: Izdatel'stvo moskovskogo universiteta, 1964), pp. 64–65. A slightly different account is offered by V. V. Zhuravlev, *Dekrety sovetskoi vlasti 1917–1920 gg. kak istoricheskii istochnik* (Moscow: Nauka, 1979), pp. 41–42.

48. *Dekrety sovetskoi vlasti*, 10 vols. (Moscow: Gosudarstvennoe izdatel'stvo politicheskoi literatury, 1957–), vol. 1, pp. 77–82. Hereafter referred to as *Dekrety*.

49. Tsyperovich, "Vospominaniia," pp. 230–31.

50. *Dekrety*, 1:77–82.

51. Dekrety, 1:77–85; N. P. Silant'ev, *Rabochii kontrol' i sovnarkhozy* (Moscow: Moskovskii rabochii, 1957), p. 62. Soviet historians' published opinions regarding the All-Russian Workers' Control Council have varied with the political winds. Some have disparagingly called it Menshevik-dominated. See Drobizhev and Medvedev, *Iz istorii sovnarkhozov*, p. 36. An expert Soviet historian informed me privately that it lacked any organizational life and was only a platform for Larin. In fact it was Larin who had suggested amending the decree by adding such an all-Russian body, which lends support to the proposition that at least one objective of the decree was to deprive the factory committee movement of any official status. See Zhuravlev, *Dekrety*, p. 43.

52. For example, Wiles, *Political Economy*, pp. 28–29.

53. *Narodnoe khoziaistvo*, no. 11, 1918, p. 22.

54. Meller and Pankratova, *Rabochee dvizhenie*, p. 321; *Izvestiia*, 16 November 1917, pp. 6–7.

55. *Pravda*, 19 November 1917, p. 1.

56. *Novyi put'*, no. 3/4, 1917, p. 26.

57. V. A. Vinogradov, *Sotsialisticheskoe obobshchestvlenie sredstv proizvodstva v promyshlennosti SSSR (1917–1918)* (Moscow: Izdatel'stvo Akademii nauk SSSR, 1955), pp. 18–19.

58. A. Lozovskii, *Rabochii kontrol'* (Peterburg [sic]: Izdatel'stvo Sotsialist, 1918), p. 37; Pankratova, *Fabzavkomy Rossii*, p. 276; Silant'ev, *Rabochii kontrol'*, pp. 77–78.

59. Vinogradov, *Sotsialisticheskoe obobshchestvlenie*, p. 36.

60. For example, the Moscow Soviet Economic Department passed a vague resolution giving control commissions the function of auditing (*uchet*) but not control (*kontrol'*). Nor did it delineate the relations between these commissions and their parent factory committees. See Silant'ev, *Rabochii kontrol'*, pp. 70–71. The Council of Workers' Control of the Central Industrial Region, in one of

the only known cases of such a council taking any action at all, issued its own practical guidelines on workers' control without once mentioning factory committees. The control-economic commissions which it discussed were to have auditing functions and to help raise productivity and support discipline, but were not to replace management or to take over enterprises. See B. F., *Rabochii kontrol': Prakticheskiia ukazaniia po vedeniiu rabochego kontrolia v promyshlennykh predpriiatiiakh* (Moscow: Izdanie soveta rabochego kontrolia tsentral'nogo promyshlennogo raiona, 1918).

61. *Novyi put'*, no. 1/2 (January), 1918, p. 5.

62. *Izvestiia*, 13 December 1917, pp. 4–5; *Novyi put'*, no. 1/2 (January), 1918, pp. 7–12; Gladkov, *Natsionalizatsiia*, pp. 102–06; *Ekonomicheskaia zhizn'*, no. 95, 1924, p. 3.

63. Remington, "Institution-Building."

64. *Novyi put'*, no. 4/5, (February), 1918, pp. 11–12; Pankratova, *Fabzavkomy Rossii*, pp. 250–51; *Vestnik professional'nykh soiuzov*, no. 1, 1918, pp. 19–20.

65. *Novyi put'*, no. 3, 1919. pp. 17–18; Pankratova, *Fabzavkomy Rossii*, pp. 265–66.

66. *Vestnik professional'nykh soiuzov*, no. 1, 1918, pp. 12–13; M. V. Kiseleva, ed., *Natsionalizatsiia promyshlennosti i organizatsiia sotsialisticheskogo proizvodstva v Petrograde (1917–1920): Dokumenty i materialy*, 2 vols (Leningrad: Izdatel'stvo leningradskogo universiteta, 1958), vol. 1, p. 177; Pankratova, *Fabzavkomy Rossii*, pp. 265–66; *Novyi put'*, no. 1 (June), 1918, p. 42.

67. Döring, *Organisationsprobleme*, pp. 72–75; *Novyi put'*, no. 1/2 (January), 1918, pp. 18–19; Kiseleva, *Natsionalizatsiia*, 1:xvii.

68. Novyi put', no. 3 (January), 1918, pp. 9–10; ibid., no. 2 (July), p. 56; Drobizhev and Medvedev, *Iz istorii sovnarkhozov*, p. 59.

69. Vestnik professional'nykh soiuzov, no. 1, 1918, pp. 5–6; Drobizhev, *Glavnyi shtab*, pp. 108–09; James Bunyan and H. H. Fisher, *The Bolshevik Revolution, 1917–1918: Documents and Materials* (Stanford: Stanford University Press, 1934), pp. 619–20; *Izvestiia*, 27 April 1918, pp. 1–2.

70. Pankratova, *Fabzavkomy Rossii*, pp. 295–96; *Novyi put'*, no. 1 (June), 1918, p. 24.

3 : *Organizing Industrial Administration*

1. Richard Pipes, *The Formation of the Soviet Union: Communism and Nationalism, 1917–1923*, rev. ed. (New York: Atheneum, 1968), p. 108.

2. The conception resembles the ideal of Byzantine architecture, which seeks to create the illusion of a building hanging from heaven rather than rising from earth. This image reflects the hierarchical way of thinking Byzantium extended to politics, art, and religion, always seeing a descending chain of repeated forms derived from a divine archetype. See Herbert Read, *Icon and Idea* (New York: Schocken Books, 1965), p. 70.

3. Sixth Party Congress, pp. 256–59.

4. Lenin, *PSS*, 36:380.

5. *Narodnoe khoziaistvo*, no. 4, 1919, p. 2.

6. Gregory Guroff, "The State and Industrialization in Russian Economic Thought, 1909–1914" (Ph.D. diss. Princeton University, 1970).

7. Lenin, *PSS, 34:308.*

8. *Narodnoe khoziaistvo*, no. 11, 1918, pp. 16–23. Larin's articles were collected and published in the Soviet Union as *Gosudarstvennyi kapitalizm voennogo vremeni v Germanii (1914–1918 gg.)* (Moscow: Gosudarstvennoe izdatel'stvo, 1928).

9. Lenin, *PSS*, 35:174–76.

10. Cf. Richard Lorenz, "Wirtschaftspolitische Alternativen der Sowjetmacht im Frühjahr und Sommer 1918," *Jahrbücher für Geschichte Osteuropas*, vol. 15, no. 2, 1967, p. 214.

11. *Sovetskaia ekonomika v 1917–1920 gg.* (Moscow: Izdatel'stvo Nauka, 1976), pp. 16–17. Zagorsky presents roughly the same figures in *State Control*, p. 11.

12. G. Tsyperovich, *Sindikaty i tresty v dorevoliutsionnoi Rossii i v SSSR: Iz istorii organizatsionnykh form promyshlennosti za posledniuiu 50 let*, 4th ed. (Leningrad: Izdatel'stvo Tekhnika i proizvodstvo, 1927), pp. 297–306.

13. Zagorsky, *State Control*, ch. 1; S. N. Prokopovich, *Voina i narodnoe khoziaistvo*, 2nd ed. (Moscow: Sovet vserossiiskikh kooperativnykh s"ezdov, 1918).

14. Lenin, *PSS*, 35:123.

15. M. M. Biziaeva, "Iz istorii organizatsii oboronnoi promyshlennosti v gody grazhdanskoi voiny (1918–1919 gg.)," in M. P. Kim, Z. A. Astapovich, and P. M. Fedosov, *Iz istorii Oktiabr'skoi Revoliutsii i sotsialisticheskogo stroitel'stva v SSSR* (Moscow: n. p., 1957), p. 116.

16. Lenin, *PSS*, 35:463–64, 178.

17. *Dekrety*, 1:232–33; Gladkov, *Ocherki*, p. 152.

18. *Novyi put'*, no. 4/5 (February), 1918, p. 1; *Dekrety*, 1:196–98.

19. *Novyi put'*, no. 3 (June), 1918, p. 24; Kiseleva, *Natsionalizatsiia*, 2:14–15.

20. V. Z. Drobizhev, "Obrazovanie sovetov narodnogo khoziaistva v moskovskom promyshlennom raione (1917–1918 gg.)," in D. K. Shelestov, ed., *Iz istorii velikoi oktiabr'skoi revoliutsii: Sbornik statei* (Moscow: Izdatel'stvo moskovskogo universiteta, 1957), p. 86; see also T. H. Rigby, "The First Proletarian Government," *British Journal of Political Science* 4 (1974): 41–42.

21. Drobizhev, "Obobshchestvlenie," pp. 56, 63.

22. A. A. Voronetskaia, "Organizatsiia vysshego soveta narodnogo khoziaistva i ego rol' v natsionalizatsii promyshlennosti," *Istoricheskie zapiski* 43 (1953): 16–17.

23. Drobizhev, "Obobshchestvlenie," pp. 60–63.

24. Drobizhev, *Glavnyi shtab*, pp. 95–99.

25. *Plenum Vysshego Soveta Narodnogo Khoziaistva, 14–23 sentiabria 1918 g.:*

Stenograficheskii otchet (Moscow: Redaktsionno-Izdatel'skii otdel VSNKh, 1919), p. 11 (hereafter called *Plenum VSNKh*); Drobizhev, "Obobshchestvlenie," pp. 57, 63.

26. Second SNKh Congress, p. 45; Drobizhev, "Obobshchestvlenie," p. 56. The accurate figures have been calculated from Soviet analysis of the data collected by the industrial census of 31 August 1918.

27. Second SNKh Congress, p. 74.

28. *Ekonomicheskaia zhizn'*, no. 245, 1919, p. 2.

29. Baevskii, *Ocherki*, pp. 17–19,

30. *Ekonomicheskaia zhizn'*, no. 95, 1924, p. 1.

31. First SNKh Congress, pp. 342–45. Also, Michael S. Farbman, *Bolshevism in Retreat* (London: W. Collins Son and Co., 1923), pp. 176–77.

32. Venediktov, *Organizatsiia*, p. 180.

33. *Tretii vserossiiskii s"ezd sovetov rabochikh, soldatskikh, i krest'ianskikh deputatov* (Peterburg: Izdatel'stvo Priboi, 1918), pp. 29–30. Hereafter called the Third Soviet Congress.

34. *Chervertyi vserossiiskii s"ezd sovetov rabochikh, krest'ianskikh, soldatskikh i kazach'ikh deputatov: Stenograficheskii otchet* (Moscow: Gosudarstvennoe izdatel'stvo, 1918), bound with the minutes of meetings of the All-Russian Central Executive Committee of the fourth session, pp. 15–16. Hereafter called the Fourth Soviet Congress.

35. V. P. Miliutin, *Istoriia ekonomicheskogo razvitiia SSSR (1917–1927)* (Moscow: Gosudarstvennoe izdatel'stvo, 1928), pp. 133–34; *Novyi put'*, no. 1 (June), 1918, p. 45; Venediktov, *Organizatsiia*, pp. 180–81.

36. A number of observers, Soviet and Western, have claimed that from some point in early 1918, a retreat or slowdown began. Stephen Cohen dates the suspension of expropriations, the measures of state capitalism, and the use of wage incentives from early April. The Soviet historian David Baevskii cites figures to show that the rate of nationalizations slowed down in March. An American socialist in Russia at this time commented that in the March-June period there was little nationalization, with moderation in other areas and an abatement in the rate of inflation. Cohen, *Bukharin*, p. 70; Baevskii, *Ocherki*, pp. 18–19; Farbman, *Bolshevism in Retreat*, p. 172.

37. *Novyi put'*, no. 3 (August), 1918, p. 4.

38. Cited in Drobizhev and Medvedev, *Iz istoriia sovnarkhozov*, p. 65.

39. *Pravda*, 23 November 1917, p. 1; Drobizhev, *Glavnyi shtab*, pp. 60–61.

40. Drobizhev, *Glavnyi shtab*, pp. 81 ff.

41. Iu. K. Avdakov and V. V. Borodin, *Proizvodstvennye ob"edineniia i ikh rol' v organizatsii upravleniia sovetskoi promyshlennosti (1917–1932 gg.)* (Moscow: Izdatel'stvo moskovskogo universiteta, 1973), pp. 8–9.

42. They called this style of work "merry anarchism." *Ekonomicheskaia zhizn'*, no. 255, 1927, p. 4.

43. Iu. Larin, *Intelligentsiia i sovety: Khoziaistvo, burzhuaziia, revoliutsiia, gosap-

parat (Moscow: Gosudarstvennoe izdatel'stvo, 1924?) pp. 6–9; Venediktov, *Organizatsiia, p. 265; Narodnoe khoziaistvo,* no. 4, 1918, p. 28; Iu. K. Avdakov, *Organizatsionno-khoziaistvennaia deiatel'nost' VSNKh v pervye gody sovetskoi vlasti, 1917–1921 gg.* (Moscow: Izdatel'stvo moskovskogo universiteta, 1971), p. 109.

44. *Narodnoe khoziaistvo,* no. 11, 1918, p. 25; *Ekonomicheskaia zhizn',* no. 255. 1927, p. 4; Drobizhev, *Glavnyi shtab,* p. 64.

45. *Plenum VSNKh,* pp. 121–2.

46. Walter Pietsch, *Revolution und Staat: Institutionen als Träger der Macht in Sowjetrussland, 1917–1922* (Cologne: Verlag Wissenschaft und Politik, 1969), p. 77.

47. The terms *raion* and *oblast'* in this context were used synonymously.

48. *Sovety narodnogo khoziaistva i planovye organy v tsentre i na mestakh, 1917–1932: Sbornik dokumentov* (Moscow: Gosudarstvennoe izdatel'stvo politicheskoi literatury, 1957), pp. 63–65.

49. A. B. Medvedev, "Razrabotka V. I. Leninym printsipov organizatsii upravleniia promyshlennosti v pervyi period sovetskoi vlasti (Oktiabr' 1917–1918 gg.)," in *O deiatel'nosti V. I. Lenina v 1917–1922 gody: Sbornik statei* (Moscow: n. p., 1958), p. 106.

50. *Sovety narodnogo khoziaistva,* p. 75.

51. Venediktov, *Organizatsiia,* pp. 549–50; Avdakov, *VSNKh,* pp. 44–47.

52. Second SNKh Congress, pp. 227–28.

53. *Ekonomicheskaia zhizn',* no. 15, 1918, p. 4; E. G. Gimpel'son, *Sovety v gody inostrannoi interventsii i grazhdanskoi voiny* (Moscow: Izdatel'stvo Nauka, 1968), pp. 333–34; Venediktov, *Organizatsiia,* p. 557; Avdakov, *VSKNh,* pp. 26–27.

54. B. M. Morozov. *Sozdanie i ukreplenie sovetskogo gosudarstvennogo apparata (noiabr' 1917 g.–mart 1919 g.)* (Moscow: Gosudarstvennoe izdatel'stvo politicheskoi literatury, 1957), p. 119.

55. Venediktov, *Organizatsiia,* p. 564; *Dekrety,* 3:520–22; Gimpel'son, *Sovety,* pp. 335–6; Gladkov, *Natsionalizatsiia,* pp. 582–3; Venediktov, *Organizatsiia,* p. 313.

56. Venediktov, *Organizatsiia,* pp. 289–92, 511–33.

57. *Ekonomicheskaia zhizn',* no. 95, 1924, p. 1; Kiseleva, *Natsionalizatsiia,* 1:154–55; Lenin, *PSS,* 35:259, 277.

58. *Novyi put',* no. 11, 1918, pp. 1–3; Arthur Ransome, *The Crisis in Russia* (London: George Allen & Unwin, 1921), p. 131.

59. Drobizhev and Medvedev, *Iz istorii sovnarkhozov,* p. 52.

60. Simon Liberman, *Building Lenin's Russia* (Chicago: University of Chicago Press, 1945), p. 2.

61. Second SNKh Congress, pp. 212–3.

62. Kiseleva, *Natsionalizatsiia,* 2:xxi–xxii; Venediktov, *Organizatsiia,* 564, 568–70.

63. A. Gurovich, "Vysshyi sovet narodnago khoziaistva: Iz vpechatlenii goda sluzhby," *Arkhiv russkoi revoliutsii* (Berlin, 1922), vol. 6, pp. 311–12.

64. *Soiuz potrebitelei*, no. 20, 1918, pp. 17–22.

65. L. A. Krol', *Za tri goda: Vospominaniia, vpechatleniia i vstrechi* (Vladivostok: Svobodnaia Rossiia, 1921), pp. 33–35.

66. Gurovich, "Vysshyi sovet," p. 311.

67. See *Plenum, VSNKh*, p. 136; *Novyi put'*, no. 4 (August), 1918, p. 31; ibid., no. 8, 1918, pp. 4–5.

68. I am grateful to H. Ray Buchanan for this idea.

69. Alexander Axelrod, *Das wirtschaftliche Ergebnis des Bolschewismus in Russland* (Olten: Verlag W. Troesch, 1920?), p. 67.

70. *Dekrety*, 4:164–66; Second SNKh Congress, pp. 227–28.

71. First SNKh Congress, pp. 102–04.

72. *Vos'moi s"ezd RKP(b), Mart 1919 goda: Protokoly* (Moscow: Gosudarstvennoe izdatel'stvo politicheskoi literatury, 1959), p. 543n. Hereafter the Eighth Party Congress.

73. Morozov, *Sozdanie*, pp. 129–30; Eighth Party Congress, p. 547n.

74. Eighth Party Congress, pp. 201–03; See also *Sed'moi vserossiiskii s"ezd sovetov rabochikh, krest'ianskikh, krasnoarmeiskikh i kazach'ikh deputatov: Stenograficheksii otchet, 5–9 dekabria 1919 g.* (Moscow: Gosudarstvennoe izdatel'stvo, 1920), p. 197. Hereafter the Seventh Soviet Congress.

75. Seventh Soviet Congress, p. 225.

76. *Vos'maia konferentsiia RKP(b), Dekabr' 1919 goda: Protokoly, 2–4 dekabria 1919 g.* (Moscow: Gosudarstvennoe izdatel'stvo politicheskoi literatury, 1961), pp. 39, 63–68, passim. Hereafter called the Eighth Party Conference.

77. *Izvestiia narodnogo komissariata finansov*, no. 9, 1919, pp. 1–3; ibid., no. 12, 1919, pp. 1–3. Note that this was not Valerian V. Obolenskii, who used the name N. Osinskii.

78. F. V. Samokhvalov, *Sovety narodnogo khoziaistva v 1917–1932 gg.* (Moscow: Izdatel'stvo Nauka, 1964), p. 76.

79. *Dekrety*, 7:182–89; Venediktov, *Organizatsiia*, pp. 440–41, 591, 581.

80. Venediktov, *Organizatsiia*, p. 549.

81. See Thomas Remington, "Trotsky, War Communism, and the Origin of the NEP," *Studies in Comparative Communism* 10 (Spring/Summer 1977); 56–57.

82. Avdakov, *VSNKh*, pp. 47–54; Avadakov and Borodin, *Proizvodstvennye ob"edineniia*, pp. 33–34.

83. F. Dan, *Dva goda skitanii (1919–1921)* (Berlin: Russische Buecherzentrale Obrazowanie, 1922), pp. 46–47.

84. E. H. Carr, *The Bolshevik Revolution, 1917–1923*, 3 vols. (Harmondsworth: Penguin Books, 1966), vol. 1, pt. III; Pipes, *Formation*.

85. Carr, *Bolshevik Revolution*, 1:138.

86. Pietsch, *Revolution und Staat*, pp. 81–82.

87. Carr, *Bolshevik Revolution*, 1:133–51.

88. First SNKh Congress, pp. 15–18, 25.

89. Bertram D. Wolfe, "The Influence of Early Military Decisions Upon the

National Structure of the Soviet Union," *American Slavic and East European Review* (1950): 169–79.

90. *Novyi put'*, no. 8, 1918, pp. 3–7.

91. Carr, *Bolshevik Revolution*, 1:287–88.

92. Quoted by Merle Fainsod, *How Russia Is Ruled* (Cambridge: Harvard University Press, 1953), p. 304.

93. Avdakov, *VSNKh*, pp. 83–96; *Dekrety*, 7:205; Carr, *Bolshevik Revolution*, 1:387–90.

4 : The Mobilization of Labor

1. Jay B. Sorenson, *The Life and Death of Soviet Trade Unionism, 1917–1928* (New York: Atherton Press, 1969), pp. 74–75.

2. Solomon M. Shvarts [Schwartz], "Sovetskii soiuz na puti k trudovoi povinnosti" (manuscript, n.d., Hoover Institituion Archives), pp. 2–7.

3. N. I. Bukharin, *Economics of the Transformation Period* (New York: Bergman Publishers, 1971), pp. 111–12.

4. Victor Serge, *Memoirs of a Revolutionary* (New York: Oxford University Press, 1967), p. 115.

5. Leon Trotsky, *The Revolution Betrayed: What Is the Soviet Union and Where Is Is It Going?* (New York: Pathfinder Press, 1972), p. 22.

6. The conflict of interpretations continues. Stephen F. Cohen finds that the "ideological" school still predominates (see his essay, "Bolshevism and Stalinism," in Tucker, *Stalinism*, p. 19), but my impression is that the military explanation has been the most forcefully argued in recent years, partly because of Cohen's persuasive work as well as the recent works by the Soviet historian E. G. Gimpel'son. Also, Jonathan Adelman has argued recently that the civil war militarized the political culture of the first generation of Bolshevik leaders, with an effect lasting well into the Stalin era. See "The Impact of Civil Wars on Communist Political Culture: The Russian and Chinese Cases" (paper presented at the APSA meeting, New York, September 1981); and "The Russian Civil War: The Formative Years" (paper presented at the AAASS meeting, Asilomar, California, September 1981).

7. Point 8 of the Communist Manifesto calls for "Equal liability of all to labor. Establishment of industrial armies, especially for agriculture" (Robert C. Tucker, *The Marx-Engels Reader* [New York: Norton, 1972], p. 352); A. L. Sidorov, *Ekonomicheskoe polozhenie Rossii v gody pervoi mirovoi voiny* (Moscow: Nauka, 1973), pp. 166–72.

8. Larin, *Gosudarstvennyi kapitalizm*, p. 6.

9. Sixth Party Congress, pp. 216–18.

10. A. A. Lipatov and N. T. Savenkov, comp., *Istoriia sovetskoi konstitutsii (v dokumentakh), 1917–1956* (Moscow: Gosudarstvennoe izdatel'stvo politicheskoi literatury, 1957), pp. 103, 146. The term for conscription, *povinnost'*, could also

be translated as obligation; for the time being, the obligation was entirely theoretical. The injunction that he who does no work should not eat originally comes from Paul's second letter to the Thessalonians, 3:10.

11. Lenin, *PSS*, 35: 174–76.

12. *Dekrety*, 3:67–71, 396–97.

13. Venediktov, *Organizatsiia*, p. 370. This measure was to apply in the first instance to nonproductive strata of the population.

14. Narodnoe khoziaistvo, no. 2, 1918, p. 21; Venediktov, *Organizatsiia*, pp. 357–58.

15. Especially in the period when VSNKh was in transition between Osinskii's and Rykov's chairmanships. See Miliutin. *Istoriia*, pp. 31–32.

16. Lorenz, "Alternativen," pp. 210–12.

17. A. Anikst, "Organizatsiia rynka truda v Rossii," in *Dva goda diktatury proletariata, 1917–1919* (Moscow: VSNKh, 1919), pp. 29–37, 38–39, 44; Kiseleva, *Natsionalizatsiia*, 2:255–62.

18. E. G. Gimpel'son, *Sovetskii rabochii klass, 1918–1920 gg.* (Moscow: Izdatel'stvo Nauka 1974), p. 63.

19. *Dekrety*, 5:37; Gimpel'son, *Sovetskii rabochii klass*, pp. 132 ff.

20. *Dekrety*, 6:318–20.

21. Remington, "Trotsky."

22. Second SNKh Congress, pp. 128–29.

23. Ransome, *Crisis*, p. 60.

24. Ibid., p. 61.

25. Venediktov, *Organizatsiia*, p. 441. See also *Novyi put'*, no. 5/6, 1920, pp. 10–12, for an account of the Petrograd SNKh's report to a visiting Italian delegation, mentioning that centralization, including one-man management, was now the cornerstone of economic policy in the spring of 1920.

26. *Dekrety*, 7:173–78; Gimpel'son, *Sovety*, pp. 352–53.

27. Ransome, *Crisis*, pp. 97–105.

28. Dan, *Skitanii*, p. 46; Baevskii, *Ocherki*, pp. 109–26.

29. Anikst, "Organizatsiia rynka," pp. 29–37.

30. Kiseleva, *Natsionalizatsiia*, 2:255–62.

31. *Dekrety*, 8:13–17, 163–64, 164–5; see also the list presented by James Bunyan, ed., *The Origin of Forced Labor in the Soviet State, 1917–1921: Documents and Materials* (Baltimore: The Johns Hopkins Press, 1967), pp. 163–64.

32. A. I. Rykov, *Stat'i i rechi*, vol. 1, *1918–1920*, ed. A. Lomov and M. Savel'ev (Moscow: Tsentral'noe upravlenie pechati VSNKh, 1926), pp. 171–75; E. G. Gimpel'son, *Velikii oktiabr' i stanovlenie sovetskoi sistemy upravleniia narodnym khoziaistvom (noiabr' 1917–1920 gg.)* (Moscow: Izdatel'stvo Nauka, 1977), p. 168.

33. *Narodnoe khoziaistvo*, no. 8, 1919, pp. 85–87.

34. *Tretii vserossiiskii s"ezd professional'nykh soiuzov, 6 aprelia 1920–13 aprelia 1920* (Moscow?: n.p., 1920?), pp. 50–51. Hereafter the Third Trade Union Congress.

35. Emma Goldman, *My Disillusionment in Russia* (Garden city: Doubleday, Page & Co., 1923), p. 181; *Pravda*, 4 January 1921, p. 4; ibid., 6 January 1921, p. 4; ibid., 18 January 1921, p. 4.

36. Sorenson, *Soviet Trade Unionism*, p. 43; V. I. Nosach, "Profsoiuzy Petrograda v period sotsialisticheskoi revoliutsii i grazhdanskoi voiny (oktiabr' 1917–1920)" (cand. diss., Moskovskaia zaoch. vyssh. shkola profdizheniia VTsSPS, Moscow, 1964), p. vii.

37. *Vestnik truda*, no. 3, 1921, pp. 8–13; Sorenson, *Soviet Trade Unionism*, pp. 82–84.

38. *Vtoroi vserossiiskii s"ezd professional'nykh soiuzov, 16–25 ianvaria 1919 g.: Stenograficheskii otchet* (Moscow: Gosudarstvennoe izdatel'stvo, 1921), pp. 46–56. Hereafter called the Second Trade Union Congress.

39. *Narodnoe khoziaistvo*, no. 5, 1918, pp. 16–20; Gladkov, *Natsionalizatsiia*, pp. 644–45.

40. *Narodnoe khoziaistvo*, no. 11, 1918, p. 64.

41. D. A. Chugaev, ed., *Rabochii klass sovetskoi Rossii v pervyi god diktatury proletariata: Sbornik dokumentov i materialov* (Moscow: Izdatel'stvo Nauka, 1964), pp. 119–20; Gimpel'son, *Velikii oktiabr'*, p. 160; *Ekonomicheskaia zhizn'*, no. 9, 1919, p. 1.

42. Gimpel'son, *Velikii oktiabr'*, pp. 268–69, 271–72.

43. *Novyi put'*, no. 1/2, 1919, pp. 5–6.

44. *Vestnik truda*, no. 4/5/6 (7/8/9), 1921, p. 4; Gimpel'son, *Velikii oktiabr'*, p. 264.

45. Gimpel'son, *Sovetskii rabochii klass*, p. 265; idem, *Velikii oktiabr'*, p. 270.

46. Gimpel'son, *Velikii oktiabr'*, p. 282.

47. *Narodnoe khoziaistvo*, no. 7/8, 1920, pp. 45–46.

48. *Vestnik truda*, no. 4/5/6, 1921, p. 4.

49. Venediktov, *Organizatsiia*, pp. 538–40.

50. *Narodnoe khoziaistvo*, no. 4, 1921, p. 47; S. A. Fediukin, *Sovetskaia vlast' i burzhuaznye spetsialisty* (Moscow: Izdatel'stvo Mysl', 1965), p. 114.

51. A. Kolontay [Kollontai], *The Workers Opposition in Russia* (Chicago: I.W.W., 1921?), pp. 14–15.

52. A. V. Krasnikova, *Na zare sovetskoi vlasti: Bol'sheviki Petrograda v pervye mesiatsy proletarskoi diktatury, noiabr' 1917–iiul' 1918 g.* (Leningrad: Lenizdat, 1963), p. 183; *Vestnik professional'nykh soiuzov*, no. 1 (5), 1919, p. 2.

53. *Vestnik truda*, no. 3 (6), 1921, p. 4.

54. Robert V. Daniels, *Conscience of the Revolution: Communist Opposition in Soviet Russia* (New York: Simon and Schuster, Clarion Books, 1969), pp. 124, 129–35; Leonard Schapiro, *Origin of the Communist Autocracy: Political Opposition in the Soviet State, First Phase, 1917–1922* (Cambridge: Harvard University Press, 1955), pp. 273–95; Richard B. Day, *Leon Trotsky and the Politics of Economic Isolation* (Cambridge: Cambridge University Press, 1973), pp. 37–44.

55. Margaret Dewar, *Labour Policy in the USSR, 1917–1928* (London: Royal Institute of International Affairs, 1956), p. 34.

56. *Vestnik professional'nykh soiuzov*, no. 1(5), 1919, pp. 11–12.

57. *Novyi put'*, no. 12, 1918, p. 5.

58. Rykov, *Stat'i i rechi*, pp. 90–91.

59. *Novyi put'*, no 1/2, 1919, pp. 87–88.

60. Schapiro, *Autocracy*, p. 255; *Ekonomicheskaia zhizn'*, no. 209, 1919, p. 1.

61. Bukharin and Preobrazhensky, *ABC*, p. 447.

62. Ibid., pp. 335–36. I have placed capitalized text into lower case.

63. Isaac Deutscher, *Soviet Trade Unions* (London: Royal Institute of International Affairs, 1950), p. 29.

64. Dewar, *Labour Policy*, p. 74; Sorenson, *Soviet Trade Unionism*, p. 83.

65. Daniels, *Conscience*, pp. 132–33.

66. Day, *Trotsky*, p. 42.

67. Carr, *Bolshevik* Revolution, 2:317–18.

68. See William Chase, "Revolutionary Enthusiasm and the Disintegration of Moscow, 1918–1921" (paper presented at the AAASS meeting, Asilomar, California, September 1981), pp. 36–37. Chase finds a similar mood among Moscow workers: a sense that the revolution was, ultimately, "theirs," but at the same time, strong discontent by early 1921.

69. Raphael R. Abramowitch, *The Soviet Revolution, 1917–1939* (New York: International Universities Press, 1962), pp. 151–52; Gregor Aronson, "Na perelome: K kharakteristike nastroenii rabochego klassa Rossii v pervuiu polovinu 1918 g." (manuscript, 1935, Hoover Institution Archives), pp. 3–4.

70. Axelrod, *Ergebnis*, pp. 37–38.

71. *Nash vek*, 28 March 1918, no. 59 (83) (newspaper in the Nikolaevskii collection, Hoover Institution Archives).

72. M. Philips Price, *My Reminiscences of the Russian Revolution* (London: Allen & Unwin, Ltd., 1921), p. 280.

73. Abramowitch, *Soviet Revolution*, pp. 153–54.

74. Fourth Factory Committee and Trade Union Conference, pp. 65–66.

75. Chugaev, *Rabochii klass*, pp. 73–74; Aronson, "Na perelome," pp. 23–24.

76. *Professional'nyi vestnik*, no. 5/6, 1918, p. 8.

77. *Novyi put'*, no. 4, 1918, pp. 25–6.

78. Aronson, "Na perelome," pp. 22–23.

79. Kiseleva, *Natsionalizatsiia*, 2:36.

80. *Novyi put'*, no. 4, 1918, pp. 1–2.

81. Ibid., no. 9/10, 1918, pp. 21, 28.

82. Venediktov, *Organizatsiia*, p. 361; Kiseleva, *Natsionalizatsiia*, 2:38–44. When the government asked the plant's former manager to return to his post, he declined, replying that only the Bolsheviks were capable of restoring discipline, being "able to take the necessary measures for raising productivity, not stopping at anything."

83. *Novyi put'*, no. 8, 1918, pp. 19–21; ibid., no. 9/10, 1918, p. 7; Kiseleva, *Natsionalizatsiia*, 2:44–52; Krasnikova, *Na zare*, p. 147.

84. Philips Price misinterpreted this movement, I believe, in calling it syndicalist (Price, *Reminiscences*, p. 280). In December 1917 the Mensheviks held a party congress uniting all factions, which declared its opposition to the Bolshevik decree on workers' control, which they considered wildly irresponsible. In its place they offered their old formula of state control. See the Menshevik newspaper *Novyi luch* for 6 December 1917 in the Nikolaevskii collection at the Hoover Institution. The newspaper of the printers' union—which long remained a persistent stronghold of Menshevism—was attacking Bolshevik experiments in building socialism as late as December 1918. See *Gazeta pechatnikov*, 30 December 1918, pp. 4–5, in the Nikolaevskii collection.

85. Chamberlin, *Russian Revolution*, 2:48; Aronson, "Na perelome," pp. 21–22; Abramovitch, *Soviet Revolution*, pp. 156–65.

86. Venediktov, *Organizatsiia*, p. 121; Aronson. "Na perelome," pp. 20–21.

87. Gimpel'son. *Sovetskii rabochii klass*, pp. 190–91, 193.

88. Ibid., pp. 124–25.

89. Chamberlin, *Russian Revolution*, 2:218, Sergey P. Melgounov, *The Red Terror in Russia* (London: J. M. Dent & Sons, 1926), pp. 49–51; Gimpel'son, *Sovetskii rabochii klass*, pp. 125–26; Biziaeva, "Iz istorii," p. 136.

90. Gimpel'son, *Sovetskii rabochii klass*, p. 125.

91. *Novyi put'*, no. 6–8, 1919, pp. 74–76.

92. Ibid., no. 10–12, 1919, pp. 60–63; Gimpel'son, *Sovetskii rabochii klass*, p. 126.

93. *Dekrety*, 5: 304–06.

94. Goldman, *My Disillusionment*, p. 109.

95. Ibid., p. 176.

96. Paul Avrich, *Kronstadt 1921* (New York: Norton, 1970), pp. 35–48; Dan, *Skitanii*, pp. 105–08.

97. Avrich, *Kronstadt*, pp. 49, 65–71.

5 : Scientific Rationalism in Bolshevik Ideology

1. V. Molotov, ed., *Kak rabochie stroiat sotsialisticheskoe khoziaistvo* (Petrograd: Izdanie SNKHSR, 1918), p. 12.

2. For example, Bukharin's book, *Economics of the Transformation Period*, expects a period in which blind market irrationality will survive before social regulation is strong enough to take over (p. 140).

3. V. I. Grinevetskii, *Poslevoennye perspektivy russkoi promyshlennosti*, 2nd ed. (Moscow: Izdatel'stvo vserossiiskogo tsentral'nogo soiuza potrebitel'skikh obshchestv, 1922), p. 37.

4. Daniel Bell, *The Coming of Post-Industrial Society: A Venture in Social Forecasting* (New York: Basic Books, 1976), p. 349; Kendall E. Bailes, "Alexei Gastev

and the Soviet Controversy over Taylorism, 1918–1924," *Soviet Studies* 29 (July 1977): 380.

5. A. A. Bogdanov, *Tektologiia: Vseobshchaia organizatsionnaia nauka*, rev. ed. (Berlin: Izdatel'stvo Z. I. Grzhebin, 1922), p. 303; N. I. Bukharin, *Ataka: Sbornik teoreticheskikh statei*, 2nd ed. (Moscow: Gosudarstvennoe izdatel'stvo, 1924), p. 239.

6. See, for example, *Kommunist*, no. 1, 1918, p. 12.

7. Lenin, *PSS*, 36:53, 167–88, 141.

8. Ibid., pp. 78–82, 188, 272, 288; Miliutin, *Istoriia*, pp. 8–9; Larin, *Intelligentsiia*, p. 11; Albert Rhys Williams, *Lenin: The Man and His Work* (New York: Scott and Seltzer, 1919), pp. 101–03.

9. *Kommunist*, no. 1, 1918, p. 12; ibid., no. 2, 1918, p. 12. Stephen Cohen overstates, I believe, Bukharin's ambivalence regarding the economic platform of the democratic Left. Cohen incorrectly states that Bukharin contributed only one article directly related to the dispute: besides the article on state capitalism in the third issue of *Kommunist*, he contributed theoretical articles (one on the need for large-scale economic development, and a clever book review of Lenin's *State and Revolution* in which Bukharin—anticipating his performance at his own show trial—used the words of his opponents to make his own points) to both the first and second issues of *Kommunist*. It is true that the tenor of these articles differs from that of Osinskii; but his subsequent theoretical searchings during War Communism flow from his attempts to reconcile the ultimately contradictory values of the technocratic and democratic wings. See Cohen, *Bukharin*, pp. 71 ff.

10. M. S. Bastrakova, *Stanovlenie sovetskoi sistemy organizatsii nauki (1917–1922)* (Moscow: Izdatel'stvo Nauka, 1973), p. 67; *Narodnoe khoziaistvo*, no. 1, 1918, pp. 5–6.

11. I. Smirnov, ed., "Dva pis'ma N. P. Gorbunova V. I. Leninu," *Novyi mir* 60 (August 1964): 278.

12. Bastrakova, *Stanovlenie*, p. 65.

13. Vladimir N. Ipatieff, *The Life of a Chemist*, ed. Xenia Joukoff Eudin, Helen Dwight Fisher, and Harold H. Fisher; trans. Vladimir Haensel and Mrs. Ralph H. Lusher (Stanford: Stanford University Press, 1946), p. 262: Jeremy Azrael, *Managerial Power and Soviet Politics* (Cambridge: Harvard University Press, 1966), pp. 30–35.

14. Bastrakova, *Stanovlenie*, p. 84.

15. Ibid., pp. 33–35, 57–58; Loren R, Graham, *The Soviet Academy of Sciences and the Communist Party, 1927–1932* (Princeton: Princeton University Press, 1967), pp. 21–22.

16. Ipatieff, *Life of a Chemist*, p. 476; N. Valentinov [Vol'skii], "Promyshlennost' v fevral'skuiu revoliutsiiu, gody voennogo kommunizma i period 1920–1928 gg." (manuscript, n.d., Hoover Institution Archives), p. 13.

17. E.g., Gurovich, "Vysshyi sovet," pp. 308–09.

18. Ipatieff, *Life of a Chemist*, p. 261.

19. Grinevetskii, *Poslevoennye perspektivy*, pp. 66, 88–90, passim.

20. Guroff, "State and Industrialization," p. 266.

21. Bastrakova, *Stanovlenie*, p. 24.

22. Second SNKh Congress, pp. 241–43; Rykov, *Stat'i i rechi*, pp. 90–91.

23. Bastrakova, *Stanovlenie*, pp. 121–27.

24. Ibid., pp. 164–65; Fediukin, *Sovetskaia vlast'*, pp. 98–101.

25. Bastrakova, *Stanovlenie*, pp. 166 ff.; Smirnov, "Dva pis'ma," pp. 276–79; Fediukin, *Sovetskaia vlast'*, p. 99; idem, *Velikii oktiabr' i intelligentsiia—iz istorii volvecheniia staroi intelligentsii v stroitel'stvo sotsializma* (Moscow: Izdatel'stvo Nauka, 1972), p. 146.

26. Bastrakova, *Stanovlenie*, pp. 161–62, 176.

27. Fediukin, *Velikii oktiabr'*, p. 164; idem, *Sovetskaia vlast'*, pp. 102–03.

28. Graham, *Academy*, pp. 30–31, 27–28; Bastrakova, *Stanovlenie*, p. 84.

29. A. E. Versman, "Die Erforschung der Bodenschäfte Russlands durch die russiche Akademie der Wissenschaften," *Das heutige Russland, 1917–1922: Wirtschaft und Kultur in der Darstellung russischen Forscher* (Berlin: L. D. Frenkel Verlag, 1923), pp. 139–45; Bastrakova, *Stanovlenie*, pp. 47–53.

30. Azrael, *Managerial Power, p. 35.*

31. Liberman, *Building Lenin's Russia*, pp. 27–29, 37, passim.

32. Fediukin, *Velikii oktiabr'*, pp. 151–52; *Krasnaia nov'*, no. 3 (7), (May 1922), pp. 211–24.

33. S. V. Utechin, "Bolsheviks and Their Allies After 1917: The Ideological Pattern," *Soviet Studies* 10 (October 1958): 129–31.

34. *Ekonomicheskaia zhizn'*, no. 254, 1919, p. 2; Liberman, *Building Lenin's Russia*, pp. 29–32.

35. *Novyi put'*, no. 7, 1920, p. 52; Gladkov, *Ocherki*, pp. 499–500; *Krasnyi arkhiv*, 95 (1939), p. 33.

36. *Novyi put'*, no. 9, 1920, p. 60; ibid., no. 10, 1920, p. 41.

37. M. P. Pavlovich, *Brestskii mir i usloviia ekonomicheskogo vozrozhdeniia Rossii* (Moscow: Izdatel'stvo VTSIK SRSKIKD, 1918), pp. 7–8.

38. Arthur Ransome, *Russia in 1919* (New York: B. W. Huebsch, 1919), pp. 97–100; Venediktov, *Organizatsiia*, 268–69.

39. Pavlovich, *Brestskii mir*, p. 50; *Plenum, VSNKh*, pp. 63–64.

40. Pavlovich, *Brestskii mir*, p. 52.

41. Ibid., ch. 7; Gladkov, *Ocherki*, p. 112.

42. Pavlovich, *Brestskii mir*, p. 60.

43. The newspaper *Ekonomicheskaia zhizn'* provided the best continuing coverage of this project. See: 1918, no. 31, p. 2; 1919, no. 6, p. 1; no. 7, p. 1; no. 14, p. 2; no. 17, p. 2; no. 23, p. 2; no. 24, p. 2; no. 26, p. 2; no. 27, p. 2; no. 77, p. 3; no. 79, p. 3; 1921, no. 12, p. 1, where the idea is brought up again as if for the first time. Also note Gurovich's recollections of the affair: "Vysshyi sovet," p. 321.

44. Venediktov, *Organizatsiia*, pp. 336–50, 506; Lubov Krassin, *Leonid Krasin: His Life and Work* (London: Skeffington and Son, Ltd., n.d.), pp. 276–77, where his widow reproduced a warm tribute from Professor Osadchii, whom Krasin had brought into the Electro-Technical Council; Gladkov, *Ocherki*, pp. 482–83.

45. Kendall E. Bailes, *Technology and Society Under Lenin and Stalin: Origins of the Soviet Technical Intelligentsia, 1917–1941* (Princeton: Princeton University Press, 1978), pp. 45–46.

46. Ipatieff, *Life of a Chemist*, pp. 271–72; *Dekrety*, 7:427–28.

47. *Resheniia partii i pravitel'stva po khoziaistvennym voprosam*, vol. 1, *1917–1928 gody* (Moscow: Izdatel' stvo politicheskoi literatury, 1967), pp. 168–69, 162.

48. Drobizhev and Medvedev, *Iz istorii sovnarkhozov*, p. 91; Gladkov, *Ocherki*, pp. 182–83.

49. Valerian V. Kuibyshev, ed., *Promyshlennost' za desiat' let (1917–1927 gg.)* Moscow: Izdanie Prezidiuma VSNKh SSSR, 1927), p. 19; Baevskii, *Ocherki*, p. 397.

50. Writing under her customary pseudonym, E. Blonina, in *Sotsialisticheskoe stroitel'stvo*, no. 2, 1919, p. 53.

51. *Sotsialisticheskoe stroitel'stvo*, no. 8–9, 1918, p. 36.

52. Gladkov, *Ocherki*, pp. 497–99.

53. *Krasnyi arkhiv*, 95 (1939), p. 31.

54. Gladkov, *Ocherki*, pp. 437–71.

55. Lenin, *PSS*, 42:157.

56. Gosudarstvennaia komissiia po elektrifikatsii Rossii, *Plan elektrifikatsii RSFSR: Vvedenie k dokladu vos'momu s"ezdu sovetov* (Moscow: n. p., 1920), pp. 9, 32, 94–129.

57. Ibid., p. 191.

58. *Novyi put'*, no. 6/7, 1918, p. 43.

59. Bell, *Post-Industrial Society*, pp. 378–408.

60. L. B. Krasin, *Dela davno minuvshikh dnei* (Moscow: Novaia Moskva, 1925), pp. 24–25.

61. G. M. Krzhizhanovskii, *Sochineniia*, 3 vols. (Moscow: Gosudarstvennoe energeticheskoe izdatel'stvo, 1933–1934?), vol. 1, pp. 80–84.

62. Charles S. Maier, "Between Taylorism and Technocracy: European Ideologies and the vision of Industrial Productivity in the 1920's," *Journal of Contemporary History* 5 (1970): 27–29.

63. Ibid., pp. 30–32.

64. Albert Rhys Williams, *Lenin: The Man and His Work* (New York: Scott and Seltzer, 1919), p. 144.

65. Camilla Gray, *The Russian Experiment in Art, 1863–1922* (New York: Harry N. Abrams, 1971), p. 200; Bailes, "Gastev," p. 375; Peter Scheibert, "Lenin, Bogdanov, and the Concept of Proletarian Culture," in Bernard W. Eissenstat, ed., *Lenin and Leninism: State, Law, and Society* (Lexington: Lexington Books, 1971), p. 200.

210 NOTES TO PAGES 138–47

66. *Pervyi vserossiiskii s"ezd professional'nykh soiuzov, 7–14 ianvaria 1918 g.: Stenograficheskii otchet* (Moscow: Izdanie VTSSPS, 1918), pp. 162–69. Hereafter cited as First Trade Union Congress.

67. First SNKh Congress, pp. 379–92, 331–4, 350.

68. *Vestnik truda*, no. 3, 1920, pp. 21–24; *Ekonomicheskaia zhizn'*, no. 73, 1919, p. 1; ibid., no. 13, 1921, p. 2; ibid., no. 15, 1921, p. 2; ibid., no. 18, 1921, p. 2; ibid., no. 30, 1921, p. 2.

69. Bailes, "Gastev," p. 380. Bailes apparently misstates the date. The institute cannot have been founded until 1921, as the articles cited in n. 68 indicate.

70. Ibid., p. 378; Kritsman, "Geroicheskii period," pp. 80–82.

71. Bukharin and Preobrazhensky, *ABC*, p. 118; N. I. Bukharin, *Historical Materialism: A System of Sociology* (New York: International Publishers, 1925), pp. 41–42.

72. N. Bukharin, *Programma Kommunistov (bol'shevikov)* (Moscow: Izdatel'stvo Kommunist, 1918), p. 35.

73. Fourth Soviet Congress, pp. 233–34.

74. Second SNKh Congress, pp. 374–75.

75. Vera S. Dunham makes a similar point about the Soviet positive hero, who must be "conversant with" both the present and future realms. *In Stalin's Time: Middleclass Values in Soviet Fiction* (Cambridge: Cambridge University Press, 1976), pp. 29–30.

76. *Oktiabr'skii perevorot i diktatura proletariata: Sbornik statei* (Moscow: Gosudarstvennoe izdatel'stvo, 1919), p. 78.

77. *Narodnoe khoziaistvo*, no. 5, 1918, pp. 1–2.

78. Bukharin, *Economics*, pp. 70–71, ch. 6.

79. Bukharin and Preobrazhensky, *ABC*, p. 118.

80. Kritsman, "Geroicheskii period," pp. 6–13; A. Stetskii, "O Geroicheskoi poeme tov. Kritsmana," *Bol'shevik*, no. 2 (18), 1925, pp. 91–94.

81. Bukharin, *Economics*, p. 69.

82. The dream of the golden age occurs in the "Dream of a Ridiculous Man," in Stavrogin's confession in *The Possessed*, and in *The Raw Youth*. It also returns in the fourth dream of Vera Pavlovna in Chernyshevskii's *What Is To Be Done?*

83. *Vestnik metallista*, no. 4/5/6, 1918, p. 21.

84. *Novyi put'*, no. 6–8, 1919, pp. 44–47.

85. *Biulleteni gosudarstvennoi komissii po elektrifikatsii Rossii*, no. 5, 1920, pp. 13–21.

86. Kolontay, *Workers Opposition*, p. 24.

87. Tenth Party Congress, p. 789.

6 : The Cudgel and the Machine

1. *Metallist*, no. 5 (13), 1919, pp. 2–3.

2. Rykov, *Stat'i i rechi*, pp. 280–81.

3. Seventh Soviet Congress, pp. 219–20; *Vestnik metallista*, no. 7/8, 1918/1919, pp. 43–45; *Novyi put'*, no. 8, 1918, pp. 3–7.

4. *Sotsialisticheskoe stroitel'stvo*, no. 6, 1919, pp. 1–3; Iu. Larin, *Proizvodstvennaia propaganda i sovetskoe khoziaistvo na rubezhe 4-ogo goda (Doklad na s"ezde politprosvetov 4 noibria 1920 g.)* (Moscow: Gosudarstvennoe izdatel'stvo, 1920), pp. 32–33; S. I. Gusev, *Edinyi khoziaistvennyi plan i edinyi khoziaistvennyi apparat* (Khar'kov: Izdatel's stvo LOIUZHA, 1920), p. 44.

5. *Novyi put'*, no. 1/2 1919, p. 90; *Ekonomicheskaia zhizn'*, no. 10, 1921, p. 1.

6. Seventh Soviet Congress, pp. 228, 239–44. Stalin similarly pointed out that since the working class still lacked experience, the state continued to need the old bureaucrats. *Ekonomicheskaia zhizn'*, no. 234, 1920, p. 2.

7. *Kommunist*, no. 4, 1918, pp. 6–8; V. Aleksandrova, *Perezhitoe (1917–1921 gg.)* (New York: Inter-University Project on the History of the Menshevik Movement, paper no. 12, September 1962), pp. 34–35; Gurovich, "Vysshyi sovet," pp. 315–16; Goldman, *My Disillusionment*, pp. 61–62.

8. The impression was not wholly inaccurate; women made up 42 percent of the VSNKh staff. *Narodnoe khoziaistvo*, no. 4, 1921, pp. 41 ff.

9. Eighth Soviet Congress, p. 220.

10. Moshe Lewin, *Lenin's Last Struggle*, trans. A. M. Sheridan Smith (New York: Vintage Books, 1970), pp. 122–23, 158; Adam B. Ulam, "Lenin's Last Phase," in Adam B. Ulam, *Ideologies and Illusions: Revolutionary Thought from Herzen to Solzhenitsyn* (Cambridge: Harvard University Press, 1976), pp. 91–104.

11. Ransome, *Crisis*, pp. 131–34.

12. Rykov, *Stat'i i rechi*, pp. 246–49.

13. Gimpel'son, *Velikii oktiabr'*, p. 289.

14. T. H. Rigby, *Communist Party Membership in the U.S.S.R., 1917–1967* (Princeton: Princeton University Press, 1968), pp. 69–87.

15. Lennard D. Gerson, *The Secret Police in Lenin's Russia* (Philadelphia: Temple University Press, 1976), pp. 115–16, 189 ff., Alexander Berkman,*The Bolshevik Myth (Diary 1920–1922)* (New York: Boni and Liveright, 1925), p. 65.

16. See the letter from an agronomist named Dukel'skii to Lenin, complaining of harassment, in *Pravda*, 28 March 1919, p. 1; also Liberman, *Building Lenin's Russia*, passim; George Solomon, *Among the Red Autocrats: My Experience in the Service of the Soviets* (New York: "Our Hope," Arno C. Gaebelin, 1935), pp. 82–83.

17. Remington, "Institution-Building."

18. Lindblom, *Politics and Markets*, ch. 5; Ipatieff, *Life of a Chemist*, p. 289; Dan, *Skitanii*, p. 16.

19. Alexander Axelrod, for example, tells how the commissar who visited his condensed milk plant and named three workers to the factor committee—thus violating the rule that factory committee members be elected—did not know that the three he chose were self-serving intriguers who employed their powers to ruin the plant's operations. *Ergebnis*, pp. 27–31.

20. Goldman, *My Disillusionment*, pp. 112–17; Gregor Aronson, "Angliiskaia rabochaia delegatsiia v Moskve" (manuscript, n.d., Hoover Institution Archives); Dan, *Skitanii*, p. 8; Serge, *Memoirs*, p. 103; Kolontay, *Workers Opposition*, p. 7.

21. Larin, *Propaganda*, p. 44.

22. *Novyi put'*, no. 9, 1919, p. 45; Gimpel'son, *Sovetskii rabochii klass*, pp. 121–22.

23. *Narodnoe khoziaistvo*, no. 4, 1921, pp. 41 ff.; Drobizhev, *Glavnyi shtab*, pp. 227–8; *Plenum VSNKh*, pp. 13, 16.

24. Gimpel'son, *Velikii oktiabr'*, pp. 259–60.

25. For example, Rykov complained in September 1918 that for several months he had been unable to obtain a correct balance sheet on the current financial situation of VSNKh's departments. When he received one on the metals industry, its figures diverged widely from those provided by the metals department itself, both in aggregate and individual categories. Rykov, *Stat'i i rechi*, p. 58. Another example concerns the number of railroad workers. The figures varied by a factor of as much as two, three, or even four, depending on whether the organ distributing food to transport workers was used, or that of the Commissariat of Communications. Gimpel'son, *Sovetskii rabochii klass*, p. 83.

26. Gimpel'son *Velikii oktiabr'*, pp. 216–7.

27. Tenth Party Congress, pp. 26–27, 411.

28. Dan, *Skitanii*, p. 96.

29. Rykov, *Stat'i i rechi*, pp. 80–81.

30. Gimpel'son, *Sovetskii rabochii klass*, p. 158. Another source gives the figure of 101 plants on army rations as of mid-March 1919. Kim et al., *Iz istorii*, p. 138. The figures on the shock sector were often internally contradictory.

31. Gimpel'son, *Sovetskii rabochii klass*, pp. 160, 161–62.

32. Avdakov and Borodin, *Proizvodstvennye ob"edineniia*, pp. 23–24; Kiseleva, *Natsionalizatsiia*, 2: xiii–xiv.

33. *Novyi put'*, no. 10 1920, pp. 25–28.

34. Baevskii, *Ocherki*, pp. 335–41.

35. Solomon Shvarts, "Politika zarabotnoi platy v sovetskoi Rossii v gody voennogo kommunizma" (manuscript, 1935, Hoover Institution Archives). pp. 14–15.

36. Gimpel'son, *Sovetskii rabochii klass*, pp. 168 ff.

37. Venediktov, *Organizatsiia*, pp. 670–71.

38. *Dekrety*, 8: 132–6.

39. Gimpel'son, *Sovetskii rabochii klass*, p. 157; idem, *Velikii oktiabr'*, pp. 190–91.

40. Tenth Party Congress, p. 293.

41. *Deviatyi s"ezd RKP(b), mart–aprel' 1920 g.* (Moscow: Partiinoe izdatel'stvo, 1934), pp. 176–77. Hereafter called the Ninth Party Congress.

42. Farbman, *Bolshevism*, pp. 184–85.

43. Robert A. Dahl and Charles E. Lindblom, *Politics, Economics, and Welfare: Planning and Politico-Economic Systems Resolved Into Basic Social Processes* (New York: Harper Torchbooks, 1963), p. 410.

44. *Ekonomicheskaia zhizn'*, no. 206, 1920, p. 1.

45. *Novyi put'*, no. 1/2, 1919, p. 41; Thomas Remington, "Varga and the Foundation of Soviet Planning," *Soviet Studies* 34 (October 1982): pp. 585–600.

46. Viktor Shklovsky, *A Sentimental Journey: Memoirs, 1917–1922*, trans. Richard Sheldon (Ithaca: Cornell University Press, 1970), p. 184.

47. Lindblom, *Politics and Markets*, ch. 5; Anthony Downs, *Inside Bureaucracy* (Boston: Little, Brown & Co., 1966), pp. 133–36.

48. Aron Katsenelenboigen, "Coloured Markets in the Soviet Union," *Soviet Studies* 29 (January 1977): 62–85.

49. Robert C. Tucker, "Swollen State, Spent Society: Stalin's Legacy to Brezhnev's Russia," *Foreign Affairs*, 60 (Winter 1981/82): 414–35.

50. *Plenum VSNKh*, pp. 115–16.

51. Rykov, *Stat'i i rechi*, pp. 52–53, 143–44.

52. Gimpel'son, *Velikii oktiabr'*, pp. 108–09.

53. *Vestnik truda*, no. 2, 1920, p. 69.

54. Drobizhev and Medvedev, *Iz istorii sovnarkhozov*, p. 156; Gimpel'son, "Voennyi kommunizm," p. 162.

55. *Souiz potrebitelei*, no. 24, 1918, pp. 10–11; Gregor Aronson, "V bor'be za edinstvo i nezavisimost' professional'nogo dvizheniia: Sud'ba professional'nogo soiuza sluzhashchikh v 1917–1920 gg." (manuscript, n.d., Hoover Institution Archives), p. 9.

56. Kritsman, "Geroicheskii period," pp. 119, 116–17.

57. *Novyi put'*, no. 9, 1919, p. 46; ibid., no. 10/12, 1919, pp. 23–4, 28.

58. Ibid., no. 14, 1919, pp. 3–6.

59. Carr, *Bolshevik Revolution*, 2: 242–43.

60. *Novyi put'*, no. 4/5, 1919, pp. 9–10, 17, 22.

61. See, for example, Goldman, *My Disillusionment*, p. 24; also Alfons Goldschmidt, *Moskau 1920: Tagebätter* (Berlin: Ernst Rowohlt Verlag, 1920), pp. 87–88; Dan, *Skitanii*, p. 35.

62. V. A. Golutvin, *Promyshlennost' pri voennom kommunizme i pri NEP'e* (Moscow: Tsentral'noe upravlenie pechati VSNKH SSSR, 1926), pp. 32–33; *Novyi put'*, no. 7, 1920, pp. 46–47.

63. Gimpel'son, *Sovetskii rabochii klass*, pp. 86–89; idem, *Velikii oktiabr'*, p. 81; Suzanne Berger, "The Traditional Sector in France and Italy," in Suzanne Berger and Michael J. Piore, *Dualism and Discontinuity in Industrial Societies* (Cambridge: Cambridge University Press, 1980), pp. 100–04.

64. *Novyi put'*, no. 10/12, 1919, pp. 41–43; *Istoriia grazhdanskoi voiny v SSSR*, vol. 4, *Reshaiushchie pobedy krasnoi armii nad ob"edinennymi silami antanty i vnutren-

nei kontrrevoliutsii (mart 1919 g.–fevral' 1920 g.) (Moscow: Gosudarstvennoe izdatel'stvo politicheskoi literatury, 1959), pp. 89–90; Gimpel'son, *Velikii oktiabr'*, p. 92.

65. *Novyi put'*, no. 12, 1920, pp. 4–5.
66. Gimpel'son, "*Voennyi kommunizm*," p. 161.
67. Venediktov, *Organizatsiia*, pp. 472–75.
68. Gimpel'son, *Sovety*, p. 359.
69. Gimpel'son, "*Voennyi kommunizm*," p. 160; *Vestnik truda*, no. 6, 1921, p. 16.
70. Eighth Soviet Congress, p. 31.
71. *Novyi put'*, no. 1 (June), 1918, p. 24; Kiseleva, *Natsionalizatsiia*, 2: 14–15.
72. *Novyi put'*, no. 11, 1920, pp. 104–07.
73. *Novyi put'*, no. 12, 1920, p. 41; *Trudy konferentsii sovnarkhozov tsentral'nogo, severnogo, i zapadnogo raionov (26–30 avgusta 1921 g.)* (Moscow: VSNKH Otdel redaktsionno-izdatel'skii, 1921), pp. 1–3; *Vestnik truda*, no. 2, 1920, pp. 61–64.
74. L. M. Spirin, *Klassy i partii v grazhdanskoi voine v Rossii (1917–1920 gg.)* (Moscow: Izdatel'stvo Mysl', 1968), pp. 318, 387; Kuibyshev, *Promyshlennost'*, pp. 3–4; *Novyi put'*, no. 9, 1920, p. 32.
75. *Novyi put'*, no. 1/2, 1919, p. 29; *Vestnik truda*, no. 3, 1921, pp. 40–43.
76. Gimpel'son, *Sovetskii rabochii klass*, p. 120; Isaac Deutscher, *The Prophet Armed: Trotsky, 1879–1921*, vol. 1 (New York: Vintage Books, 1965), p. 512; idem, *The Prophet Unarmed: Trotsky, 1921–1929*, vol. 2 (New York: Vintage Books, n.d.), pp. 6–22.

7 : Mobilization and the Evolution of Soviet Politics

1. *Novyi put'*, no. 3 (August), 1918, p. 6.
2. Gimpel'son, *Velikii oktiabr'*, p. 209.
3. *Ekonomicheskaia zhizn'*, no. 245, 1919, p. 1; *Novyi put'*, no. 11, 1920, pp. 3–7.
4. *Krasnaia nov'*, no. 1 (5), 1922, p. 200.
5. Kritsman, "Geroicheskii period." p. 98; *Krasnaia nov'*, no. 4, 1921, p. 154. Note that this Bogdanov was not A. A. Bogdanov (Malinovskii), the organizational systems theorist, but P. A. Bogdanov, a leader of the construction workers' trade union and later the chairman of VSNKh.
6. Tenth Party Congress, pp. 407, 409–11.
7. I. V. Stalin, *Sochineniia*, 13 vols. (Moscow: Gosurdarstvennoe izdatel'stvo politicheskoi literatury, 1946–1951), vol. 11, pp. 161–64.
8. Cohen, *Bukharin*, p. 207.
9. Lewin, "Society, State, and Ideology."
10. Sheila Fitzpatrick, "Cultural Revolution as Class War," in Sheila Fitzpatrick, ed., *Cultural Revolution in Russia, 1928–1931* (Bloomington: Indiana University Press, 1978); Bailes, *Technology and Society*, part 3.
11. Stalin, *Sochineniia*, 13:29–41.

12. Robert C. Tucker, "Stalinism as Revolution from Above," in Robert C. Tucker, *Stalinism*, pp. 93–95.

13. Bailes, *Technology and Society*, pp. 173 ff; Fitzpatrick, "Cultural Revolution," p. 37.

14. Nicholas S. Timasheff, *The Great Retreat* (New York: E. P. Dutton & Co., 1946), provided an early interpretation of the Stalin era along these lines.

15. Dunham, *In Stalin's Time*, pp. 11 ff.

16. George W. Breslauer, *Khrushchev and Brezhnev as Leaders: Building Authority in Soviet Politics* (London: George Allen & Unwin, 1982); also see T. H. Rigby, "Politics in the Mono-Organizational Society," in Andrew C. Janos, ed., *Authoritarian Politics in Communist Europe: Uniformity and Diversity in One-Party States* (Berkeley: Institute of International Studies, University of California, 1976), pp. 36 ff; idem, "Stalinism and the Mono-Organizational Society," in Tucker, *Stalinism*.

17. Seweryn Bialer, *Stalin's Successors: Leadership, Stability and Change in the Soviet Union* (Cambridge: Cambridge University Press, 1981), pp. 50–51.

18. Robert E. Blackwell, Jr., "Cadres Policy in the Brezhnev Era," *Problems of Communism* 28 (March–April 1979): 38. Blackwell speaks of a "creeping institutionalization" of the political struggle.

19. L. I. Brezhnev, *Voprosy upravleniia ekonomikoi razvitogo sotsialisticheskogo obshchestva: Rechi, doklady, vystupleniia* (Moscow: Politizdat, 1976), p. 16; V. G. Afanas'ev, *The Scientific Management of Society* (Moscow: Progress Publishers, 1971). A recent review of the Soviet project to centralize and systematize all economic planning and management in a massive national computer network (OGAS) is found in William J. Conyngham, "Technology and Decision-Making: Some Aspects of the Development of OGAS" *Slavic Review* 39 (September 1980): 426–445.

20. Jerry F. Hough and Merle Fainsod, *How the Soviet Union Is Governed* (Cambridge: Harvard University Press, 1979), pp. 298 ff. An extensive study of citizen participation in local government is Theodore H. Friedgut, *Political Participation in the USSR* (Princeton: Princeton University Press, 1979).

21. V. G. Britvin, "Sotsiologicheskaia sluzhba predpriiatiia i problemy povysheniia effektivnosti sotsiologicheskikh issledovanii," *Sotsiologicheskie issledovaniia*, no. 4 (1980), p. 145; V. G. Baikova, *Ideologicheskaia rabota KPSS v usloviiakh razvitogo sotsializma* (Moscow: Mysl', 1977), p. 189; N. Vainonen, "Byt' khoziainom: Chto eto znachit?" *Zhurnalist*, no. 2 (1982), p. 42; T. M. Novikova, "Obshchestvennaia deiatel'nost' v biudzhete vremeni promyshlennykh rabochikh," *Sotsiologicheskie issledovaniia*, no. 2 (1981), pp. 80–84; Sergei Runov, "Samaia skuchnaia tema, ili kuda smotrit obshchestvennost'," *Zhurnalist*, no. 12 (December 1981), p. 55.

22. Friedgut, *Participation*, pp. 308–12; also see Ellen P. Mickiewicz, *Media and the Russian Public* (New York: Praeger Publishers, 1981), ch. 8, "The Super-Activists: Communist Party Members," pp. 118–31.

23. Friedgut, *Participation*, pp. 15–16.
24. Bialer, *Stalin's Successors*, ch. 9.
25. Hough and Fainsod, p. 266; Alexander Shtromas, *Political Change and Social Development: The Case of the Soviet Union* (Frankfurt: Peter Lang, 1981), pp. 100–01; Thomas Remington, "Organizational Competence in Communist Systems" (paper delivered at the APSA meeting, New York, September 1981); see also the interesting discussion by Alexander Yanov, *Detente After Brezhnev: The Domestic Roots of Soviet Foreign Policy* (Berkeley: Institute of International Studies, University of California, 1977), pp. 3–5.
26. Zygmunt Bauman, *Socialism: The Active Utopia* (New York: Holmes and Meier, 1976), p. 81. Bauman discusses the absence of a "sustaining" public sector outside the state in socialist societies, but does not see dissident culture as a surrogate for such a public.
27. Cf. Howard L. Biddulph, "Soviet Intellectual Dissent as a Political Counter-Culture," *Western Political Quarterly* 25 (September 1972): 522–33; also Iurii Glazov, "Chto zhe takoe demokraticheskoe dvizhenie v SSSR?" *Novyi zhurnal* 109 (1972): 224–34.
28. Note, for example, the joint Central Committee, Council of Ministers, and VTsSPS decree, "O dal'neishem ukreplenii trudovoi distsipliny i sokrashchenii tekuchesti kadrov v narodnom khoziastve," *Kommunist,* 1980, no. 2.
29. Evidence for this may be found in Andropov's address at the Central Committee Plenum of 22 November 1982 (*Pravda,* 23 November 1982); his meeting with the Moscow machine builders, reported in *Pravda,* 1 February 1983; finally the joint Central Committee, Council of Ministers, and VTsSPS decree on strengthening labor discipline, published in *Pravda,* 7 August 1983.

Index

Academy of Sciences, 120–21, 123, 125

Adelman, Jonathan, 202*n*

All-Russian Conference of Entrepreneurial Organizations, 34

All-Russian Factory Committee Congress, 30, 31

All-Russian Workers' Control Council, 196*n*

Andropov, Yuri, 185

Armand, Inessa (E. Blonina), 133

Azrael, Jeremy, 124

Baevskii, David, 6

Bagging, 166

Bednota, 5

Blonina, E. *See* Armand, Inessa

Bogdanov (Malinovskii), A. A., 114

Bolshevism: and capitalist marketplace, 113–14; and collective bargaining, 78–79; as cultural revolution, 179–80; and economic federalism, 74–75; and industrialization through electrification, 133–34; and labor-management relations, 78–79; and militarization, 3; and nationalism through centralized state power, 119–20; planned industrialization in, 114–15; pragmatic rules of, 7; and radical decentralization, 24–25; rebuilding

centralized state by, 48–49; socialism questioned in, 177; and the Stalin revolution, 180–81; and state of industry, 54–55; theory of social organization in, 114, 125; unity and centralization of authority in, 91–92. *See also* Industrialization; Mobilization; Scientific rationalism; Socialism; Soviet politics; War Communism

Brezhnev, Leonid, and rationalization, 184–85

Bukharin, Nikolai: on collective vs. single-person management, 87; on Democratic Left, 116, 139; on labor mobilization, 80; on new ruling class, 114–15, 116; and social integration, 179; and state capitalism, 16–17; on statification, 99

Bureaucratism, 147–50

Center vs. locality conflict, 69–74

Central Aero-Hydrodynamics Institute, 125

Central control: and bagging, 166; and the black market, 167–68; bureaucracies as instrument of, 150; and the Cheka, 151; and Commissariat for State Control, 151–52; final collapse of, 173–75; and fuel and food crisis, 174; and *glavki,*

Liberman, Simon, 125
Lomov (Oppokov), G. I., 14, 75, 128
Lozovskii, A. L., 36, 138, 160
Lur'e, M. *See* Larin, M.

Malinovskii. *See* Bogdanov, A. A.
Mensheviks, 28, 102, 206*n*
Military-Revolutionary Committee
(MRC), 56
Miliutin, V. P., 14, 28–29, 59
Mobilization: acceptance of institutional hierarchy in, 181–82; after World War II, 182; collapse of, 12–13, 177–78; control of industrial administration during, 18–19; and intelligentsia, 182–83; and Khrushchev, 183–85; and political authority, 187; of private markets, 163–75; process of, 11–12; Shliapnikov on, 146–47; under Stalin, 179, 180–83; of working-class organizations, 12, 18. *See also* Bolshevism; Industrialization; Socialism; Soviet politics; Statification; War Communism
Molotov, V., 45, 59
MRC. *See* Military-Revolutionary Committee

Narodnoe khoziaistvo, 90, 141
National Congresses, 1917–1921, 3
Nationalization: approval of, 58–59; central control of, 51–63; central plan for, 55–57; by commissars, 62; demobilization plan for, 54–55; expropriations, 56, 60; Lenin on local takeovers, 59; Rykov on, 58; slow process of, 59–60; of stock companies, 56; by Supreme Economic Council, 57–63; by workers' groups, 56–57
National unity, and economic control, 16

Nauchno-tekhnicheski otdel (Scientific-Technical Department), 121–23
New Economic Policy (NEP), 176, 177
Ninth Party Congress: on economic plan of Trotsky, 73–74; on electrification, 131–32; on *glavki* and *sovnarkhoz* powers, 73
Northern Economic Council, 45–46, 148–49
Novyi put'. *See* Northern Economic Council
NTO. *See* Nauchno-tekhnicheski otdel

Obolenskii, L., 72
Obshchestvennost' (civil society), 182, 186
Oppokov. *See* Lomov, G. I.
Osinskii, N., 60, 61; on center-locality conflict, 70–71; and Commissariat for Internal Affairs, 62; on socialist construction, 141; on workers' control, 28, 29, 40

Pavlovich, M. P., 127–30
Petrograd Central Council of Factory Committees, 35–37, 38–39, 43–44
Petrograd economic exhibition, 171–73
Postwar Perspectives of Russian Industry (Grinevetskii), 119–20

Radek, Karl, 14, 75
Ransome, Arthur, 87, 88–89
Rationalization. *See* Mobilization
Regional (*oblast'*) councils, 63–65
Remeslenniki (craftsmen), 168
Rykov, A. I., 58, 99, 114, 147, 165, 212*n*

Sapronov, T. V., 71
Savel'ev, 40, 60

glavki and *sovnarkhozy*, 63, 69, 73; and nationalization, 57–63; planning workers' control, 31; and regional councils, 63–64; specialists employed by, 95–96
Szamuely, Laszlo, 8

Taylor, Frederick, and Taylorism, 137
Technocratic Left, 136–45
Tektologiia (Bogdanov), 114
Tenth Party Congress, 3, 100–01
Ter-Oganesov, V. T., 120–21
Third Soviet Congress, 59, 82
Third *Sovnarkhoz* Congress, 73
Trade unions: administrative functions of, 94; collective bargaining in, 78–79; and consolidation by industry, 94–97; decline in membership of, 94–96; great trade-union controversy, 97–100; in industrial administration, 94–96; and Menshevism, 92–93; role of, 92–101; and statification, 93, 98–99. *See also* Statification; Worker protest; Workers' control
Trotsky, Leon: on collective vs. single-person management, 86; economic plan of, 73–74; on the great trade-union controversy, 97–98, 100; on labor mobilization, 86; and War Communism, 81
Tsander, F. A., 125

Uchet (auditing), 196n

Valentinov, Nikolai, 119
Varga, Evgenii, 149
Vernadskii, V. I., 120, 123–24
Volga-Don Canal, 128

Volga cataracts, 129–30, 133
Voskresnik (donation of labor on Sunday), 89

War Communism, 3, 5–18, 80–81, 111–12. *See also* Bolshevik ideology; Industrialization; Mobilization; Socialism; Soviet politics
Williams, Albert Rhys, 115
Worker protest: against Brest-Litovsk treaty, 102–03; against dissolution of Constituent Assembly, 101–02; at Putilov works, 103–04, 106–07, 109–10; by railroad workers, 103; by strikes, 105, 107, 108, 111. *See also* Factory committees, Mobilization; Statification; Trade unions; Workers' control
Workers' control: as anarchism, 30; and centralization, 24, 29; Chubar' on, 31; and decree of November 1917, 41–42; as function of state, 46–47; Kritsman on, 30; Larin on, 30–31; Miliutin on, 28–29, 30; Osinskii on, 28, 29; as party slogan, 28; and Petrograd Central Council of Factory Committees, 32; planned by Supreme Economic Council, 31; of production and distribution, 28, 29; Schwartz on, 27; Skrypnik on, 29, 31; in social democracy, 23–24. *See also* Factory committees; Mobilization; Statification; Trade unions; Worker protest
Workers' Opposition, 100

Zhivotov, 42
Zinoviev, Grigorii, 76–77, 112, 149–50, 176